• • •

Unintended Consequences

STUDIES ON THE IMPACT OF THE ILLEGAL DRUG TRADE
LaMond Tullis, Series Editor

•　　•　　•

A Project of the
United Nations Research Institute
for Social Development (UNRISD)
and the
United Nations University (UNU)

Volume 1   *Bolivia and Coca: A Study in Dependency,*
James Painter

Volume 2   *Political Economy and Illegal Drugs in Colombia,*
Francisco E. Thoumi

Volume 3   *Mexico's "War" on Drugs: Causes and Consequences,*
María Celia Toro

Volume 4   *Unintended Consequences: Illegal Drugs and Drug
Policies in Nine Countries,* LaMond Tullis

Volume 5   *Marijuana in the "Third World": Appalachia, U.S.A.,*
Richard R. Clayton and William Estep

Volume 6   *The Burmese Connection: Illegal Drugs in the Golden
Triangle,* Ronald Renard

UNINTENDED CONSEQUENCES

• • •

Illegal Drugs and Drug Policies in Nine Countries

LaMond Tullis

LYNNE
RIENNER
PUBLISHERS

BOULDER
LONDON

Published in the United States of America in 1995 by
Lynne Rienner Publishers, Inc.
1800 30th Street, Boulder, Colorado 80301

and in the United Kingdom by
Lynne Rienner Publishers, Inc.
3 Henrietta Street, Covent Garden, London WC2E 8LU

Library of Congress Cataloging-in-Publication Data
Tullis, LaMond, 1935–
   Unintended consequences: illegal drugs and drug policies in nine
countries / LaMond Tullis.
   p.   cm.—(Studies on the impact of the illegal drug trade;
v. 4)
   Includes bibliographical references and index.
   ISBN 1-55587-549-1 (alk. paper)
   1. Drug traffic. 2. Narcotics, Control of. I. Title.
II. Series.
HV5801.T785   1995
363.4'5'—dc20   95-3464
                                                        CIP

British Cataloguing in Publication Data
A Cataloguing in Publication record for this book
is available from the British Library.

Distributed in Japan and Southeast Asia by:
The United Nations University Press
The United Nations University
53-70, Jingumae 5-chome
Shibuya-ku, Tokyo 150
ISBN 92-808-0891-5

Contents

· · ·

Preface   vii

Introduction   1

1   Drugs, Illegality, and Crime   7

    Illegality, 7
    What Is the Drugs-Crime Nexus? 8
    Illustrations, 20
    Summary and Conclusions, 27

2   Drug Production and Consumption   35

    Estimating Production Figures, 36
    Current Production in Nine Countries, 39
    Current Consumption in Nine Countries, 49
    Summary and Conclusions, 58

3   Drug Trafficking   65

    Colombia, 66
    Peru, 70
    Bolivia, 71
    Mexico, 74
    Thailand, 75
    Laos, 77
    Myanmar/Burma, 80
    Pakistan, 81
    Summary and Conclusions, 83

4   Drug-Control Efforts and Their Effectiveness   89

    Colombia, 92
    Peru, 95
    Bolivia, 99
    Mexico, 104
    Thailand, 107
    Laos, 111

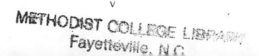

      Myanmar/Burma, 113
      Pakistan, 116
      Kentucky, U.S., 120
      How Effective Have Drug-Control Efforts Been? 122

5   Unintended Socioeconomic and Political Effects   135

      Conceptual Considerations, 135
      Colombia, 140
      Bolivia, 155
      Summary and Conclusions, 170

6   What Ought to Be Done?
    Consequences of Action and Inaction   177

      Reducing Drug Abuse and International Demand, 184
      Other Harm-Reduction Efforts in
        Net Consumer Countries, 188
      Principal Producer Countries' Options to Reduce Harm, 191
      Harm-Reduction Consequences of Altering the
        International Prohibition Regime, 200
      Summary and Conclusions, 204

Bibliography   211
Index   223
About the Book and Author   228
About the United Nations Research Institute for Social Development
    (UNRISD) and the United Nations University (UNU)   229

Preface

• • •

This integrative and interpretive volume draws on observations and inferences from nine country studies (Peru, Colombia, Bolivia, Mexico, Thailand, Myanmar/Burma, Laos, Pakistan, and Kentucky, U.S.[1]) commissioned by the United Nations Research Institute for Social Development (UNRISD) and the United Nations University (UNU).[2] Those studies and this volume address the socioeconomic and political consequences of the production, consumption, and trade of certain illegal psychoactive drugs. They examine the impact of the laws and policies designed to criminalize, discourage, thwart, or otherwise deal with those illegal activities, and they offer observations regarding potential impacts of likely future illicit-drug policies. Of course, this volume cannot—and does not—deal with every rich detail contained in the individual country-study reports. Readers are therefore urged to consult those reports for a wide range of social, economic, political, and anthropological information.

As the list of country studies implies, the geographic focus is on principal "producer" or "trafficking" countries or regions generally classified as "developing" or "less developed." Nevertheless, because impacts on such countries inevitably relate to illegal international trade with principal consuming countries, these are also given appropriate review. It must be noted, of course, that in recent years the distinctions between producing and consuming countries have materially decreased. All countries affected by illicit drugs are now consumers *and* producers.

Although there has been much debate about the impact of illicit-drug consumption and drug-control policies in industrialized countries, especially the United States, much less is known (either in quantitative or qualitative terms) about the impact of drug production, consumption, and trade in developing countries, particularly in those most noted for being large producers or transiters. By the same token, as Dharam Ghai has noted, "while policy discussions, proposals and actions have concentrated for the most part on methods to control the production and trade in drugs, much less attention has been given to efforts to influence the demand for them. It was because of these biases in the policy discussions and the relative paucity of information on the wide-ranging social and economic consequences of the production and consumption of illicit drugs in developing countries that UNRISD decided to launch research on this topic."[3]

Although numerous licit and illicit drugs are noted in the literature (principally in terms of how they affect the central nervous system[4] or affect behavior in different "sets" and "settings"[5]), our studies are confined to certain illicit drugs currently significant in international transactions—cocaine, opium, heroin, and several kinds of cannabis preparations, including marijuana, ganja, and hashish.[6] These illicit drugs appear to be the most significant socially, economically, politically, and internationally. Of the countries or regions reported in the UNRISD/UNU country-studies series, "designer drugs" (e.g., methamphetamines, methcathinone) appear to be significant only for Pakistan.

With the country studies and this integrative volume we have sought to make a responsible contribution to an understanding of what is happening with illicit coca, opium, and cannabis derivatives; why it is happening; and what kinds of public policy options may be open to address consequences judged to be both unfortunate and deleterious.

UNRISD initiated the country-study research project in February 1989. Shortly thereafter UNU became a joint sponsor. The Department of Political Science and the David M. Kennedy Center for International Studies at Brigham Young University have also tendered substantial support. The Center of International Studies at Princeton University provided office space and library facilities while I was a visiting research fellow there during the 1990–1991 academic year. Also, the United Nations Drug Control Programme (UNDCP) provided funding for an authors' conference and has given publication support.

The country-study project has been developed in three phases. The first, which consists of a literature survey and an annotated bibliography of 2,058 items, was completed in 1991.[7] The second consists of the individually authored country studies either now published or in various stages of preparation. The third is the integrative work represented by this volume.

Aside from conducting field, archival, and other research for the country studies, the authors met at two workshops. In May 1991, UNRISD hosted a two-day authors' workshop in Geneva for discussions concerning approach and format for the country studies. An authors' workshop underwritten by UNDCP was held in Vienna in August 1992 to discuss and refine the drafts.

For this volume, I am grateful to the country-study authors for their data, their insightful analyses, and their thoughtful consideration of policy options that may yet be open to the international community as it continues to struggle with psychoactive drugs, prohibition laws, and the socioeconomic and political effects of both. Three outside reviewers and other readers have helped me develop some of the arguments and refine the presentation as well as discard excess baggage. Although I cannot hold the readers responsible for the book's weaknesses, its strengths acknowledge an abundant debt. My special thanks to Susan Manning Sims, who read and critiqued the entire manuscript, and to Larry Borowsky, who made me say the same thing in fewer words.

LaMond Tullis

Notes

1. The respective authors are Elena Alvarez (Peru), Francisco Thoumi (Colombia), James Painter (Bolivia), María Celia Toro (Mexico), Anchalee Singhanetra-Renard (Thailand), Ronald Renard (Myanmar/Burma), Daniel Henning (Laos), Doris Buddenberg (Pakistan), and Richard Clayton and William Estep (Kentucky, U.S.).

2. As of this writing, the Bolivia, Colombia, and Mexico studies have been published by Lynne Rienner Publishers, the Kentucky and Myanmar/Burma studies are in press, and the remainder are in various draft stages.

3. Dharam Ghai, preface to LaMond Tullis, "Illicit Drug Taking and Prohibition Laws: Public Consequences and the Reform of Public Policy in the United States," UNRISD Discussion Paper, April 1991.

4. See, for example, Terrence C. Cox, et al., *Drugs and Drug Abuse: A Reference Text* (Toronto: Addiction Research Foundation, 1983) and Ernest L. Abel, *Drugs and Sex: A Bibliography* (Westport, Conn.: Greenwood Press, 1983).

5. See, for example, James M. Corry and Peter Cimbolic, *Drugs: Facts, Alternatives, Decisions* (Belmont, Calif.: Wadsworth Publishing Company, 1985) and Norman Zinberg, *Set and Setting: The Basis for Controlled Intoxicant Use* (New Haven, Conn.: Yale University Press, 1984).

6. An extensive sampling of the literature describing each of these drugs and their respective properties may be found in LaMond Tullis, *Handbook of Research on the Illicit Drug Traffic: Socioeconomic and Political Consequences* (Westport, Conn.: Greenwood Press, 1991), xvii–xxviii, 3–43.

7. Ibid., i–xxviii, 1–641.

Introduction

• • •

The woman was perhaps in her late twenties or early thirties. Nattily dressed in a sloppy leather jacket and faded blue jeans with holes in the knees and carrying a tattered leather suitcase, she stood in front of me at a foreign-exchange window in Geneva's international airport in July 1992. I wanted to exchange U.S. currency for Swiss francs. I had two $100 bills to change and a few more in reserve. I hoped she would have enough to get by, but I wondered. Her clothes could be bought at Goodwill Industries in my country for less than $25. And the suitcase? The latch appeared to be broken, requiring the case to be held together with two leather straps buckled at the top, near the handle. The young woman spoke in French but with a heavy Spanish accent.

I noticed her present her passport and another document to the teller. The man consulted his files and then said something to the woman, who lifted her case to the counter and began to undo the buckles. Strange, I thought. And I was in a hurry. But the other line was longer, so I stayed on.

The woman opened the case, revealing at least thirty stacks of U.S. bills. Each stack, perhaps ten to twelve centimeters high, was topped with a $100 bill. With the assistance of an automatic counting machine, the teller began to number the bills. It looked as though there would be a long delay. I queued up in the other line. Five minutes later, when I exchanged my two bills, the teller was still counting. When I passed by the exchange window fifteen minutes later, he was counting still.

Assuming each bill in each stack to be U.S. $100, and assuming the stacking rate to be about 150 bills/centimeter, I calculate the tattered and battered suitcase to have held approximately $5 million. Whose money? Who was the woman working for? What security arrangements attended her travels? Into whose account was the money going? What was the teller thinking? I know what I was thinking—that the teller was counting "dirty" money, at least money that someone wanted to hide. I guessed that it was Colombian drug money.

Whether Colombian drug money or not, by most estimates illicit-drug trafficking is one of the world's most substantial illegal money earners. Of the U.S. $1 trillion that some people think course the coffers of organized crime annually (almost as much as the U.S. annual federal budget),[1] organizations involved in the illicit-drug trade are thought to pick up around $300 billion.[2] Cut the figures in half. Allow the principal illicit-drug traffickers to collect only around $150 billion annually, an amount probably well within the mark of reality. In U.S. $100 bills, it would take 30,000 suitcases of the kind I observed at Geneva's foreign-exchange window to carry it.

There is no confirmation of any of these amounts, of course, and the oft-quoted figures may simply be repetitive hyperventilating. But between 1975 and 1989 the Colombian traffickers alone appear to have amassed from their cocaine trade between U.S. $39 and $66 billion, depending on assumptions about revenues and investment returns.[3] This amount comfortably relates to Colombia's reported 1991 GNP of U.S. $40 billion,[4] which gives some indication of the potential power of Colombia's drug traffickers vis-à-vis the state itself. A UN observer estimates that the retail value of illicit-drug trafficking exceeds the international trade in oil and is second only to the international weapons trade.[5] Another study shows that late-1980s consumer expenditures on illicit drugs in the United States alone likely exceeded the gross domestic product of eighty-eight different countries.[6] In whatever range, considerable money is paid globally for illegal drugs, quite certainly more than U.S. $100 billion annually, perhaps even the oft-quoted U.S. $300 billion. In response, new "mafias," in Michael Elliott's words, "have popped up as if the earth had been sown with dragons' teeth."[7]

Why do people produce and traffic illicit drugs? How are they able to do so? At first blush one might suppose that the large amount of money made in servicing consumer demand is solely responsible. Surely, money and the power that goes with it account for trafficking and much production. But other answers must be found in society. These relate to how a society is structured, how political power is accrued and wielded within it, how economic policy is applied, how the economy performs, and how resistant the cultural fabric is to the use of public office for private gain.

If answers to why people produce and traffic in illicit drugs are complex, why people *consume* those drugs and thereby help create an atmosphere of massive criminal behavior is an equally complex issue. Do consumers seek to rebel? To escape? To cope? To survive? To register resignation and defeat? To belong? Simply to stimulate pleasure sensors? Depending on place and circumstance, all queries may be answered "yes." Thus, the drive to consume drugs may have sociopsychological explanations, psychological/genetic explanations, or structural explanations dealing with supply and socioeconomic circumstances.

Unintended Consequences: Illegal Drugs and Drug Policies in Nine Countries does not pretend to answer all of these questions. It and the nine country-study reports from which it draws information do focus on the socioeconomic and political consequences of the illegal production, consumption, and trade of coca, cannabis, and opium derivatives. The orienting questions that have driven this research project since its inception remain intact: What illicit drug activities (including production, trafficking, and consumption) occur in major producer or transiting regions? What effects do those activities have on the regions' socioeconomic and political fabric? What drug-control and allied activities are being carried out to countermand those effects? To what degree are the activities successful? And what are the unintended consequences of their application? How might the deleterious effects of production, consumption, trade, and drug-control laws be mitigated?

The answers, insofar as answers are possible, are not to be found in any single discipline, method, theory, frame of reference, or value preference. Although country-study authors have approached the discussion from their own disciplines—economics, political science, political economy, history, environmental studies—they have tried to be sensitive to the need for cross-disciplinary integration. They have sought, through meetings, discussions, workshops, and seminars, to embrace an extremely complex subject realistically, both generally and in the countries studied—Peru, Bolivia, Colombia, Mexico, Pakistan, Thailand, Laos, Myanmar/Burma, and Kentucky, U.S.

Production, consumption, trade, and countervailing laws have all combined to impact peoples and countries around the world in ways that invite thoughtful analyses and a reconsideration of present illicit-drug policies. Accordingly, the purpose of this volume and associated country studies is to examine the socioeconomic and political consequences not only of the illicit-drug trade but also of drug-control policy instruments designed to thwart it.

Even though the production and consumption of illicit drugs have been part of the international scene for many decades, new and aggressive production and marketing efforts now affect the economic, social, personal, and political lives of millions of people. In this drama, cocaine and crack have been increasingly involved. That and the growing consumption of heroin (used more and more in conjunction with cocaine) are sure to present additional public-health and safety issues in the final five years of the twentieth century—and no doubt beyond.

The effects of massive illegal drug transactions range in some countries from economic prosperity and enhanced employment opportunities to environmental degradation, distorted economies and social structures, militarized societies, troubled health-care systems, subverted governments and national value systems, terrorized populations, and increasing human misery. Transnationally, the traffic affects international processes and institutions, as weak states and private actors become relatively more powerful. Thus, the huge volume and the vast sums of money and profits associated with the trade have imposed interesting, frequently serious, consequences on countries' political, economic, and social conditions as well as on their transnational relations.

Although understandable variations exist in estimates of production, consumption, and trade, on four matters there is substantial agreement: (1) the production of marijuana, heroin, and especially cocaine/crack is increasing;[8] (2) cocaine traffickers, now finding their supply substantially exceeding current market demand in the United States, are vigorously opening new markets in Canada, Great Britain, and the countries of Europe (with Spain and Italy serving as principal ports of entry); (3) the increasing supply of illicit drugs relative to current demand heightens violence as international drug syndicates and domestic gangs battle over market turf; and, (4) the policy instruments designed so far to curtail the demand for, suppress the traffic in, and control the supply of illicit drugs have not produced satisfactory results. Observers increasingly believe that successful solutions to drug problems, whether in countries that produce more than they consume (net producers or exporters) or in countries that consume more than they produce (net consumers), will be found only in international cooperation that addresses demand, supply, trade, and the policy instruments that make all three illegal.

Illicit drugs are a global phenomenon with transnational characteristics. Production and trafficking, and perhaps even some consumption of these drugs, may be understood in large part through the lens of a business enterprise. That the business is in most cases illegal simply evokes a mirror image of much that is normal. Suppliers (traffickers) identify a marketable product, give incentives to (or place sanctions upon) growers to ensure availability, pursue markets and market advantage by advertising and by outdoing (or undoing) the competition, stay ahead of legal obstacles through technological and product innovation, engage in domestic political processes as a powerful interest group, train and discipline employees, diversify economically, earn profits, and repatriate capital.

Small-time growers plant coca bushes in Peru, Bolivia, and elsewhere in Latin America. They cultivate opium poppies in Guatemala,

Mexico, Colombia, Lebanon, Afghanistan, Myanmar/Burma, Pakistan, Laos, Thailand, China, Khazikstan, Turkmenistan, and other countries. And business enterprises ranging from multinational syndicates to individual weekend farmers grow cannabis plants in virtually every nation on the planet. From these sources, domestic and transnational enterprises begin the task of refining, packaging, and shipping cocaine and heroin (and, at times, marijuana) to consumers worldwide. Petty merchants at home and abroad busily work to supply a sea of ready consumers, secure more customers, account for sales proceeds, and apply drug-law discipline to wayward souls, including those who may try to pilfer from the cash register or muscle in on protected market shares.

To a greater or lesser degree, countries across the globe have declared business transactions involving cocaine, heroin, and marijuana illegal. But when the transactions continued, drug control through law enforcement was expanded and upgraded. Law-enforcement efforts are directed at growers (eradicating their crops or offering them economic incentives to engage in normal economic activities), at traffickers (incarcerating them, confiscating their product at points of origin or international borders, and seizing their money and other assets), and at consumers (applying various measures, from social pressure, as practiced in the Netherlands, to mandatory jail or death, as in Malaysia). But growers still grow, traffickers still traffic, and consumers still consume—more so than ever before.

Successful business enterprises framed in illegality rouse the worst imaginable social and political outcomes. They infiltrate otherwise legitimate bureaucracies, buy public decisions, make alliances with terrorists, threaten or launch intimidating violent attacks on any who choose not to stand aside, create antistates wholly outside the rule of law, and contribute to sundry economic and social effects inimical to civilized life.

Lately there has been growing disillusionment with the effectiveness of drug-control efforts and increasing anxiety about the ills the drug trade spawns—vast criminal organizations that behave as enterprise capitalists unfettered not only by law or its enforcement but also by cultural standards that civilized society requires for its permanence. Thus, people have begun to speak of hallucinogenic drugs as part of a historical human condition that cannot be avoided, only controlled. The search is therefore on "reducing harm"—the harm done by drugs and by the prohibition laws designed to control them.

Unintended Consequences: Illegal Drugs and Drug Policies in Nine Countries explores the unfolding global drama and infers specific policy options for Bolivia and Colombia, countries that represent regions that produce and market illegal drugs. Bolivia specializes in growing coca, the agricultural precursor to cocaine, and Colombia specializes in marketing the product worldwide. Neither is afflicted by heavy consumption. But that could change. Examination of the two countries offers insights into what can and cannot be done about illegal drugs in developing or less developed countries; hence these countries receive greater emphasis here.

In the ensuing pages, I (1) examine the contexts in which drugs are illegal; (2) describe production, consumption, trafficking, and drug-control efforts in the nine countries studied; (3) analyze the effectiveness of drug-control laws in reducing demand and supply; (4) analyze some of the socioeconomic and political effects of production, consumption, trafficking, and efforts to control all three; and (5) discuss prescriptions—policy options and recommendations.

Notes

1. Russell Watson, "Death on the Spot," *Newsweek*, 13 December 1993, 18.

2. Raphael Francis Perl, "Congress and International Drug Policy," *Extensions* (A Journal of the Carl Albert Congressional Research and Studies Center [U.S.]), Fall 1993, 6–9.

3. Francisco Thoumi, *Political Economy and Illegal Drugs in Colombia* (Boulder, Colo.: Lynne Rienner Publishers, 1994), 183–195; 196–197.

4. World Bank, *World Development Report 1993* (New York: Oxford University Press, 1992), 238.

5. United Nations, Conference Room Paper No. 1, 13 October 1989, prepared for the Joint Meetings of the Committee for Programme and Co-ordination and the Administrative Committee on Co-ordination, 24th series, New York, 16–18 October 1989, no. 89–24360.

6. See LaMond Tullis, "Cocaine and Food: Likely Effects of a Burgeoning Transnational Industry on Food Production in Bolivia and Peru," in *Pursuing Food Security*, W. Ladd Hollist and F. LaMond Tullis, eds. (Boulder, Colo.: Lynne Rienner Publishers, 1987), 250.

7. Michael Elliott et al., "Global Mafia," *Newsweek*, 13 December 1993, 22.

8. Illustrative is information from *Latin America Weekly Report*, 11 August 1994, 354–355:

> Apart from a statistical squabble, this is what the various sources tell us about the way the South American drug business is evolving: The area devoted to coca plantations in Bolivia has increased by 1,200 hectares in the last year; The Bolivian industry is expanding downstream: In Chapare there are an estimated 10,000 "labs" producing basic paste, with a capacity of 350 to 400 kilos a day; coca cultivation in Colombia has moved from the Andean region towards the Orinoco and Amazon lowlands (60% is now located in Guaviare and Putumayo); the south of Ayacucho has become the key drug-trafficking centre in Peru: Colombian traffickers are financing the introduction of opium poppy; Venezuela is fast becoming a producer as well as a transit country: In July alone the army destroyed 330 hectares of coca, opium poppy and marijuana plantations in the far west of the country.

... 1 ...

Drugs, Illegality, and Crime

Legal drugs invoke pharmaceutical discussions about effects and side effects. Illegal drugs force examination of additional subjects, including where production, trafficking, and consumption are occurring and under what circumstances. Thus, a consideration of "drugs and crime" is a necessary prelude to considering everything else about illicit drugs.

Illegal drugs—whether produced, consumed, or trafficked—and crime walk hand in hand. This is so in part because of drug-control laws, in part because of some drugs' psychopharmacological properties (how they affect pleasure, motor, and mood sensors), and in part because of the nature of a given culture and society and how traffickers choose—or are permitted—to operate in such cultures and societies. Drug-control laws and illegal-drug consumption combine to create a worldwide black market in which awesome amounts of money are made and widespread criminal behavior occurs.

Applying and avoiding the law in relationship to addiction, abuse, and pleasure seeking from drugs' psychopharmacological properties appear to induce most drug-related criminal behavior. Of all criminal activity associated with the illegal-drug trade—from production and consumption to trafficking—trafficking is by far the most consequential because of the amount of underground money concentrated in relatively few hands and because of the way many traffickers choose to spend or invest it.[1]

Illegality

Some drugs are illegal by definition—national, state, and provincial legislatures and some dictatorships have so designated them. Among these are cocaine, heroin, various forms of cannabis, and many "designer drugs" such as methamphetamine. Producing, consuming, and trading these drugs are now illegal or are sharply curtailed in most countries, a position seconded by international conventions and multilateral treaties.[2] Efforts by law-enforcement agents to apply antidrug laws and by people in the illegal-drug business to avoid those laws create crimes—providing or consuming an illegal product, or illegally depriving, disrupting, or destroying people, property, and institutions in the process of servicing or prohibiting a market.

Were it not for the laws, the production, consumption, and trade of drugs would not be illegal and therefore not criminal. But crimes might still result. Drug-related crimes derive from more than simple legislative artifacts that parliaments may make and unmake according to their political will. Some addictive drugs (e.g., crack cocaine) have psychopharmacological properties that may induce violent behavior against children, spouses, the unborn, and random bystanders.[3] Even if drugs were legal, wholesalers might vie for markets and territory, spreading some of the violence and corruption that now accompany the illegal trade. Thus, whether from some drugs' psychopharmacological properties or from the fact that production, trafficking, and consumption are illegal and sometimes accompanied by marketing violence, crimes are committed. The large amount of money associated with producing, trading, consuming, and proscribing illicit drugs makes the magnitude of criminal behavior and its consequences of more than passing note.

What Is the Drugs-Crime Nexus?

In principal consuming areas such as North America and Western Europe, it is now almost popular to refer to a tripartite classification scheme of psychopharmacological effects, economic-compulsive drives, and systemic violence to identify the relationship of drugs to crime, particularly violent crime against people and property.[4] The psychopharmacological dimension, particularly with crack cocaine,[5] relates to people's becoming irrational, excited, agitated, impulsive, uncontrollably angry, and physically abusive, even to the point of committing murder. The economic-compulsive dimension is associated with criminal acts to obtain money for personal drug consumption (e.g., through burglaries and robberies). The systemic dimension relates to drug syndicates, associations, gangs, and smugglers protecting their product or turf from law-enforcement officials or from each other by whatever means necessary.

We should add a fourth dimension to this standard tripartite analysis of crime and drugs. This relates to police forces, militaries, drug-enforcement agents, border-patrol officers, judges, and politicians at all levels who either seek personal gain from public office or otherwise allow themselves to be corrupted by greed and rationalization. This part of the drugs-crime nexus is becoming more troublesome globally because personal resistance to underground money appears to be declining. For example, in mid-1994 tears were shed and recriminations made in Thailand as Thai legislators became enmeshed in U.S. drug charges.[6] Corporate and state drug-related crimes appear to be increasing globally because illicit-drug money finds "legitimate" havens and outlets in countries where administrative and political personnel are allied with the traffic. A few years ago it was Bolivia, then Panama. Now it is thought to be Haiti and perhaps more than one country in East Asia. No nation appears to be immune from this corruption-drugs relationship, not even the United States of America.[7] Let us call this the "corruption-criminality" connection, thereby creating a quadripartite classification—*psychopharmacological, economic-compulsive, systemic,* and *corruptive.*

With these categories in mind, let us consider the various ways in which criminality may be related to illicit drugs (aside from the simple fact that prohibition by definition criminalizes production, trade, and consumption).[8] Insofar as psychopharmacological connections exist (as, for example, with crack cocaine), the relationship is fairly straightforward. People consume crack cocaine, and they sometimes get agitated and violent and hurt others or themselves. Violence directed against others is usually termed criminal. However, not all drugs have violence-producing psychopharmacological effects. Indeed, the set and setting for drug taking may even contribute to a reduction in social violence. In the 1960s, for example, marijuana consumption in the United States and Western Europe was associated with subcultures that eschewed violence, particularly the violence of the Vietnam War. Love and peace became symbols not only of a drug subculture but of antiviolence.

In considering psychopharmacology and the criminality of violence directed toward others, one must keep in mind that drug *use* and drug *abuse* produce overhead consequences for society that are light years apart. Occasional consumption of cocaine or crack by a small fragment of a country's population likely produces few generalized social harms. Drug abuse by a substantial portion of a country's population—particularly of cocaine or crack—cannot be viewed in such benign terms.[9]

Regarding economic-compulsive relationships (people stealing in order to buy drugs), on the basis of empirical evidence hardly anyone dares assert definitive causal connections[10] except when crack is involved.[11] Some observers conclude that drug taking does not cause crime, particularly property crime, so much as it accelerates it, mostly among poor drug takers in countries whose criminal laws have driven up drug prices the most. "It's the high prices of drugs on the black market that create an incentive to property crime, writes Lana Harrison."[12] Thus, there likely exists a spurious relationship between illicit-drug use and property crime in the sense that both are often related to other causes. However, hardly anyone denies the accelerator effect of drugs on crime.

Some observers blame society for "structural conditions" (e.g., poverty) that push people into both crime and drugs[13] or observe that "deviant behaviors occur within the context of a general deviance syndrome"[14] (whatever the cause of that syndrome). Be that as it may, drug use, particularly drug abuse in across-the-board prohibition countries, increases and sustains criminal behavior. Money and addiction make more money and more drugs necessary.[15] Inasmuch as prices tend to be highest in prohibition countries with the most stringent laws, more money and probably more crime are required to service abuse or addiction there.

Criminality associated with systemic violence shifts our attention away from consumers to major, midsize, and even some small traffickers. There is a certain bravado associated with the lifestyle of major traffickers that makes systemic violence and violent risk taking an intrinsic part of the way they do business. This behavior is related to money and what major traffickers do with it. Aside from engaging in conspicuous consumption (e.g., private zoos in remote hamlets), making sanitized business investments in normal economies, and developing modern service-based regional strongholds (e.g., Khun Sa in Homong, Myanmar[16]), major and midsize traffickers frequently infiltrate and corrupt regional and national governments; make alliances with terrorist organizations or antistate groups; assassinate uncooperative people and murder unfortunate bystanders; intimidate judges, law-enforcement agents, and ordinary citizens; and work to create an antistate wholly outside the rule of any semblance of national law. Beyond that, their predations cheapen life, destroy families, and emasculate culture and social norms[17]—all in the name of making drugs available to ready consumers.

Petty street vendors are frequently far removed from such impacts, and we should allow that such a massive assault on civilized decency cannot necessarily be attributed to them. Nevertheless, it appears the isolated entrepreneurial streetcorner vendor is increasingly being replaced by network vendors ultimately tied to major and middle-ranking traffickers. Insofar as this is true, one would expect almost all trafficking to hasten processes of social disorganization. The assaults on government—even allowing that some governments may be worthy of assault and their laws appropriately subverted—create considerable social and economic overhead and institutional waste and debris, an effect particularly pronounced in countries enjoying a modicum of legitimate government and rule of law. Many people view most of these activities as criminal.

Many traffickers are masters at committing systemic violence and at corrupting public institutions and people. Police forces, judiciaries, military officers, politicians, people of all walks of life are known to subvert public honor for private gain. The perceived gravity of the corruptive-criminality connection is, of course, culturally specific; some cultures are more tolerant than others of private gains associated with public service. Nevertheless, it appears that drug barons have characteristically exceeded the norm that divides honor from dishonor in virtually every country in which they have operated, even bringing presidents and military commanders into their influence, if not employ (e.g., in Bolivia, 1980–1982; in Haiti until late 1994).

Crimes by Drug Abusers

Various criminal mixes of the above categories—psychopharmacological, economic-compulsive, systemic, corruptive—are found among drug abusers throughout the world, with most of the evidence focusing on the economic-compulsive category—that is, drug abuse associated with robberies, thefts, burglaries, and so forth—or, in the case of crack cocaine abusers, violence against others, including the unborn.[18] In the economic-compulsive category there are wide variations throughout the world. Cultural, social, and economic differences may account for some of those variations.

In Germany, for example, and perhaps in most of Western Europe, not much crime appears to be associated with economic compulsion. Perhaps this may be explained because Germans prefer heroin (ultimately a sedative) and are entitled to social welfare and medical support at public expense, thereby enabling them to use personal earnings to support their addiction and reducing the need for criminal incomes. Most crimes that German heroin addicts do commit, when they feel compelled to commit them, are "petty"—shoplifting, burglary, robbery—not the kind of violent criminal activity characteristic of drug addicts, for example, in the United States.[19] Moreover, in Germany, heroin addicts tend not to be traffickers involved in systemic crimes of violence. The same can be said of illegal drug users in Australia, where there is little evidence that a drug-consumption/crime nexus exists except with respect to petty crime.[20]

In the Netherlands, particularly in Amsterdam, which is noted for its liberal social-welfare and drug policies (welfare support is relatively high; drug costs are low), a close connection between illegal drug use and criminality is observed. However, the connection is not psychopharmacological or economic-compulsive so much as it is driven by social conditions associated with drug taking. On the whole, these produce a pretty benign form of criminality.[21] By contrast, chronic users in New York City and Liverpool are much more prone to predatory crime.[22]

In China, drug trafficking, drug abuse, and drug-related crimes have grown exponentially since the early 1980s.[23] The overland trafficking out of the Golden Triangle through China to international market connections (mostly in Hong Kong) has spilled over to local consumers. China's policy of "killing the chicken to frighten the monkey"[24] has driven up illegal-drug prices to the point where the country's new generation of addicts resorts to extensive property crime to obtain its drug-consumption money.[25]

Many consumers in principal illicit-drug-producing countries—from the street urchins of Peru recently addicted to *bazuco*[26] to the old opium consumers in the highlands of Laos, Burma, and Thailand who still enjoy their favorite smoke or chew—earn their drug money in the employ of traffickers. At multiple stages along the route of a labor-intensive enterprise, people take their pay in illegal drugs, consuming a part, selling a part. Some would call this criminal activity. Others would observe that desperate people, living literally on the margin of existence, simply try to stay alive by selling their services.

Since perhaps 1990, new forms of criminal activity among drug consumers have been noted, certainly in the United States but also in other countries. These activities relate to initiation ceremonies and turf-defense networks associated with youth gangs.[27] Many social scientists have concluded that youth gangs have become a substitute for family, that as real families disintegrate through parental failures, cultural breakdown, or economically imposed hardships, children look for—indeed, desperately seek—alternative forms of association. Youth gangs have become family for street urchins in Lima, São Paulo, Bangkok, Los Angeles, and New York. Gangs that act as pseudo-families are certainly not new; Charles Dickens noted this phenomenon in nineteenth-century England.[28] At that time, such "families" turned to petty theft to survive. Today they frequently turn to drugs, violence (sometimes even homicide), and major theft as ritualized ceremonies of belonging and obligation that have little to do with real issues of temporal survival but a lot to do with gaining a sense of community in disintegrating societies.

Gangs and drugs are therefore related, but perhaps in the spurious way that economic compulsion and drugs are related—a straight causal connection does not always exist. Nevertheless, when drugs and gangs combine, one can be virtually certain that criminal behavior will also be found. Further, criminal activity becomes more pronounced in communities and nations that offer people more rhetoric than substance to drive their hopes and life's ambitions and that run low on coercive capabilities.

For whatever reason people abuse drugs (through chronic use and/or addiction), the criminality associated with that abuse drives an internationally integrated enterprise that involves growers and, usually, major traffickers. Absent consumers, no growers or traffickers would surface. Consumers, least thought of as criminals (the extent of their criminality is relatively small compared to that of traffickers), nevertheless constitute the critical element in a business that is criminal by definition and is associated with social and political externalities viewed as being criminal. Regardless of what drives consumers, they—and the criminalizing laws—are the principal engines that keep drug-related crime alive and well.

Crimes by Traffickers

Among drug abusers, the high correlation between drug use and crime is in part definitional (e.g., "taking illegal drugs is a crime"), in part direct (e.g., crack cocaine causes violent behavior), in part causally ambiguous (e.g., whether drug taking causes economic-compulsive crime or prior criminality causes drug taking), and in part associational (e.g., youth gangs). Among traffickers, however, the drugs-crime connection is quite straightforward. Though social scientists disagree over why people are drawn into trafficking, there is no argument that a drugs-crime nexus exists among people so engaged. The draw is money, and the pursuit of it—especially among major traffickers pushing cocaine and heroin—evokes every criminal act that falls within the analytical categories discussed above (i.e., psychopharmacological, economic-compulsive, systemic, and corruptive), with the preponderance of the direct impact occurring in the systemic and corruptive categories.

Even allowing for the marijuana industry, more decentralized and less prone to syndication and violence, in many geographical areas there is more money to be made in illegal drugs than in any other available pursuit, despite the risk and loss factors associated with an illegal trade. Drug money buys the peasant a new quality of life, one to be defended at all costs. At the other end of the spectrum, it also provides the wherewithal for some terrorist groups to prosecute political demands (e.g., Peru's Sendero Luminoso [Shining Path]). Both political terrorists and major traffickers in cocaine and heroin are world-class criminals who deprive, hurt, maim, and destroy out of business necessity or political ambition. Most people consider this to be criminal, and much of the criminality is funded by profits from illegal drugs.

Traffickers' criminality is thus linked to the third (systemic violence) and fourth (corruptive) categories, as is their related criminal support system, which focuses on acquiring, securing, laundering, and safely guarding money and getting and preserving positions of power. Traffickers, not consumers, commit most drug-related homicides.[29] Traffickers, not consumers, use the billions at their command to attempt—largely successfully—to corrupt, subvert, or eliminate institutions and people who stand in their way. In Colombia, for example, the value of a human life is U.S. $13, the going price for a hired killer (*sicario*) to snuff it out. The going value of an entire political system may be less than the value of a country's illegal-drug traffic, as Bolivia discovered in the early 1980s when the narco-barons took it over[30] and in 1994 when still another of its past presidents was indicted on charges of drug running while in office.[31]

A major international news magazine is alarmed at the prospects.[32] In the United States, murder, robbery, and assault reached record levels in 1980 and then began a cyclical decline (other peaks occurred in 1850, 1900, and 1960). "Then," as Ted Robert Gurr notes, "fueled by the crack cocaine epidemic, violent crime climbed back up: A new murder record was set in 1992, even though the total numbers of youths—the cohort most associated with crime—was dropping."[33] There has been an increase in random murder, in the depreciation of life, in general assaults on people's dignity. Much of this has been fueled by criminal drug organizations battling for markets and turf, particularly in the United States's inner cities. The spillover effect even has children killing children.

> No single event has contributed more to the recent contagion of violence than the wide availability of crack cocaine in American cities by the mid-to-late 1980s. It inspired the explosive growth of gangs, which became surrogate families to the emotionally wounded children of desolate communities. The lure of unimaginable wealth attracted many of the best, brightest, most enterprising and most charismatic young men to the drug trade—and also those who looked up to them. The drug itself prompted some to kill without remorse while high and made others desperate enough to do anything to find money for the next hit. Finally, the drug profits fueled a prodigious arms race on America's streets; that led competitors to solidify markets or settle differences with an awesome toll in bloodshed.[34]

The most extensive varieties of drug-related violence and large-scale criminal behavior—usually part of the systemic dimension—are attached to major drug-distribution networks, as traffickers and smugglers jockey to push their wares. This level of criminality is more widespread in areas where formal and informal social controls are absent or ineffective, where traditionally high rates of interpersonal violence exist, and where large numbers of people are economically disadvantaged.[35] Petty traffickers who, of themselves, may well shun systemic violence are soon caught in the spider's web of large-scale turf battles. They either join and become part of the enterprise, drop out, move on, or are eliminated.

Criminality does not end with these more sensational and personal acts of depriving, hurting, maiming, and destroying. Even the "benign" repatriation of drug traffickers' capital through illegal money laundering—whether this entails investment in legitimate enterprise or disbursement to cover business debts in the underground economy—contributes to criminality. Beyond that, drug traffickers corrupt the state or individuals who run it in order to improve product movement and access to intelligence, protect persons and property, allow for easier repatriation of money, and build respectability through political influence. Corruptive criminality is accordingly a second major hallmark of major and middle-ranking traffickers and perhaps of a number of lesser ones as well.

Experience bred in conflict has honed leadership and discipline among criminal organizations worldwide. The new organizations are much more sophisticated than the old ones of the Sicilian mafia or Medellín "cartel" type. One international news magazine fears they have become the "global mafia," a new monolithic threat capable of invoking fears such as those stirred up by East-West rhetoric about communism and capitalism,[36] criminal conspiracies whose combined intelligence, firepower, and will for violence exceed the capacity of some governments to restrain or counter them.

Some of these groups, flushed with money from the drug trade, have sufficient resources to buy nuclear weapons. Can they get them? The U.S. CIA allows for that possibility and takes note of missing weapons-grade plutonium from the former Soviet republics.[37] In August 1994 the press gave wide coverage to a case in which weapons-grade plutonium, presumably from the former USSR, had turned up in Germany in the hands of criminal elements. More recently, Seymour M. Hersh argued that organized crime has Russia much more firmly in grasp than ever reported and that the government's control over its nuclear weapons and materials has been seriously eroded.[38] Can New York, London, or Tokyo be held hostage? At some point, yes. Illegal drugs—their production, trade, consumption, and control—appear to be contributing to this possibility. You can buy anything in this world with enough money and enough time.

The new organized criminals have become so strong and so wealthy partly as a consequence of three global changes or trends that have brought unparalleled prosperity to the world in the wake of a reduction in international trade barriers. These positive, helpful global changes are (1) the development of computer and communications technology and their dissemination worldwide; (2) the collapse of communism; and (3) the declining significance of national borders around the globe. The opportunities for progress created by these three developments have contributed to—indeed, facilitated— the meteoric rise in the number of international criminals. The enormous profits from the illicit-drug trade and other smuggling operations now bankroll the most efficient crime organizations the world has probably ever seen.[39]

The criminal adoption of high-tech computer and communications technology worldwide—including fax machines, cellular telephones, and encryption techniques that would make the German Enigma Machine of World War II[40] look like child's play—has facilitated the expansion of global trade and the protection of industrial secrets. Multinationals, beholden to no country, quickly find and exploit locations of comparative advantage, protecting their secrets from the prying eyes of competitors and governments. Money moves from country to country in unprecedented amounts over "wires" (some say up to U.S. $1 billion per day in crime money alone[41]), through satellites, and via underground cables.

Such technology creates a safe, near foolproof way for drug traffickers needing to launder vast quantities of money. New cellular phones each week (to hamper call tracing), funds bounced through a dozen banks in less than a day, and an electronic collection system that aggregates diverse deposits to a single source in ways virtually impossible to trace—this is a perfect formula for the clandestine transactions that constitute the calling cards of the big-time illicit-drug traffickers.[42] By the same devices, major traffickers buy arms, hire paramilitary personnel, invest in legitimate businesses worldwide, pay bribes, and collect on their political capital.[43]

The collapse of communism,[44] beginning in 1989, has also facilitated organized crime and has been an unprecedented boon to drug traffickers, who must smuggle both product and cash across national borders. For one thing, people in Eastern Europe and the republics of the former USSR have suddenly found that the profit motive is not a cardinal sin. However, lacking a tradition of both moral and institutional restraint on capitalism's tendencies to run amok, some people pursue quick fixes and profits, and, in this, drug trafficking is a highly attractive option.

Weak governments and porous borders facilitate the drug traffickers in Eastern Europe and former Soviet republics. Governments have neither the political will nor institutional capability to secure their borders against the tenacious efforts of drug traffickers and other smugglers. In Iron Curtain times, traffic was light, almost everything was searched, and public officials seemed not to mind heaping inconveniences, indignities, and injustices upon anyone's person or product, drug merchants included. But all that has now changed. Communist laws that once deterred do so no longer. Being an expression of morally and economically bankrupt regimes, they lack legitimacy. Moreover, the new regimes are trying to encourage, not discourage, trade and investment and consequently have cut down on border inspections.

Not surprisingly, the fact that there are no laws against money laundering, fraud, or organized crime on the books in many ex-communist countries is helpful to anyone looking for a quick profit, including some Russian emigrés returning to countries where much activity that is criminal in any real sense of the word is technically legal.[45] Fortunes are being made, and a lot of common people feel left out. The situation is a ready magnet for the less scrupulous and the more success-at-any-cost[46] categories in which drug smugglers excel.

Aside from technology and the collapse of communism, a third contemporary international factor facilitating drug traffickers' work is the declining significance of national borders worldwide. With few exceptions (Cubans, Chinese, North Koreans, and perhaps Vietnamese), most people have political license to exit their homelands at their pleasure. Those who have virtually unfettered travel privileges frequently carry whatever they desire without much fear of detection, even granting that some nationals are targeted for unusual observation (e.g., Nigerians entering the United States because of their past courier services to East Asian heroin traffickers).[47] Moreover, it is increasingly easy to transship illegal products through unsuspecting countries, disguising both product and provenance. Mexico is a large transshipment country for South American cocaine destined for the U.S. market.[48] Likewise, Russia is becoming an important transshipment country for heroin originating in the Golden Crescent (Afghanistan and Pakistan, principally) and headed for Western Europe. Russia has even taken on some notoriety regarding cocaine. A ton of the product from Colombia, packaged to look like canned meat destined for Finland, was recently seized in St. Petersburg.[49] Illegal drugs, aliens, and prostitutes all move relatively easily across scores of national borders. Thus, the substantial decline of border significance in Western Europe since 1992 has opened the whole region to ready and quick movement of products, including cocaine, heroin, marijuana, and methamphetamines.

Beyond that region, observers do not marvel that Estonia, with no major raw materials of its own, has become the world's sixth largest copper exporter—most of it contraband.[50] German stolen-car rings, prostitution rackets, drug networks, arms caches, people smuggling, and the use of compliance techniques (learned from the CIA and KGB) on suppliers and distributors—these are some of the consequences of the declining significance of national borders worldwide. In the Western Hemisphere, the North American Free Trade Agreement (NAFTA) and other trade-liberalization agreements will make smuggling easier than ever and will probably contribute to a continuing decline in the wholesale price of cocaine and heroin in the U.S. market.

Being efficient and intelligent and having an eye to the long term, drug traffickers and their organizations continuously seek to diversify their investments and find new markets. They invest in legitimate business whenever they can. High-rise apartments in Miami and the French Riviera are said to be popular. Banks in Panama and the Cayman Islands, real estate everywhere, cattle ranches in the far reaches of Colombia—these are just some of the places to which sanitized underground money finds its way.

Import-export businesses help with money laundering, itself facilitated by banks in the Baltic republics and elsewhere that ask no questions and readily convert funds to tradable international bills. This has been a fortuitous circumstance for drug traffickers, as traditional hot-money depositories in countries such as Switzerland and Luxembourg have been forced to tighten their regulations.

As for new markets, Eastern Europe has beckoned. People long under the yoke of a bureaucracy that preached but hardly practiced restraint on passions and appetites have adopted everything Western. This, coupled with the socioeconomic and sociopsychological trauma of the transition to capitalism, has unfortunately, contributed to illicit-drug taking. In order to service this new market, they have developed ports of entry for their cocaine through Spain and Italy, which they judge to be especially lax in maritime border security.[51]

New technology that aids clandestine activity and conceals the fruits of its labor, the collapse of communism, and the declining significance of national borders worldwide have combined with the developed world's apparently insatiable appetite for drugs, especially cocaine, to produce an interesting by-product—the most efficient crime organizations in history. All this has increased global criminality probably by several orders of magnitude, especially in areas noted for systemic violence and corruption.

Crimes by Producers

The drugs-crime nexus among producers (particularly growers of the opium poppy and coca bush) and petty refiners differs from those of consumers and traffickers. More than any other group, these individuals are driven by economic imperatives little appreciated by the world's middle classes and elite.

The principal drug-growing countries or regions (e.g., Peru, Bolivia, Mexico, Afghanistan, Myanmar/Burma, Laos) and drug-refining countries (e.g., Pakistan, Thailand, Colombia) are among the most impoverished and economically stagnant on the planet, making their citizens prone to involvement in the illicit-drug business. The range of economic-growth opportunities for such citizens is frequently highly constricted. In some places, increasing population density on fixed land resources continues to negatively impact both people's well-being and their environment.[52] Also, national income-distribution indicators show a heavy urban bias.[53] The peasants naturally look for the best options open to them, frequently gravitating to informal or underground economies,[54] including illegal drugs.

In many areas—at least during start-up times—illegal-drug growers can make from ten to fifty times more in provisioning the illegal-drug market than they can in any other agricultural pursuit.[55] Accordingly, either in seeking better opportunities or out of sheer economic desperation, growers and the urban poor who aspire to be growers migrate to regions both isolated and propitious to cultivate —sometimes after first uprooting traditional crops—coca, opium, and cannabis for local and international drug-consumption markets. Poverty and the absence of alternative income pursuits therefore contribute to criminal involvement in the drug trade.

Sometimes the growers' search for new opportunities is facilitated by mainstream development strategies and institutions (both in their success and in their failure at the macroeconomic level). At other times economic imperatives, some of which may be associated with macroeconomic conditions brought on by recession, adjustment programs, and changed economic models (e.g., liberalization), are contributing factors. As for political imperatives, some are associated with regional insurgent or terrorist groups who use drug money to finance their operations (e.g., Sendero Luminoso in Peru). In the latter case it must be noted that growers, especially in Peru's Upper Huallaga Valley and regions of Myanmar once controlled by Khun Sa, are "ordered" to grow drug crops, for which economic returns may be lower than they once were. Insurgent guerrillas or terrorist groups appropriate much of the surplus for their own operations, perpetuating rural poverty along with drug production.

Illustrations

Traffickers

Because the most consequential criminality is associated with traffickers, specific mention of several groups is warranted.[56] Early in the current drug-use wave, much illegal-drug distribution was akin to a cottage industry—small-time traffickers, including tourists, picking up a few hundred grams of heroin or cocaine or a kilo of marijuana from a producer and distributing the product directly to casual but trusted contacts and personal friends, who in turn passed along small amounts, some of it for financial gain. Some traffic is still carried out that way. However, trafficking is increasingly organized, particularly at the production, wholesale, and middleman levels, pronouncedly so for cocaine and heroin (less so for marijuana). This appears to have pushed most small-time dealers into strictly retail street sales. Even here there is evidence that organization is taking place, at least in the United States; isolated cottage-industry street vendors who buy from a wholesaler and then peddle their wares may be in decline as more elaborate distribution networks supplant them. For example, some dealers now use children as fronts in order to take advantage of lenient juvenile crime laws that often apply even to young people heavily and purposefully engaged in adult crimes.[57]

Given the nearly universal illegality of trafficking in drugs, it is understandable that the descriptor for organized drug groups is organized crime. It is difficult to imagine any organized criminal group not having at least a portion of its operations dedicated to drug trafficking; the income is enormous, and until recently prospects for additional income have been staggering. Elaborate organizations are by no means new. Some large, vertically integrated, multinational, illicit-drug-distribution organizations existed as early as the 1930s. For example, the French Connection (between refiners and traffickers headquartered in Marseilles and opium growers in Turkey) supplied heroin to U.S. addicts from the 1930s until 1973, when an international law-enforcement effort not only destroyed the French laboratories but ultimately put Turkish opium growers out of business.[58] The resulting shortage of heroin enabled Mexican, Pakistani, and Asian traffickers to penetrate the U.S. market as well as to increase production to cover supply shortages elsewhere.

Whereas earlier drug-trafficking groups were put out of business by law-enforcement efforts or eclipsed by later comers—there being no shortage of people willing to organize to meet market demand—the old Sicilian mafia lives on. Drug-dealing branches, damaged from time to time, nevertheless are highly effective, particularly in the heroin market, where they control a worldwide network. The Sicilian mafia is also trying to carve out territorial control for itself in several cocaine markets.[59]

A good many later comers to the illegal-drug trade are also alive and well: the Chinese Triads,[60] which are beginning to replace traditional organized crime networks in the Asian heroin market;[61] the Mexican mafia, which specializes in cocaine, marijuana, and Mexican heroin;[62] the Colombian Cali cocaine syndicate, which, although somewhat loosely structured, nevertheless exports discriminate violence—as opposed to the now-defunct Medellín's *in*discriminate violence—along with its product and efficient organization wherever it operates;[63] the Japanese Yakuza, which are now pushing narcotics (principally heroin), with networks in Hawaii and the western United States; the Jamaican Posses, who have a high propensity for violence and traffic in large volumes of drugs (wholesale and retail) and firearms throughout the United States and the Caribbean;[64] and, strictly within the United States, the Aryan Brotherhood and the Texas syndicate,[65] along with additional statewide and many small regional groups. All these later comers to the illegal-drug scene are increasingly gravitating to sophisticated organization and distribution techniques, using all the high technology available to law-enforcement agencies as a protective countermeasure to increasingly refined law-enforcement efforts.[66]

North America, as a consuming society, appears to be well laced with organized traffickers, both large and small. Heavy consuming societies elsewhere also appear to be undergoing increasing tendencies toward drug-traffic organization. One encounters references to Australia, where the Chinese Triads are setting up their heroin network,[67] to the United Kingdom, where the Triads are also thought to be at work,[68] to Spain and Italy, where the Colombians have established "ports of entry" for the rest of Europe and work in collaboration with conventional Italian mafiosi,[69] to Holland, where pushers in Amsterdam's booming drug market now offer free home delivery; and to the former Soviet Union, whose own peculiar regime of denial and forceful "curtain" vis-à-vis unwanted Western entrants were nevertheless no match for determined drug-trafficking organizations, even before the Soviet Union's economic crises weakened its internal control.

Aside from the trafficking organizations that extend into or are based in principal consumer countries, evidence of substantial organized production and marketing networks exists for most of the producer or transiting countries not discussed above—such as Peru, Bolivia, Myanmar/Burma, Pakistan, Afghanistan, Thailand, and Laos.

Sophisticated organizations either have existed or appear to be crop-ping up in countries peripheral to the drug trade—Cuba, Honduras, Venezuela, Brazil, the Bahamas, Paraguay, Costa Rica, Nigeria, Turkey, Canada, Turks and Caicos Islands, Panama, Bulgaria, El Sal-vador, Argentina, Nicaragua, and Haiti.

A frequent query is whether terrorist or insurgent groups, to fi-nance their operations, to prosecute an ideological position, to gain political support, or to undermine an existing government, are really allied with drug-trafficking organizations—or whether the organiza-tions themselves are involved in terrorist activities. This seems par-ticularly important to sort out, given that many governments have long argued that such links and activities do indeed exist. A number of terrorist or insurgent organizations deal in drugs for pragmatic reasons, regardless of whatever else drives them.[70] Several, particu-larly in the coca-growing regions of South America, support the co-caine trade to bolster political positions and to acquire operating funds, even though they may be ideologically opposed to the drug trade itself.

The best example of this latter variety is the fearsome Sendero Luminoso in Peru, only partially defanged since Peruvian security forces captured its maximum leader, Amibael Guzmán, in 1992.[71] This band of guerrillas entered the Upper Huallaga Valley, Peru's principal coca-growing region, as early as 1984 and successfully turned regional opinion against a U.S.-backed coca-eradication pro-gram into a campaign of antigovernment violence. In the process, the guerrillas gained something of a sanctuary and substantial peas-ant support. It is of considerable interest that whenever Sendero Lu-minoso took over a village, it cleaned up streets, improved public services, and imposed a bloody but effective brand of justice in a re-gion that the central Peruvian government, as far as municipal ser-vices and public administration were concerned, had largely aban-doned. The guerrillas, by protecting the peasants, facilitated the production of drugs for sale but prohibited drug use in the areas they controlled.

Colombian political terrorists are thought to have financed much of their operations through the drug trade, which caused some "conventional" drug barons to explode in retribution.[72] "Drug terrorism" by the Medellín syndicate followed in a futile effort to find a secure position for itself in Colombian society.[73] Colombia has had a long wave of political terrorism, beginning in the 1940s and continuing to the present—*La Violencia.* But in its early manifesta-tions it was a rural phenomenon that left the cities largely unscathed. Today's drug-related variety has impacted Colombia's inner political sanctuaries, a situation perhaps on hold since the death of Pablo Escobar, although some outside observers doubt it.[74] An Ecuadorian terrorist group, said to be working in coordination with groups in Colombia and Peru, also reportedly has cooperated with regional drug traffickers.[75] At least one Colombian drug syndicate armed Bolivian peasants in an effort to keep coca producers operating[76] and even paid Colombian rebel groups, such as M-19 guerrillas, to protect syndicate laboratories and to eliminate domestic opposition.[77]

Separatist terrorists in Sri Lanka are said to have become engaged in drug traffic in order to finance their arms and ammunition purchases.[78] The U.S.-supported contras in Central America were repeatedly accused of linking with drug traffickers in order to supplement their U.S. subsidies,[79] just as the rebels of Afghanistan did during the Soviet Union's occupation of their homeland.[80] A not-so-ideologically motivated terrorist group has protected the new surge of opium poppy growing in western Guatemala.[81]

Some drug-financed insurgent groups, particularly in Myanmar/Burma, are involved in a civil war, although a determined Burmese military offensive seems finally to have cornered the fabled Khun Sa. However, it is unlikely that his fall—if he falls—will have much impact on the Golden Triangle's booming opium production.[82] Some fear that the enormous profits from the drug trade will attract terrorist groups into the principal consuming countries, such as the United States. Thus, there is concern that the drug/terrorism connection will increasingly encourage such groups to force agendas on governments, destabilize democracies, spawn anarchy, and export revolution.[83] Those fears notwithstanding, most drug-related violence in the principal consuming countries still seems to be conducted among and between drug organizations and pushers as they struggle for market shares and experience heightened internal "leadership challenges" within their ranks. The better organized and, perhaps, more vertically integrated a group is, the more likely it is to be able to prosecute its interests vigorously—particularly when societies take strong countermeasures to protect their own affairs.

These trafficker activities must be cast against the national political fabric if their consequences are to be understood. Where political institutions are relatively strong, traffickers appear to exert a troubling but not strongly disrupting influence on national life, although considerable disruption can occur locally, as in U.S. inner cities. In institutionally weak countries such as Colombia, Peru, Afghanistan, and Myanmar/Burma, however, drug traffickers take center stage and impose a struggle for a nation's institutional life, for discrete subnational territory, and for control over the lives of many citizens. It therefore appears that those who can organize and fund the activity of crime in institutionally weak states enjoy the most power. The drug trade has found near perfect homes around the planet.[84]

The cocaine syndicates seem to be the most efficient and profitable criminal organizations. However, this may derive not so much from impressive marketing organization (the heroin groups likely get the nod here) as from the increased global demand for cocaine. Moreover, owing to accidents of history and geography, cocaine production is currently relatively localized in Colombia, Peru, and Bolivia, not spread throughout the world.[85] Vertical integration is therefore more possible, and control, even from "loose cartels," is more easily accomplished. Should the demand for cocaine subside, Colombia's syndicates—their profits notwithstanding—would fall on abundantly hard times. In the meantime, however, they are strong enough to be more than just a troubling influence on Colombia's national life.

Marijuana traffickers are the least globally organized (even though marijuana is more widely used), a fact associated with marijuana's worldwide production pattern ("anybody can grow it anywhere") and with what looks to be marijuana traffickers' relatively reduced power against and threat to societies that have criminalized their work.

Drug demand produced the drug marketers; antidrug laws turned them into national and international criminals who have copied the behavior of age-old criminal organizations. The social, economic, and political havoc they have heaped on producer and consumer societies has few parallels; in the process, their chiefs and numerous subalterns have become fabulously rich. Drug organizations' success lies partly in the relative failure of drug-control policies intended to cripple their abilities and incapacitate their criminal offshoots. Some traffickers are caught (e.g., Pablo Escobar), and some of their organizations are crippled or put out of business. However, drug traffickers are like the fabled Greek Hydra, whose capacity for replenishing severed heads has long captured the imagination.

Every country with significant production and consumption of illegal drugs has its array of traffickers. As long as significant international market demand exists and as long as criminalizing laws remain in place, it seems inevitable that the countries will continue to have an abundance of traffickers and numerous pretenders to the throne standing just offstage, all of them criminals in fact or criminals in the making.

Producers

Given the economic imperatives, with some significant periodic and regional exceptions,[86] and given a continuing buoyant international market demand, producers have generally been involved in a rapid-growth industry. On the whole, growers and small-time cottage-industry processors have reaped considerable benefits from the illegal-drug trade because some of the vast income that major traffickers accrue has spilled over to them. At the producer level, the illicit-drug industry is labor intensive, decentralized, growth-pole oriented, cottage-industry promoting, and foreign-exchange earning—desirable features of rural development in economically stagnating areas. Even under illicit marketing conditions, the drug traffic heavily infuses capital into backwater areas, turning frontier towns into regional shopping centers and improving employment at many levels.[87]

Income linkages develop among the lower classes, spreading the drug trade's benefits throughout many rural societies. For example, food produced in South America's Andean villages finds its way into coca-growing regions in exchange for money, coca, and cocaine. Impoverished hamlets thereby become commercial providers of the foodstuffs required for the specialized coca-growing to continue. While the "caloric exchange ratio"—that is, the ratio of food exported to benefits received—is relatively exploitative of the highland peasants,[88] it appears to be less than the alternative exploitation that highlanders have historically suffered. In any event, villagers now engage in the trade with abandon.

This array of economic benefits that comes from supplying an international market has become quite substantial in some areas. If the benefits originated in a legitimate economic development model, the world would herald them as a positive sign of progress and improvement in the lesser-developed regions of countries such as Peru, Bolivia, Colombia, Mexico, Myanmar/Burma, Guatemala, Jamaica, Thailand, Laos, Afghanistan, Pakistan, and Lebanon. Although the income source is criticized, several million "common" people heretofore marginalized from their countries' national societies, economies, and polities have benefited from international illegal-drug sales. They have earned more money, experienced more social mobility, and exercised more power over their destiny and that of their children than perhaps at any time in this century.

That is a considerable motivation under ordinary times. But these times have not been ordinary. With the winding down of the socialist engine of development and a relaxation in East-West struggles, some of the countries where the world's illegal drugs are grown have begun to experiment with new growth models. The most popular has derived from neoclassical economics and has called for major macro-restructuring of economies—removal of budgetary deficits, letting the national currency float on the world market, rationalizing the tax base, ceasing food subsidies, massively cutting inflation, extensively privatizing the economy. In the long term, in some countries these procedures have shown promise at the macro level—GNP has grown, international trade has increased, investments are being made for the long term in the domestic economy, and so forth. However, in the short run (and perhaps the medium run and conceivably the long term also, absent positive public policy) this "medicine" for ailing capitalist and ex-socialist countries in many instances has massively constricted economies, worsened the distribution of national incomes, and placed tens of millions of people's economic well-being at risk.[89] This has driven a lot of people into underground economies; one of the most flourishing is illegal drugs.

The political overtones have been interesting. For example, it has been said that the coca trade saved Bolivia from internal explosion as its economy contracted from the mid-1980s, throwing hundreds of thousands of people out of work. Had miners, unemployed students, and white-collar government workers just out of a job not had coca growing to turn to, they could easily have resorted to the violence so prevalent elsewhere when these transformations occur. Up to 20 percent of Bolivia's real GNP is related to illegal drugs.

Peru was not so lucky. Although a lot of Peruvians turned to growing illegal-drug crops and entered other kinds of illegal economies, the general economic mess left by the Alán García regime, the continuing relative tenacity of Sendero Luminoso, and the inability of the current Alberto Fujimori government to reconcile peace, nondemocratic government, and international respectability have conspired to make life for probably a majority of Peruvians a continuing challenge.

There are downsides for producers, of course. Illegal drugs have all the trappings of a boom-and-bust economy, just as do other forms of contraband (e.g., Colombian emeralds and African animal products) and sugar, coffee, tobacco, and military arms, all of which depend on consumer whims and governmental controls. Some coca-growing regions have already experienced severe economic depression as production expanded or as traffickers altered their purchasing habits, either out of political necessity or marketing preference. Moreover, being small cogs in a large trade, growers are sometimes caught in political dilemmas in which their profit margins are squeezed, making them eager candidates for cultivation of *legal* crops. But regional political overlords—themselves in the drug business—prevent them from doing so.

There are other downsides, too. No environmental safety standards accompany the use of highly toxic chemicals in refining. The skin from the legs of some Peruvian *pisadores* (people who use their bare feet to stomp a mixture of coca leaves and petrochemicals to release cocaine alkaloids) has fallen off like skin from a boiled tomato. Some children are becoming addicted to drugs their parents produce. In some areas institutionalized terror has been replaced by an even more pernicious brand of insurgent terror. But the economic imperative lives on. Social and political disorganization, if not disintegration, in the wake of demographic changes and national economic failures cause desperate people to take desperate measures. Growing drug crops, even under conditions of high risk and great inconvenience, is one of them.

Summary and Conclusions

Crime and drugs walk hand in hand, either from the drugs' pharmacological effects, the economic-compulsive drives of drug abusers, the systemic violence so characteristic of traffickers' protecting turf and opening new markets, or the corrupting influence of drug money on public people and institutions. Of all criminality, the trafficker-related systemic and corruptive varieties are most consequential for countries and peoples. Those kinds of crime appear to be on the increase globally today. Drug-funded criminal organizations are increasing in size, sophistication, and strength. Experience bred in conflict has honed leadership and disciplined the rank and file among criminal organizations worldwide.

Three global transformations now facilitate trafficker criminality: development of computer and communications technology and their worldwide dissemination, the collapse of communism, and the declining significance of national borders around the planet. All have facilitated the development of integrated criminal organizations, whose operations span the globe.

Notes

1. See the special reports in *U.S. News and World Report,* 17 January 1994, and *Newsweek,* 13 December 1993.

2. For an extended discussion, see LaMond Tullis, *Handbook of Research on the Illicit Drug Traffic: Socioeconomic and Political Consequences* (Westport, Conn.: Greenwood Press, 1991), 97–102.

3. James Q. Wilson and John J. DiIulio Jr., "Crackdown," *The New Republic,* 10 July 1989, 21–25.

4. The originator is Paul J. Goldstein, "The Drugs-Violence Nexus: A Tripartite Conceptual Framework," *Journal of Drug Issues* 15 (1985), 493–506.

See commentaries by Mario De La Rosa, Elizabeth Y. Lambert, and Bernard Gropper, eds., *Drugs and Violence: Causes, Correlates, and Consequences*, NIDA Research Monograph 103 (Washington, D.C.: U.S. Government Printing Office, 1990).

5. See Wilson and DiIulio Jr., "Crackdown," 21.

6. Philip Shenon, "Thai Legislators Are Enmeshed in Drug Charges by the U.S.," *New York Times*, 26 May 1994, 5.

7. See, for example, Victoria Irwin, "Drugs and Police: Cities Probe the Corruption Connection," *Christian Science Monitor*, 30 September 1986; John Kendall, "Drugs, Money Add Up to Temptation for Police," *Los Angeles Times*, 20 December 1988, 3; Jim Schachter, "Customs Service Cleans House in a Drive on Drug Corruption," *Los Angeles Times*, 16 June 1987, 3; and "Slice of Vice: More Miami Cops Arrested," *Time*, 8 January 1986, 72. Interested readers will also want to consult the standard reference volume by Michael Tonry and James Q. Wilson, eds., *Drugs and Crime*, vol. 13 of *Crime and Justice: A Review of Research* (Chicago: University of Chicago Press, 1990).

8. See the discussion by Martin Grapendaal, Ed Leuw, and Hans Nelen, "Drugs and Crime in an Accommodating Social Context: The Situation in Amsterdam," *Contemporary Drug Problems*, Summer 1992, 303–326.

9. See chapter 6 of LaMond Tullis, *Handbook of Research on the Illicit Drug Traffic: Socioeconomic and Political Consequences* (Westport, Conn.: Greenwood Press, 1991), 185–208. Considerations involve social, economic, and political externalities tied to certain occupations and to impacts on fetuses.

10. See, for example, Tonry and Wilson, *Drugs and Crime*. The various authors are able to describe the patterns in which drugs and crimes are interlinked more confidently than they are able to explain them.

11. Wilson and DiIulio, "Crackdown," 21.

12. Lana D. Harrison, "International Perspectives on the Interface of Drug Use and Criminal Behavior," *Contemporary Drug Problems*, Summer 1992, 188–189.

13. Ibid., 193.

14. Lana D. Harrison, "The Drug-Crime Nexus in the USA," *Contemporary Drug Problems*, Summer 1992, 205.

15. Duane C. McBride and Clyde B. McCoy, "The Drugs-Crime Relationship: An Analytical Framework," *The Prison Journal* 73:3–4 (September/December 1993), 257–278.

16. Bertil Lintner, "Opium War," *Far Eastern Economic Review*, 20 January 1994, 23.

17. Tullis, *Handbook*, 64–72. For dismaying facts about the United States, see *U.S. News and World Report*, 17 January 1994, 22–41.

18. For a discussion about fetuses and references to the literature, see Tullis, *Handbook*, 197–198.

19. Karl-Heinz Reuband, "Drug Addiction and Crime in West Germany: A Review of the Empirical Evidence," *Contemporary Drug Problems*, Summer 1992, 327–349.

20. Stephen Mugford, "Licit and Illicit Drug Use, Health Costs and the 'Crime Connection' in Australia: Public Views and Policy Implications," *Contemporary Drug Problems*, Summer 1992, 381.

21. Grapendaal, Leuw, and Nelen, "Drugs and Crime," 313.

22. Ibid.

23. Yao Jianguo, "Yunnan: China's Anti-Drug Outpost," *Beijing Review*, 26 August–1 September, 1991.

24. Dali L. Yang, "Illegal Drugs, Policy Change, and State Power: The Case of Contemporary China," *Journal of Contemporary China* 4 (Fall 1993), 28.

25. Ibid., 22.

26. *Bazuco* is semirefined cocaine mixed with tobacco and contains many petrochemical and other impurities.

27. See, for example, Seth Faison, "U.S. Says 17 in Bronx Gang Rented Rights to Sell Heroin," *New York Times*, 27 May 1994, A12.

28. Charles Dickens, *Oliver Twist* (Paris: Hachette, 1870).

29. Henry H. Brownstein, Hari R. Shiledar Baxi, Paul J. Goldstein, and Patrick J. Ryan, "The Relationship of Drugs, Drug Trafficking, and Drug Traffickers to Homicide," *Journal of Crime and Justice* 15:1 (1992), 25–44.

30. See, for example, "Cocaine: The Military Connection," *Latin American Regional Reports*, 29 August 1980, 5–6; and Richard B. Craig, "Illicit Drug Traffic: Implications for South American Source Countries," *Journal of Interamerican Studies and World Affairs* 29 (Summer 1987), 1–35.

31. CNN reported on 20 March 1994 that ex-president Paz Zamora had been indicted.

32. *U.S. News and World Report*, 17 January 1994, 22–41.

33. Cited in ibid., 26.

34. Ibid., 37.

35. James J. Collins, "Summary Thoughts About Drugs and Violence," in Mario De La Rosa, Elizabeth Y. Lambert, and Bernard Gropper, eds., *Drugs and Violence: Causes, Correlates, and Consequences*, NIDA Research Monograph 103, (Washington, D.C.: U.S. Government Printing Office, 1990).

36. Michael Elliott et al., "Global Mafia," *Newsweek*, 13 December 1993, 22.

37. Ibid., 22.

38. Seymour M. Hersh, "The Wild East," *Atlantic Monthly*, June 1994, 61–82. See also Claire Sterling, "Redfellas: The Growing Power of Russia's Mob," *The New Republic*, 11 April 1994, 19–27.

39. In a rare display of analytical prowess, *Newsweek* allowed Michael Elliott et al. ("Global Mafia") to explore these commonly noted categories. For this section I am drawing on their work as well as that of Steven Flynn, *The Transnational Drug Challenge and the New World Order*, Report of the CSIS Project on the Global Drug Trade in the Post–Cold War Era (Washington, D.C.: Center for Strategic and International Studies, 1993).

40. Wladyslaw Kozaczuk, *Enigma: How the German Machine Cipher Was Broken, and How It Was Read by the Allies in World War Two*, trans. by Christopher Kasparek (Frederick, Md.: University Publications of America, 1984).

41. Russell Watson, "Death on the Spot," *Newsweek*, 13 December 1993, 19.

42. See, for example, "Money Laundering: Who's Involved, How It Works, and Where It's Spreading," *Business Week*, 18 March 1985, 74.

43. See Flynn, *Transnational Drug Challenge*.

44. Instructive reports are found in Daniel Chirot, ed., *The Crisis of Leninism and the Decline of the Left: The Revolutions of 1989* (Seattle: University of Washington Press, 1991).

45. Elliott, "Global Mafia," 26.

46. See Celestine Bohlen, "For New Russia, a New Breed of Swindler," *New York Times*, 17 March 1994, A1.

47. See Tullis, *Handbook*, 80, note 37.

48. See, for example, Brook Larmer, "Colombians Take Over 'Coke' Trade in Mexico," *Christian Science Monitor,* 9 January 1989, 1; William Branigin, "The Mexican Connection," *Washington Post Weekly,* 14–20 March 1988, 7; Camille Groedidler, "Mexico Becoming Center of Drug Traffic Despite Anti-Drug Drive," *Christian Science Monitor,* 11 January 1984, 9; William Overend, "Cocaine Floods Southland via Colombia-Mexico Link," *Los Angeles Times,* 31 December 1987; and Michael Wines, "Traffic in Cocaine Reported Surging Weeks after Colombian Crackdown," *New York Times,* 1 November 1989, A10.

49. Elliott, "Global Mafia," 25.

50. Ibid.

51. "U.S. Interdiction Efforts Forcing Coke Shipments to Europe, OC Commissioners Report," *Crime Control Digest,* 21 October 1985, 2–3.

52. Growing populations on fixed land bases sometimes leave new generations unable to provide sufficient caloric intake to sustain life, or at least life that can be marginally enjoyed while pursuing traditionally available income-generating opportunities. Not all drug-growing areas are pressured on this point.

53. See, in general, UNDP, *Human Development Report 1993* (New York: Oxford University Press, 1993).

54. The best theoretical discussion is by Hernando de Soto, *The Other Path: The Invisible Revolution in the Third World* (New York: Harper & Row, 1989).

55. See the discussions in LaMond Tullis, "Cocaine and Food: Likely Effects of a Burgeoning Transnational Industry on Food Production in Bolivia and Peru," in W. Ladd Hollist and LaMond Tullis, eds., *Pursuing Food Security: Strategies and Obstacles in Africa, Asia, Latin America, and the Middle East* (Boulder, Colo.: Lynne Rienner Publishers, 1987), Table 12.2, p. 255; Jeffrey Franks, "La economía de la coca en Bolivia: ¿Plaga o salvación?" *Informe Confidencial,* June 1991, 23 (Table 6) (La Paz: Muller Associates); and Federico Aguiló, "Movilidad Espacial y Movilidad Social Generada for el Narcotráfico," in *Efectos del Narcotráfico* (La Paz: ILDIS, 1988), 68. James Painter reports that in Bolivia the ratio is nineteen times higher from coca than from the second most profitable crop (citrus) in the Chapare at the time of his survey. See *Bolivia and Coca: A Study in Dependency* (Boulder, Colo.: Lynne Rienner Publishers, 1994), 10.

56. For extended discussion, see Tullis, *Handbook,* Chapter 4.

57. See Gina Kolata, "In Cities, Poor Families Are Dying of Crack," *New York Times,* 1989.

58. John Bacon discusses the French Connection and those who dominated it and speculates about a possible resurrection of the French criminal underworld ["Is the French Connection Really Dead?" *Drug Enforcement,* Summer 1981, 19–21]. The negotiations between the United States and Turkey and the effectiveness of the opium-ban laws in Turkey following the demise of the French Connection are discussed in two U.S. congressional hearings—U.S. Congress, House Committee on International Relations, Subcommittee on Future Foreign Policy Research and Development, "The Effectiveness of Turkish Opium Control," *Ninety-Fourth Congress, First Session* (Washington, D.C.: U.S. Government Printing Office, 1975) and U.S. Congress, House Committee on Foreign Affairs, "Turkish Opium Ban Negotiations," *Ninety-Third Congress, Second Session* (Washington, D.C.: U.S. Government Printing Office, 1974).

59. Sean M. McWeeney, "The Sicilian Mafia and Its Impact on the United States," *FBI Law Enforcement Bulletin*, February 1987, 1–9, reviews the Sicilian mafia's relationship to heroin and cocaine trafficking.

60. Frank Robertson, *Triangle of Death: The Inside Story of the Triads—The Chinese Mafia* (London: Routledge and K. Paul, 1977) characterizes the Chinese Triads as criminal offshoots of a once vast patriotic organization formed to rid China of its despotic overlords and to establish a republic. The original Triad society still exists, the author says, in fragmented form in Hong Kong and in almost every sizable Chinese overseas community. Although the overwhelming majority of its members are lawful, hardworking citizens, there is a criminal minority, organized into some 1,500 gangs worldwide. The criminal offshoots from Hong Kong—extremely closely knit brotherhoods, difficult to penetrate—are specializing in heroin distribution in Great Britain, all of Europe, and the United States. See Fenton Bresler, *The Trail of the Triads: An Investigation into International Crime* (London: Weidenfeld and Nicolson, 1980).

61. Keith B. Richburg, "More Heroin Said to Enter U.S. from Asia; Chinese Gangs Replacing Traditional Organized Crime Networks," *Washington Post*, 16 March 1988, A16. These Chinese groups now dominate the New York heroin trade, made possible not only by their own aggressive marketing strategies but also by the weakening of traditional organized crime there through generational divisions and a series of major prosecutions. A vacuum developed, and the Triads filled it. See Peter Kerr, "Chinese Now Dominate New York Heroin Trade," *New York Times*, 9 August 1987, B1.

62. In general, in Mexico, organizations are mentioned by their leaders' names or simply as "families." For example, William Overend speaks of "seven major drug families of Mexico" who developed a partnership with Colombian syndicates to use Mexico as a transshipment point for cocaine in transit to the United States and Canada ("Cocaine Floods Southland via Colombia-Mexico Link," *Los Angeles Times*, 31 December 1987). One of these is the Herrera Family. See Peter A. Lupsha, "Drug Trafficking: Mexico and Colombia in Comparative Perspective," *Journal of International Affairs*, 35:1 (1981), 95–115.

63. Discussions of the Colombian syndicates have fallen in both applied (e.g., examination of their impact on society and on both supply-side and demand-side drug traffic) and theoretical categories (e.g., whether they are vertically integrated in a conventional business sense or by intimidation and terror—there being hardly any disagreement that some kind of vertical integration exists). Discussions concern how many syndicates there are, what their international characteristics are, how much legitimate business enterprise they are taking over, the degree to which they are corrupting the judicial and political systems (particularly of Colombia), their economic impact on the larger society, who their principals are, how powerful and rich they are, and so forth.

64. See Phillip C. McGuire, "Jamaican Posses: A Call for Cooperation among Law Enforcement Agencies," *Police Chief*, January 1988, 20. Bernard D. Headly, "War in 'Babylon': Dynamics of the Jamaican Informal Drug Economy," *Social Justice* 15:3–4 (1988): 61–86, argues that "dependent development" in Jamaica has produced such a scarcity of socially acceptable work that a substantial part of the Jamaican population has been economically marginalized. To extricate itself from that marginalization, some Jamaicans join gangs, emigrate to the United States, and become involved in the international drug traffic. It

is thought that the Posses working in the United States have about 10,000 members.

65. The Aryan Brotherhood and the Texas syndicate, along with many other groups, are discussed in the President's Commission on Organized Crime, *The Impact: Organized Crime Today,* Report to the President and the Attorney General (Washington, D.C.: The Commission, 1986).

66. See, for example, Michael Mecham, "Drug Smugglers Prove Elusive Targets for Interdiction Forces," *Aviation Week and Space Technology,* 30 January 1989, 34–36; and William Carley, "Losing Battle: U.S. Air War on Drugs So Far Fails to Stem Caribbean Smuggling," *Wall Street Journal,* 20 October 1988.

67. See Carl Robinson, "The Day of the Triads: Hong Kong's Gangs Move in on Australia," *Newsweek,* 7 November 1988, 72; and Stephen Brookes, "Chinese Mafia Takes Vice Abroad," *Insight,* 24 April 1989, 34–36.

68. Fenton Bresler, *The Chinese Mafia: An Investigation into International Crime* (New York: Stein and Day, 1981).

69. Cathy Booth, "Tentacles of the Octopus; The Mafia Brings Europe's Worst Drug Epidemic Home," *Time,* 12 December 1988, 48; Karen Wolman, "Europe's Cocaine Boom Confounds Antidrug War," *Christian Science Monitor,* 19 June, 1989, 1–2.

70. See, for example, James Adams, *The Financing of Terror* (London: New English Library, 1986). Robert Cribb shows how the Indonesian independence movement (1945–1949) was financed in large part through the sale of opium when the Dutch trade blockade suppressed normal commerce in rubber and sugar ("Opium and the Indonesian Revolution," *Modern Asian Studies,* 22:4 [1988], 701–722). Grant Wardlaw argues strongly against the linkages being understood in political or ideological terms. Drug connections exist, on the whole, for practical economic reasons rather than ideological ones ("Linkages Between the Illegal Drugs Traffic and Terrorism," *Conflict Quarterly,* Summer 1988, 5–26).

71. James Brooke, "The Rebels Lose Leaders, but Give Peru No Peace," *New York Times,* 5 February 1993, A3.

72. Scott B. MacDonald, *Mountain High, White Avalanche: Cocaine and Power in the Andean States and Panama* (New York: Praeger, 1989).

73. See, for example, Leslie Wirpsa, "Colombian Mafia Hurt by Testimony of Key Deserter," *Miami Herald,* 12 June 1989, 4A.

74. See the Associated Press release of late May 1994 by Andrew Selsky ("Colombia Balks at U.S. Pressure to Escalate Drug War"). My source is the *Daily Herald* (Utah), 26 May 1994, A6.

75. Robert Thomas Baratta, "Political Violence in Ecuador and the AVC," *Terrorism* 10 (1987), 165–174.

76. See Dave Miller, "Drug Mafia Arms Campesinos," *Latinamerica Press,* 14 July 1988, 6; and "Probing into the Underworld," *Latin America Regional Reports,* 4 March 1983, 3–4.

77. Timothy Ross, "Colombia Goes after Drug Barons," *Christian Science Monitor,* 12 January 1987, 9.

78. See D. P. Kumarasingha, "Drugs—A Growing Problem in Sri Lanka," *Forensic Science International* 36 (1988), 283–284.

79. Jonathan Kwitny, "Money, Drugs and the Contras," *The Nation,* 29 August 1987, 1.

80. See Mary Thornton, "Sales of Opium Reportedly Fund Afghan Rebels, *Washington Post,* 17 December 1983, A32.

81. Wilson Ring, "Opium Production Rises in Guatemala Mountains," *Washington Post*, 30 June 1989, A25.

82. Lintner, "Opium War," 22–26.

83. This point is advanced by Michael Satchell, "Narcotics: Terror's New Ally," *U.S. News and World Report*, 4 May 1987, 30–37. Mark S. Steinitz, "Insurgents, Terrorists, and the Drug Trade," *Washington Quarterly*, 8:4 (1985), 141–156, examines the evidence of terrorist involvement in the drug trade with respect to Latin America, Southeast Asia, the Middle East, and Europe, examining the factors behind the linkages and, in particular, the changing patterns of the international drug scene that have brought insurgency, terrorism, and the drug trade into closer geographical proximity.

84. The point is vividly driven home for Colombia by Francisco Thoumi, *Political Economy and Illegal Drugs in Colombia* (Boulder, Colo.: Lynne Rienner Publishers, 1994). The same point can be raised for Khun Sa's relative success in Myanmar/Burma.

85. Yale historian David Musto reported at the Workshop on the International Implications of the Transnational Drug Phenomenon, 18–19 April 1994, Philadelphia, Pennsylvania, that following a turn-of-the-century crackdown on cocaine in the Western Hemisphere, growers moved production to Indonesia. I do not know if Indonesian coca bushes are currently involved in production for international trade. It seems unlikely.

86. These have occurred, for example, when significant but almost always temporary governmental trade-suppression assaults on traffickers or internal wars among the traffickers themselves (e.g., Medellín and Cali cocaine syndicates) have removed traffickers from their normal purchase/pickup routes.

87. Tullis, "Cocaine and Food," 257–258.

88. Edmundo Morales, "Land Reform, Social Change, and Modernization in the National Periphery: A Study of Five Villages in the Northeastern Andes of Peru," Ph.D. dissertation, City University of New York, 1983. Morales holds, nevertheless, that "the direct economic relationship between peasants, the urban poor and the underworld brings a plethora of negative effects that disturb the traditional life in the countryside" (p. 136).

89. See, in general, UNDP, *Human Development Report 1993* and World Bank, *World Development Report 1980*.

... 2 ...

Drug Production and Consumption

In Chapter 1 we saw that crime and drugs walk hand in hand, either from the drugs' pharmacological effects, the economic-compulsive drives of drug abusers, the systemic violence associated with traffickers, or the corrupting influence of drug money on people and institutions. How much drug-related crime might exist relates therefore not only to traffickers (who are responsible for most of the socially and politically significant crime) but also to producers and consumers. Inasmuch as international counterinitiatives to deal with illicit drugs focus on producers and consumers as well as traffickers, it is important to know how much global production and consumption may exist. On some more or less realistic estimate rests the credibility, if not validity, of policy measures, both actual and proposed.

Unfortunately, the importance of assembling realistic data is substantially greater than the capacity to do so, at least at the present time. How much illegal drug production and consumption may be occurring globally is simply not known at any acceptable level of accuracy, and establishing universally agreed-upon estimates appears not to be possible. Too many factors and too many unproven assumptions enter into the calculations. Moreover, different observers give the assumptions different weightings, which obviously biases estimated production and consumption outcomes, sometimes substantially. Nevertheless, on the basis of considered "best guesses," some quantitative and comparative information is advanced in this chapter for the countries studied under the United Nations Research Institute for Social Development/United Nations University (UNRISD/ UNU) project. These data lay the groundwork for the policy discussions advanced in subsequent chapters.

With the exception of significant marijuana production in the United States (some of which appears to be exported), most illicit drugs destined for international trade originate in less developed countries or regions. Peru, Bolivia, and Colombia account for more than 98 percent of the world's cocaine supply.[1] The Golden Crescent (Pakistan, Afghanistan, Iran), the Golden Triangle (Myanmar/Burma, Laos, Thailand), and Mexico account for the vast majority of illegal opiates (opium, morphine, heroin) traded internationally, although Lebanon's Bekaa Valley, Colombia, and Guatemala are fast becoming major producers. Cannabis (e.g., marijuana, ganja, hashish) is produced in most parts of the world. Cannabis entering the U.S. market comes principally from Colombia, Mexico, Jamaica, supplementing U.S. domestic crops. Some worldwide exports emanate from Thailand, Morocco, Lebanon, and Iran.

Drugs exported from these net-producing nations are usually bound for markets in industrialized countries. The United States is by far the largest single consumer of illicit drugs, although European countries and the new republics of the former USSR report significantly increased usage. Heroin is, and has been, used nominally in all Western European countries for many decades. However, with a cocaine glut on their hands, Colombian traffickers have vigorously worked to make Europe into an illegal multidrug market. Having successfully gained a foothold there, they expanded east. The USSR began to note the penetration of cocaine into its own borderlands even before the 1989 collapse of communism opened Eastern Europe for greater smuggling of illicit drugs and other contraband. Canada and Australia have also recorded increased consumption of illicit drugs.

In the past, less developed countries have produced but tended not to consume drugs destined for the illicit international market. Now, however, domestic consumption is increasing in almost all supplier countries (e.g., Peru, Bolivia, and Colombia where smoking a mixture of coca paste and tobacco—*bazuco*—has become more popular). Myanmar/Burma, Thailand, Laos, Iran, and Pakistan all note considerable problems with new waves of opium and heroin addiction, and opiate addiction has once again emerged as a public concern in China. Consumption is no longer an exclusive demand problem of the industrialized countries. It has become a global phenomenon.

Estimating Production Figures

The countries of the UNRISD/UNU study (Bolivia, Peru, Colombia, Mexico, Thailand, Myanmar/Burma, Laos, Pakistan, and Kentucky, U.S.) are not, of course, the only significant countries involved in illicit drug production. Other countries increasingly figure as important actors in the international drug trade. For example, the Bekaa Valley of Lebanon, a region under the de facto control of the Syrians, is a significant producer of opium, heroin, and hashish. Morocco figures heavily in cannabis, Guatemala increasingly in heroin. Venezuela and Chile appear to have significantly entered the cocaine-processing market, and Paraguay may become a major producer of coca. Hong Kong is a large transiting area for East Asian heroin, and China has begun to show significant increases in illicit drug production in all but cocaine. However, discussable data are scarcer for these countries than for the nations under study.

The production of botanically based drugs is both licit and illicit. Considerable legitimate production occurs for medical and scientific purposes. India is a large producer of licit opium. Bolivia and Peru produce between them about 20,000 tons of legal coca leaves each year, some of which are consumed locally as part of traditional culture, the balance being used industrially (e.g., for flavoring in Coca-Cola) and medically (e.g., production of novocaine).

Production estimates for legal drug crops are naturally much more accurate than for illegal ones. Even under the best of circumstances, illicit-drug production figures are only gross estimates, in part because of the clandestine nature of much of the drug trade. The problem is complicated further, however, and in no small way by the political ends such estimates are intended to serve. In Bolivia's case, James Painter notes that U.S. government officials tend to underestimate production, whereas Bolivian officials overestimate it because "they are involved in constant and delicate negotiations over the levels of international aid, or compensation, to be paid for coca eradication."[2] Moreover, some have suggested that "the U.S. government increases its estimates of the number of hectares under cultivation when it is opting for a repressive or militarized strategy and drops them when Bolivia is pushing for economic compensation for the reduction of its coca."[3] Similar phenomena are noted in the other studies.[4]

Lack of access to information from the industry (e.g., with quarterly corporate reports) greatly complicates the task of compiling production data. Nevertheless, governments, private agencies, and the United Nations make estimates based on seizures, aerial and ground surveys, consumption trends, and assumptions underlying agricultural data analyses.

In recent years, increasing reliance has been placed on production estimates as a basis for formulating public policy. But consider the general problem of agricultural data gathering and the specific complications this poses for estimating illicit-crop production. Most of the countries under study here have a diversified geography and topography that hinders data gathering; the agricultural holdings are generally small and encompass a variety of agricultural pursuits that are not readily distinguishable with respect to their illegality; many of the agricultural units are located in remote areas (frequently outside the control of central governments); and most of the countries lack both funding and expert personnel to conduct accurate surveys. Considering, additionally, the proclivity of illicit-drug-crop growers to settle in very remote areas, to protect their crops with force if necessary, and to convince government authorities that "nothing is happening here, so don't bother us," one understands a little more adequately some of the practical detriments to gathering accurate production figures.

How much illicit-drug production exists? No one really knows. Every conclusion is based on a series of estimates. Those estimates may be intelligent appraisals underwritten by high technology, or they may simply be guesses. International agencies attempt to refine the intelligent estimates. In the countries under study here, refined estimates are made by the U.S. Agency for International Development (USAID), the U.S. State Department, the United States National Narcotics Intelligence Consumers Committee (NNICC), the United Nations International Drug Control Programme (UNDCP), and the United Nations Development Programme (UNDP). Not unexpectedly, estimates advanced even by the international agencies have varied substantially for some countries.

In general, production estimates are made from ground surveys where possible (usually on a sampling basis) and from aerial photographs of known producing areas when ground sampling is impractical or too dangerous. An approximate number of acres or hectares (1 hectare = 2.43 acres) sown to illegal crops is thus obtained. Yields per hectare are estimated, and then total production estimates are calculated. The U.S. State Department uses this high-technology method overlaid by the two assumptions (hectarage and yields) mentioned. The department usually comes up with the lowest, or most conservative, results from among those making estimates. The validity of production estimates in dangerous areas—which includes most areas where illicit drugs are grown—hinges not only on high-tech devices such as sophisticated aerial photography but also an overlay of yield estimates and other factors. Yet the question remains: How valid are the yield estimates?

Crop yields may fluctuate widely—between 1 and 3 metric tons per hectare (mt/ha) of coca in Peru, for example—depending on climatic conditions, age and variety of the plant, elevation, and sundry cropping and production conditions.[5] Thus, Elena Alvarez's survey of production studies in Peru shows a wide variation in estimates.[6] On hectarage, the estimates range between 166,500 and 115,630 hectares.[7]

Yield estimates range from 0.96 to 3.4 mt/ha. In Bolivia, the hectarage differences are smaller (between 50,300 and 47,644 for 1990),[8] but variance in the other parameters remains. Estimates for other countries show even greater variance.

Clearly, informed guesses are better than no guesses. But, given the softness of the assumptions and the data, one might legitimately expect real production to depart from estimated production by a considerable margin. That, of course, distorts the "downstream" estimates of economic and other impacts for any given country, complicating efforts to implement an effective production-control program.

Crop production uncertainties are just one perturbing factor in gauging the amount of illegal drugs being produced. The alkaloid content of any given precursor plant is not a given; it varies according to cultivation practices, climatic conditions and microzones, plant subspecies, and harvesting practices. One must make estimates about that content. In the case of coca leaves, the cocaine content is known to vary widely, from about 0.25 percent to 1.5 percent, thereby throwing a large "wild card" into estimates of actual cocaine derived from the estimated crop production, itself subject to numerous assumptions. Moreover, the leaves, whatever their recoverable alkaloid content at the time of picking, quickly (within a matter of days) lose much of their potency. Any delay in processing the leaves (which might arise, for example, if a successful trafficker interdiction program happens to be underway) can therefore add additional uncertainties to the production figures.

Estimates of actual drug production in any given country therefore derive from assumptions about the hectarage dedicated to an illicit crop, about the yield per hectare of that crop, about its alkaloid content, and about intangible factors such as harvesting efficiency, wastage, and spoilage.

With those caveats in mind—each having been weighed carefully by the country-study authors—the studies report production figure ranges of agricultural harvests, semi- or fully refined products, or both, as discussed below and summarized in Table 2.1. The figures given are mid-ranges of probable real production. For purposes of comparison, U.S. State Department Bureau of International Narcotics figures for 1993, where available, are given in parentheses in each cell of Table 2.1.

Current Production in Nine Countries

Bolivia[9] is a principal producer of coca. In recent years more and more coca, cocaine paste, and cocaine hydrochloride have been processed there. Until the 1940s almost all Bolivian coca—around 97

Table 2.1 Illicit-Drug Production in Nine Countries

Gross Estimates, Illicit-Drug Production
(in metric tons)

	Coca	Cocaine	Opium	Heroin	Cannabis
Peru	200,000 (155,500)	75?	NKP	NKP	NKP
Bolivia	100,000 (84,400)	72	NKP	NKP	NKP
Colombia	30,000 (31,700)	175	? (160)[a]	? (20)	10,000 (4,125)
Mexico	NKP	(?)[b]	(62)[c] (49)[c]	(6)[c]	(6,280)[c]
Myanmar/ Burma	NKP	NKP	2,300 (2,280)	130	?
Laos	NKP	NKP	250 (230)	30 (19)	?
Thailand	NKP	NKP	40 (42)[d]	?	?
Pakistan	NKP	NKP	165–300 (175)	60 (55)[e]	? ?
Kentucky, U.S.	NKP	NKP	NKP	NKP	275–352

Notes: Codes: NKP = No Known Production; () Production as reported by U.S. Department of State, Bureau of International Narcotics Matters, *International Narcotics Control Strategy Report* (INCSR), April 1994. Other figures are estimates from the country-study reports.

a. *INCSR 1993,* 110, lists 20,000 hectares of potentially harvestable opium in 1992, up from 1,344 in 1991. The State Department estimates that each cultivated hectare is capable of yielding 8 kilograms of opium gum, which has the potential to produce 1 kilogram of heroin (p. 108). Thus, heroin conversion is estimated at 1 kilogram per hectare. The estimates for 1993 are unchanged (*INCSR 1994,* 108).

b. Cocaine production does exist, as evidenced by the destruction of one cocaine-processing lab in 1991. Four labs were destroyed in 1992, but Mexican authorities did not specify whether they were heroin- or cocaine-processing facilities.

c. *INCSR 1994,* 163, lists the 1990 opium figure for Mexico as 62. *INCSR 1991* estimated the heroin yield for 1990 to be 6.2 tons. The 1993 estimate is 49 metric tons (*INCSR 1994,* 161). By State Department estimates, from 1989–1992, opium cultivation dropped from 6,600 hectares to 3,310 hectares but rose in 1993 to 3,960 hectares. Average yields in Mexico are said to be 12–15 kilograms/hectare (*INCSR 1993,* 166). Marijuana production for 1989 is lised as 35,050 hectares, down from 53,900 hectares in 1989 with a probable further decline to about 11,220 hectares in 1993 and usable plant yield of 6,280 metric tons. If *INCSR* figures are correct, this indicates a considerable drop in production.

d. *INCSR 1994,* 298, lists the 1990 figure as 40 metric tons, declining to 24 in 1992 but rising to 42 metric tons in 1993.

e. *INCSR 1993,* p. 247, lists this figure as the amount consumed in country. As others have said that Pakistan is now self-sufficient in heroin production (and also exports it), one must assume that the real figure is probably much higher than 55 metric tons.

percent—was grown in a region called the Yungas, an 11,000-square-kilometer area located northeast of Bolivia's capital, La Paz.[10] The residual remainder was produced in Cochabamba (2 percent) and Santa Cruz (1 percent). A more recently colonized area, the Chapare, has since overtaken all other regions in coca-growing importance. It now accounts for more than three-quarters of the country's plantings. James Painter notes that "as early as 1963, the Chapare was producing nearly 3,500 tons of coca from only 1,300 hectares [2.69 mt/ha] compared to the 1,400 tons from the 1,700 hectares in the Yungas [.82mt/ha]. By 1970 the Chapare accounted for 83 percent of national production (of 8,500 tons) from just 850 hectares more of coca."[11] In 1993 the region probably produced more than 80,000 metric tons.

After 1970 there was a spectacular increase in international demand for cocaine. The Chapare, with its vast flatlands that required no terracing (as in the Yungas), responded to satisfy the need. By the mid-1970s the area was producing all but 1,300 tons of Bolivia's national production of 27,000 tons of coca. Thereafter, the Chapare continued to share in increased output, which also picked up in Cochabamba, Santa Cruz, and the Yungas, reaching more than 150,000 tons in 1987, then falling to 116,000 tons in 1990, according to Bolivian national figures,[12] and to perhaps 100,000 tons in 1992. Although all observers allowed for considerable increase in hectarage and tonnage over the years before the decline that began after 1987, the U.S. State Department placed the 1990 figures at 77,000 tons and the 1993 figures at 84,400,[13] thus emphasizing the uncertainty of estimates.

Until the late 1980s, when processing labs began to operate in Bolivia, almost all the agricultural coca production was shipped to Colombia for processing into cocaine. Bolivia's entry into a value-added market was facilitated by the 1989 internal wars in Colombia that thwarted traffickers' mobility there for a while.

Peru,[14] like Bolivia, grows coca, not opium or cannabis. Phenomena similar to those observed in Bolivia have been at work in Peru. Since Inca times, coca has been grown around Cuzco, but production expanded to other regions—principally the Upper Huallaga Valley—in response to the rising international demand for cocaine in the 1970s and 1980s. Most studies about Peruvian coca production have been carried out in the Upper Huallaga Valley. Inferences are made for the whole country based principally on those studies and are subject to all the variations, uncertainties, and arguable assumptions noted above. All things considered, the most likely hectarage figure for Peruvian illegal coca (17,914 hectares are grown legally[15]) is around 200,000,[16] even though the U.S. State Department's calculations are considerably lower (129,000 hectares, dropping to 108,800 in 1993 due to blight and aging coca plants).[17]

Allowing for wide variations in estimates as well as the actual condition in reality, the average yield per hectare throughout the country is probably in the neighborhood of 1.8 metric tons (the range from various estimators is 1–3.8 metric tons),[18] bringing illegal coca production to around 360,000 metric tons. This figure is considerably higher than the State Department's 1992 estimate of 223,900 metric tons (and 1993 estimate of 155,500 due mainly to blight).[19] The above hectarage and tonnage figures were 20 to 50 percent higher than the U.S. State Department allowed as being realistic in reports issued before 1992[20] and 55 to 61 percent higher than the department's 1993 report allows.[21] These discrepancies heighten the realization that no one has a firm grasp on production realities with these illegal crops.

From the 1970s to the mid-1980s, almost all of Peru's coca harvest was shipped to Colombia to be processed, either as raw leaf or as coca paste. After August 1989, when internal war erupted between the Colombian government and the drug traffickers, Peru, like Bolivia, increasingly processed its own coca base into cocaine base and cocaine hydrochloride for shipment to consuming centers.[22]

Some coca leaf is grown in Colombia[23] (on the order of 30,000 metric tons derived from 38,000 hectares of land), mostly in the southern part of the country.[24] Marijuana is still grown in Colombia (1,700–10,000 metric tons[25]), and reports that opium is harvested in various regions have been verified. The 1992 opium harvest was probably around 160 metric tons, making Colombia a world-class opium producer.[26] Most of the opium was probably converted to heroin in Colombian laboratories. However, Colombia is best known as the world's cocaine-processing and illicit-trafficking center.

Francisco Thoumi points out the array of imponderables associated with estimates about Colombia.[27] In 1988, the last year for which four studies report comparable data, the estimated export volume of cocaine to the United States and Europe ranged from 52 to 310 metric tons.[28] The amount of cocaine produced for local consumption, primarily in the form of bazuco, is not given. The U.S. State Department estimates 1990 production of cocaine and cocaine base to be 132 metric tons,[29] a conjecture it totally dropped in its 1993 report. Perhaps 175 metric tons may be a reasonable estimate of production for 1992.

In the late 1970s and early 1980s, Colombia was probably the world's most significant cannabis producer, and although production had fallen considerably by 1992, it may have increased substantially during the 1993 crop year.[30] Today, as with the other drug crops, marijuana production figures vary widely, with most estimates of the cultivated area (other than those from the U.S. State Department) being around 10,000 hectares.[31] The U.S. State Department placed 1992 hectarage at closer to 2,000,[32] having accorded considerable efficacy to aerial herbicidal spraying and manual eradication programs, but reduced its optimism in this regard for 1993, when its estimate increased to 5,000 hectares.[33] Assuming a 1 mt/ha ratio, and accepting an estimate of 10,000 hectares under cultivation, Colombia may be producing around 10,000 metric tons of marijuana each year. If State Department figures are given higher credibility, marijuana production would be around half that.

Prior to 1991, no estimates were given for opium or heroin production in Colombia, although it was widely affirmed that both were being produced. The opium poppy migrated to Colombia (and to Guatemala) in the late 1980s in response to aerial herbicidal spraying programs in Mexico, which was a major poppy producer.

In Mexico,[34] no coca is grown, and few, if any, cocaine production laboratories are in operation, although the country is a principal transshipment territory for South American cocaine destined for the U.S. market. Considerable marijuana is grown in the country, however (somewhere between 8,000 and 40,000 metric tons). Mexico also continues to be a significant producer of opium (perhaps 60 metric tons) and heroin (perhaps 6 metric tons), herbicidal spraying notwithstanding. The principal export market for Mexican marijuana and heroin is the United States.

Relying on estimates by others, Celia Toro concludes that 450 tons of cocaine from Colombia, Peru, and Bolivia may have entered the U.S. market in 1988 (a figure considerably higher than nominal production figures from South America [322 metric tons], would seem to allow, again emphasizing the uncertainty of figures). Of that 300–450 metric tons, about a third was transited through Mexican territory.[35] Toro does not give an independent production analysis for marijuana, opium, and heroin.

The U.S. State Department estimates that for 1990 Mexico produced nearly 40,000 metric tons of marijuana from about 42,000 hectares of cultivated cannabis, 62 metric tons of opium from the 5,000 hectares of opium poppy that escaped eradication (4,650 hectares were eradicated), and 6.2 metric tons of heroin.[36] For 1992 the opium figures are 40 tons from 3,000 hectares (nearly 7,000 hectares were eradicated). These estimates do not coincide with those produced by independent scholars, but they do have the weight of both conservatism and intelligence reports on their side. As in the cases of other countries, they might be interpreted as being the minimum likely figures for Mexico.

Thailand,[37] historically a significant producer of opium and heroin, is likely now a net illicit-drug importer in order to satisfy its own consumption needs. At the same time, it remains a major transiting country for heroin processed in hill-country border areas of Laos and Myanmar/Burma and continues to produce a small amount of opium (around 40 metric tons in 1993).[38] It also has processing laboratories to refine opium from Myanmar/Burma and Laos into heroin. It is thus a major trafficking country for the world market.

In Thailand, opium poppy is grown almost exclusively in the northern hill country. Since 1987, 4,000 hectares or less of opium poppy have been cultivated each year, about half of which have been eradicated. For 1990 the Thai government reported production of 20 tons,[39] a fairly small amount considering Thailand's reputation as a transshipment and consuming country. The U.S. State Department placed the 1990 figure at closer to 46 tons.[40] Because of significant eradication underway in Thailand, we might hazard a guess of around 22 tons for 1992. However, since 1992, harvestable cultivation has probably increased.[41] Nonetheless, the opium production estimate for Thailand probably remains lower than domestic consumption.[42]

Cannabis, a relatively new commercial crop in Thailand, is grown everywhere in the country, with current production apparently moving from small peasant growers to large plantations. It is not known how much cannabis Thailand produces, although production clearly exceeds domestic market demand. Thailand is therefore a marijuana exporter.[43] It is also a cannabis-transiting country. In 1987 law enforcement officials destroyed nearly 3,000 tons of cannabis, most of which appeared to originate outside Thailand. Seizure figures have dropped dramatically since 1987 (85 metric tons in 1992),[44] but there is no suggestion as to what this may mean with respect to Thailand's cannabis-production statistics.

Myanmar/Burma[45] is arguably the world's leading producer of opium, but it is one of the most difficult in which to gather statistics because of the uncooperative nature of the present government. Even if officials were more open, they would probably not be able to produce reliable data, because most illicit Burmese opium is grown in mountainous areas that have been under the control of insurgents. Indeed, large portions of Myanmar/Burma have not had effective central government control since independence in 1948.

The U.S. State Department estimates that from the 1989 crop year Myanmar/Burma produced 2,300 tons of opium, either to be consumed locally (400 tons), exported (300 tons), or refined into heroin (1,600 tons). From available tonnage either used or stockpiled (opium keeps for a long time), nearly 130 tons of heroin were thought to have been produced in the clandestine laboratories that operate in the hill country, largely bordering on Thailand, for easy export to the world market.[46] The tenuous nature of these estimates is exemplified by the fact that the State Department withdrew its classification scheme in its 1993 report, advancing for 1992 only that 2,280 metric tons of opium were produced, with 280 tons lost or seized, 150 tons consumed, and 300 metric tons exported.[47] The 1994 report suggests a modest increase in hectares cultivated and yields obtained (165,800 hectares in successful production; 2,575 metric tons of opium potentially yielded).[48]

Despite their usual conservatism, U.S. State Department figures are much higher—by a factor of ten—than those the government of Myanmar/Burma (the State Law and Order Council, or SLORC) wants to accept. Ronald Renard notes that

> there are, of course, technical reasons why the estimates by SLORC and the United States vary so widely. Estimating opium production is simply not an easy job. Besides reticence of growers and traders to reveal production data, access to the growing areas in the remote areas in Upper Burma where the poppy is grown is difficult, and yields are subject to wide variation from year to year and even in different parts of the same growing area.
>
> Aerial photography can help. But even the sophisticated French satellite imagery used to estimate opium production in Thailand has reportedly been unable to provide exact answers in that country. Factors such as the short "window" during which there is no cloud cover in the area and the inability of the satellite to vary its orbit so as to take images of the sharp ridges on which opium is grown and which also obscure the poppies have impeded the success of this promising technique. As a result, the answer will never be resolved to everybody's satisfaction until field checking in the opium growing areas of Burma can be conducted. Given the unsettled conditions in much of this area, however, that day will not come anytime soon, particularly in the Burmese area of the Golden Triangle where field estimation techniques have not yet been implemented.
>
> Furthermore, Burma's unsettled conditions in which even SLORC does not enjoy access to much of the country obstructs opium production knowledge. Thus even were SLORC willing to conduct a thorough survey of opium producing areas, the task would be formidable.[49]

The technical reasons for disparate production estimates probably do not account for all the variance noted between SLORC and U.S. State Department figures. Some of the variance may well be attached to the political agendas of each government, an observation that may also be placed upon the insurgent groups working to prevent SLORC from gaining access to anything in territories they control.[50] Renard holds that the reasons for these political agendas are rooted in the history of drug use in Burma over the past 150 years, in which Buddhist traditionalists have sought either to control—or, failing there, to downplay—Burma's drug-consumption problems.

Until recently, Laos[51] has been relatively isolated from the rest of the world, with the result that little data is available on drug production there. As in Thailand and Myanmar/Burma, illicit-drug production flourishes in the hill country, collectively is known as the Golden Triangle, which borders on those two countries.

The attractiveness of the hill country derives from topography, migration, and demographics. Approximately 70 percent of Laos is broken into highland enclaves isolated by mountain ranges. No central government has been able to exercise complete control over the activity of the forty-seven ethnic groups scattered throughout these districts.[52] Compounding this difficulty is China's Yunnan Province, which lies on Laos's northern border and historically has been a source of intensive opium production and trade. Immigrants from Yunnan brought opium production technology to Laos in the nineteenth century.[53] This transfer was intensified when Hmong tribesmen, who had a self-developed opium-production technology, invaded Laos from southern China and Vietnam in the first quarter of the twentieth century.[54]

In early 1990, the Lao National Commission for Drug Control and Supervision reported that reliable information on opium cultivation and production was not available, although it did estimate that between 3 and 5 kilograms of opium per hectare (kg/ha) were harvested from an unknown number of hectares. A U.S. government internal paper argues that the yield was closer to 9 kg/ha in Houaphan Province, where growing conditions are extremely ideal.[55]

The U.S. State Department estimates that in 1989 nearly 400 metric tons of opium were produced from more than 40,000 hectares dedicated to opium cultivation.[56] By 1990 production apparently had fallen off by a third, to around 275 metric tons from 30,000 hectares of cultivated poppy. Production in 1992 may have been in the neighborhood of 250 metric tons[57] and could be dropping today.[58] Most of this poppy apparently goes to Thailand for processing, although evidence indicates that China has become a transshipment country for Laotian opium headed for processing in Hong Kong.

The above figures sharply contrast with the Lao National Commission's reluctant late-1990 estimates of about 60 metric tons of opium produced.[59] The commission reasoned that poppy growing is hard work that restricts a family to approximately 1 hectare or less, from which the following calculations derive:

If one assumes that between 60% and 90% of all Lao Soung house-holds are opium producers and cultivate about 80% of all opium poppies in the Lao People's Democratic Republic, with Lao Loum and Lao Theung producing the remaining 20%, the total area under opium poppy cultivation should be between 15,000 and 16,000 hectares with total annual yield of 60 to 65.[60]

So much for estimates.

Heroin definitely has been produced in Laos; clandestine production laboratories there have been located and destroyed.[61] Around 30 metric tons of heroin may have been produced in 1988,[62] and perhaps 19 metric tons in 1992.[63] A small amount of marijuana is produced in Laos, as evidenced mostly by a few seizures (e.g., 1,200 kilograms in Vientiane Province in 1990).[64]

In Pakistan,[65] cannabis has been produced from time immemorial[66] and opium as early as the twelfth century A.D., starting with Muslim rule and continuing with the British in South Asia—in accordance with the development of growing empires' administrative and revenue systems.[67] Historically, most opium produced in Pakistan appears to have been destined for export because, traditionally, per capita opium consumption has never been as high as in, say, Thailand, Myanmar/Burma, or (probably) Laos.

Today, Pakistan produces opium in its remote, federally administered but politically autonomous tribal areas in the Northwest Frontier Province (NWFP). The U.S. State Department estimates 1992 opium production to be 175 tons from more than 8,000 hectares of cultivated poppy that escaped eradication (977 hectares were eradicated).[68] In 1993 both hectarage and tonnage may have slightly dropped (6,280 hectares; 140 metric tons).[69]

Beginning in 1979 and extending to the present, systematic, large-scale heroin production has been undertaken in Pakistan. By all acknowledgments, the early laboratories were crude and primitive, consisting mostly of assorted barrels, buckets, pans, and perhaps some glassware. But many were capable of producing 50 kilograms or more of heroin per week, drawing down opium stocks by around 600 kilograms per week per laboratory.[70] More recently, because of the rapid growth of heroin consumption in Pakistan, the country has imported large stocks of opium from Afghanistan and elsewhere to meet the increasing domestic demand and international marketing opportunities. It is likely that Pakistani heroin chemists can no longer meet domestic demand, much of which appears to be satisfied by large-scale smuggling across the Pakistan-Afghanistan border,[71] principally through the Khyber Agency southwest of Peshawar and through other inaccessible tribal areas of the NWFP.

As for estimates of heroin production, for 1990 the U.S. State Department lists 58 metric tons produced within Pakistan, nearly 4 tons seized, and 112 metric tons consumed domestically by the more than a million Pakistani heroin addicts.[72] That much consumption would require considerable heroin importing if the figure of 58 tons produced is reasonably reliable.

Contrary to conditions in Laos, where both opium and heroin production have apparently declined, through 1992 Pakistan demonstrated a robust capacity to increase production and international marketing. Output probably increased 25 percent from 1989 to 1990.[73] However, in 1993 production may have leveled off or declined slightly.

In 1992, 188 tons of marijuana were seized in Pakistan, giving credence to the belief that considerable cannabis production occurs there. However, not even the U.S. State Department dares hazard a guess as to how much is produced.[74]

Aside from being a major drug producer, Pakistan is also an important transshipment country, aided by being centrally located in the convergence of the Golden Crescent that comprises the conjoining regions of Iran, Afghanistan, and Pakistan. Pakistani heroin is sold worldwide.

Finally, we turn to Kentucky, U.S.[75] in our survey of representative drug producers and traffickers. Although the Appalachian region of Kentucky has been a transshipment point for illegal drugs for a long time, starting with alcohol during the Prohibition era and continuing with cocaine today, in terms of illicit crops it is most noted for marijuana production. The country study by Richard Clayton and William Estep contains an elaborate discussion of production estimates and the disconcerting assumptions that underlie them. The figure of roughly 300 tons in Table 2.1 above is based on an overall U.S. production estimate of 1,800 to 2,300 metric tons (assuming approximately half a kilogram of marijuana from each plant cultivated and a 50 percent survival rate from annual eradication programs), with Kentucky having 15.4 percent of the total.[76] In 1991, Kentucky was the highest-ranking U.S. state for marijuana production. In that year, 809,366 cultivated plants were destroyed in Kentucky and 5,257,486 eradicated nationwide. Kentucky does not produce opium, heroin, or cocaine.

Eastern Kentucky—Appalachia—has both human and geographic conditions that favor contemporary marijuana production. Many of the relatively isolated families in the Kentucky hills have members who gained expertise running illegal liquor during Prohibition. Moreover, the hills and hollows themselves present a kind of "closedness" that lends itself well to clandestine activity such as illicit-drug production.

Current Consumption in Nine Countries

In the United States, which is a principal consumer of every known legal and illegal psychoactive drug, systematic and quite sophisticated national surveys are undertaken each year to attempt to determine the number of drug users and the type and quantity of illicit drugs consumed. In some instances this can be broken down by state (e.g., Kentucky, U.S.). Such surveys have a host of well-known methodological problems, but the data and the annual analyses appear to better reflect reality than would anthropological micro-studies or qualitative accounts, however valuable and useful these are.[77]

In contrast, in most of the countries under study here only qualitative observations, if not sheer guesses, about consumption are available. At times even this is complicated by political interests. Some governments do not want to portray their people as being addicted to drugs. By the same token, foreign governments and international institutions often worry that illicit-drug supplies in principal producer countries will, in fact, "leak" into their own populations and create nations of addicts (which, in some cases, has occurred). These governments are likely to overestimate the problem as a means to try to control it.

These caveats aside, and granted that some countries may in fact be experiencing a decline in consumption, almost everyone considers that *global* illicit-drug use, independent of population growth, has increased in the 1980s and 1990s and is likely to increase for some time yet. From the qualitative information contained in the country-study reports, there is strong reason to suppose that illicit-drug use is rising in all the countries except the United States, in some instances at a rapid pace.

In Bolivia, which is a principal coca producer but which also shows increased vertical integration of the industry (by processing coca into coca paste and cocaine), the government organization CONAPRE (Consejo Nacional de Prevención Integral del Uso Indebido de Drogas—National Council on Drug Abuse Prevention and Education) estimated that consumption of cocaine base (semi-refined cocaine) and cocaine had increased 54 percent from 1980 to 1988. Still, in the worst case, according to CONAPRE's estimates, no more than 1.7 percent of the population had tried a refined coca derivative. By contrast, the U.S. embassy in La Paz estimates that 6 to 7 percent of the urban population smokes cocaine base every day, consuming around 20 tons of cocaine a year, equivalent to somewhere between 4 and 9 percent of all the cocaine base produced in the country in 1990.[78] Various studies that have attempted to produce quantitative information suggest that between 5,000 and 240,000 Bolivians are habitual users of a refined coca derivative.[79]

James Painter reports that "more neutral observers are virtually unanimous in saying that the studies carried out so far—which are many—fall short in some way of giving an accurate figure, whether it be due to the small size of the sample, the methodologies used, the type of people questioned, or the funding for the study."[80] Hard data are spotty but striking—for example, calls to the *A Ti* drug hotline in Bolivia increased from 20 a month in April 1988 to 500 a month toward the end of 1989.[81] Many of the studies present a qualitative picture of drug abuse among street children, highly visible in the country's drug-production and -trafficking centers—Santa Cruz, Cochabamba, and Trinidad. "Personal testimonies show the ready availability of cocaine base and other drugs at cheap prices on the streets of these cities," Painter notes.[82] The ready availability of cocaine derivatives at cheap prices has apparently contributed to an increase in consumption, particularly among younger males.

Lest one jump too readily at a supply-side interpretation of consumption and gravitate to the facile policy conclusions that derive therefrom, one ought to take to heart Painter's trenchant caveat:

> But it is also the case that Bolivia would probably have a drug-user problem whether or not it was a producer country. Urban life for young people in economically marginal areas of Santa Cruz, La Paz and Cochabamba is plagued by many of the social problems—lack of employment and poor housing, health care and schools, to name the most obvious—that would make children vulnerable anywhere in the world. And it is worth remembering that marijuana—in some studies, the most popular drug among young users—is not known to be grown in Bolivia.[83]

In Mexico, a principal producer of marijuana and heroin and a major transiting country for cocaine, drug consumption is not considered the most urgent illicit-drug problem,[84] but it is nevertheless of growing concern to national authorities. Celia Toro's country-study report conveys an interesting picture. Based on all available consumption information, including a national household survey conducted for the first time in 1988,[85] several comparative (but not longitudinal) inferences can be made. Among U.S. and Mexican respondents who have ever used drugs in the course of their lifetime, the percentage of Mexicans is less than one-tenth that in the United States.[86]

According to the 1988 survey, marijuana is the drug of choice in Mexico, particularly among the 18–25 age group. Within that Mexican group, 4.31 percent declared they had smoked marijuana at least once, compared to a U.S. figure of 52.2 percent for the same age group. Toro shows that the highest prevalence of cocaine use is within the same age group (18–25) in both countries: 0.52 percent in Mexico and 19.4 percent in the United States.[87] Of the total Mexican population, 2.99 percent had used marijuana, 0.33 percent had tried cocaine, and 0.11 percent had experimented with heroin.[88] Regular use (i.e., during the previous thirty days) is considerably lower: 0.54 percent of the Mexican population smoked marijuana, and 0.14 percent used cocaine. The number of heroin users appears to be insignificant.[89] Marijuana is followed in abuse by tranquilizers and inhalants. Over the past ten years, the inhalation of solvents and the use of cocaine have shown the most rapid growth.[90] Marijuana consumption is also rising, albeit less rapidly.

The highest rates of drug use have been reported in Mexico's northwestern region[91] (an opium poppy–cultivation area). Toro says that "most Mexican users of heroin either lived in this area or obtained the drug for the first time in this region or while in the United States."[92] Considering other countries in Latin America,[93] the lowest reported rates ever for marijuana and cocaine use are found in Mexico and Costa Rica, the highest in Colombia.[94]

Notwithstanding the overall paucity of national studies on illicit-drug use in Mexico, all the qualitative evidence points to a positive correlation between the new availability of cocaine in the 1980s and a corresponding increased use among Mexicans in the 1980s and 1990s. Toro says that "officials at the Mexican Attorney General's Office believe that the recent increase in the use of cocaine among Mexicans is explained by the fact that cocaine dealers are crossing through Mexican territory in order to reach U.S. consumers; either cocaine traffickers pay in kind for transportation and other services or they are launching an aggressive marketing strategy to gain new markets for their merchandise."[95]

Even here, however, there are contrary views both about consumption and what causes it. Some epidemiologists claim that supply-driven drug consumption does not hold in the Mexican case: "In contrast to findings for other countries, perceived availability has not correlated strongly with drug use in Mexico."[96] Neither is poverty itself causally linked to drug abuse. In Mexico, the most important factor correlated with drug abuse is the disintegration of the family.[97]

Toro allows that both positions—supply and family dissolution—may drive illicit-drug consumption. Cocaine traffickers are trying to find new markets—Mexico has good possibilities—and the social disintegration affecting large numbers of youth and young adults makes them available for "alternative value pursuits"—namely, illicit-drug consumption. Toro opines that the most serious drug-use-related problem in Mexico is not marijuana, cocaine, or heroin but minors' inhalation of solvents. In a survey of street children under eighteen in a southern section of Mexico City, 22 percent acknowledged daily use of solvents as against only 1.5 percent reporting daily use of marijuana. The same survey showed that 36 percent of homeless children routinely inhaled solvents.[98]

In Colombia, a principal producer of cocaine and marijuana (and secondary producer of coca, opium poppy, and heroin), marijuana consumption rose dramatically during the 1970s, when the country became a chief supplier for the U.S. market after crops in Mexico had been sprayed with herbicides. The first empirical study of usage in Colombia took place in June 1972.[99] A population sample taken in Medellín (a subsequent principal center for cocaine traffickers and processors) revealed that 5 percent of the people were heavy users of marijuana and 1.9 percent of narcotics, LSD, solvents, psychoactive mushrooms, and other drugs (aside from cigarettes and alcohol). Many people no doubt were multiple drug users, although the study did not make distinctions. Later studies[100] confirmed an increasingly heavy usage in Medellín and other urban centers. In the 1980s and 1990s this abuse involved bazuco and cocaine. Alarmingly, later studies showed that 13.8 percent of the men and 2.2 percent of the women aged 12–64 were alcoholics and that another 12.1 percent and 2.4 percent were at high risk of becoming so. Many of these men and women became multiple drug users.

Among illegal drugs, marijuana continues to be the most commonly consumed, involving around 1.1 percent of the population, mostly males.[101] Bazuco is highly addictive and appears to be a drug of choice among increasing numbers of teenagers. In Colombia, bazuco smoking is often associated with multiple addictions and is linked to violence, criminality, and other problems. Francisco Thoumi notes that "bazuco consumption is a social clandestine activity in the slums, and is closely associated with violence and the *sicario* [hired killer] industry. However, bazuco consumption is not widespread and it is concentrated in clearly identified social groups—mainly young, very poor urban dwellers and perhaps some rich young people associated with the illegal PSAD [drug] trade."[102]

Everyone Thoumi interviewed in Colombia—health officials and researchers—concurred that cocaine is consumed in Colombia but that as of 1992 it had not yet become an epidemiological problem because it was used mostly as a "social drug" in conjunction with alcohol. "Frequently, the main purpose of cocaine is to mitigate some of the undesired effects of alcohol, and to allow the user to continue consuming alcohol, or to make it easier to drive a car," Thoumi found. "No doubt both of these uses can be very dangerous, but there is still a consensus among the health officials interviewed that the nature of cocaine consumption in Colombia, and the characteristics of society, make it unlikely that a cocaine epidemic will develop in the future."[103] The current low prices for cocaine in Colombia (70 percent pure cocaine retails for about $3 per gram) make it unlikely that demand will rise as a function of any price declines.

The above information is impressionistic, of course, but conclusions that Colombia, a major cocaine producer, will not likely experience a cocaine-consumption epidemic are supported by a recent study by Estupiñán and Torres de Galvis (1990), based on detailed interviews with 7,165 urban residents aged 15–59. These authors, working from a risk index created for each person interviewed, concluded that about 8.5 percent of the population faces a high risk of becoming marijuana users, 4.3 percent of becoming bazuco users, and 2.7 percent of becoming cocaine users.[104]

Thoumi shows that Colombia has a serious drug problem but that most of it is tied to legal psychoactive drugs, mostly alcohol. As in Mexico, consumers of marijuana and cocaine (and perhaps heroin, too) as a percentage of population are far fewer in Colombia than in the United States. The increased usage in the 1980s and 1990s has concerned many people, but, as in Mexico, Colombia's authorities and opinion makers see matters other than addiction as the country's key illicit-drug concerns. Alcoholism and the high levels of violence in Colombian society are among those more important concerns, as are economic problems (unemployment, underemployment, poverty) and the threat to national security posed by the drug traffickers.

In Peru, the world's largest producer of coca and an increasingly important producer of cocaine, there is no current epidemic of addiction to cocaine base or to cocaine, but usage is growing and addiction problems could become severe.[105] There are differences in terms of illicit-drug consumption according to regions, with major urban areas showing a marked increase; as yet, however, consumption levels even there do not appear to be significant. Elena Alvarez notes separate drug-use patterns for Lima and the provinces:

> In the Lima pattern, there is a higher, though not very significant, prevalence of consumption of illicit drugs, such as coca paste, cocaine, and marijuana; in the provincial pattern, in contrast, consumption of non-prescription pharmaceutical products is the norm,

such as analgesics, cough syrups, expectorants and tranquilizers. Also, the "provincial" pattern includes coca leaf chewing and the taking of hallucinogenic substances.[106]

The Lima drug-use pattern includes a class distribution, with cocaine consumption becoming a growing problem among upper-class teenagers. Coca-paste smoking appears to be spreading among coca producers in the Upper Huallaga Valley and elsewhere where export-production is emphasized. Many parents in the illicit-drug-growing areas fear that their children may become major consumers of the products grown and produced for export.[107]

As in Colombia, Mexico, and to some extent Bolivia, the pervasive presence of illicit drugs in Peru has not resulted in major addiction problems, although pockets of individuals and certain areas have been more widely affected than others (e.g., homeless children, teenagers, marginalized people, and hired hands in the traffickers' enterprise who are sometimes paid in kind). All the country studies indicate that usage and to some extent addiction are increasing, although not yet to the point of being a major concern to governments and law-enforcement officials. However, health officials see a problem looming on the horizon and are not so sanguine.

Thailand produces a small amount of opium and heroin and probably more significant amounts of cannabis but is a world-class transiting country for opium and heroin entering the world market from Myanmar/Burma and Laos. Consumption here historically has been considered (probably accurately), a problem for minority groups in the hills. Lately, however, both opium and heroin addiction have been increasing, especially in urban areas. Unlike countries in Latin America, which have nominally troublesome illicit-drug use, Thailand has a significant consumption problem. The effects are compounded by the fact that so many users are congregated in Bangkok, where drugs are joined by wholesale illicit sex, with an accompanying rapid and extensive transmission of AIDS. In Thailand's case, illegal drugs, random sex, and AIDS correlate. The consequences of all this are beginning to fan out from Bangkok to affect the entire country.

The Thailand Development Research Institute (TRDI), arguably the most prestigious and respected institute of its kind in Thailand, published a report in 1991 estimating that Thailand had between 495,900 and 747,100 narcotics addicts, of which about 150,000 to 335,000 were addicted to heroin.[108] Other scholars have disputed these figures.[109] Given that dispute, it is instructive to review the method by which the two TRDI authors came up with the above estimates. Anchalee Singhanetra-Renard notes that

Ammar and Chaiyut based their estimate on a number of data sources, including the work of Anek and Thanawan who used the Key Informant Survey System (KISS) to estimate the number of addicts (to all types of narcotics including amphetamines) per population of 100,000 and the rate of addiction during the year 1984–1985. Using data from a survey of four provinces, one in each region but not including Bangkok, Anek and Thanawan found that the highest incidence in these four provinces was 1,500 addicts per 100,000 population in Lampang. Ammar and Chaiyut then used this study to estimate the rate of usage for the entire country, Bangkok included. For Bangkok, they made the assumption that if Lampang was 1,500, the rate in Bangkok should range from 2,000 to 5,000 per 100,000. They justify this estimate by stating this amount would equal about 45 percent of the total opium addicts in the country. This is proportionately less than the number of opium addicts who registered with the government in 1959 to receive treatment when Sarit declared opium illegal. Since quite a few addicts did not register at that time, this estimate of 5,000 does not seem high. However, the fact that the opium addicts registering in 1959 had been engaging in a legal practice while today's heroin addicts are not and the two figures may not be completely comparable with the result that 5,000 is quite likely too high. The total estimated narcotics addicts in Thailand for 1989 were then estimated at from 495,900 to 747,100.[110]

Singhanetra-Renard estimates the number of persons addicted to cannabis, heroin, and opium to be more than 400,000.[111]

Addicts aside, many Thais other than members of hill tribes apparently consume illicit drugs casually. With these assumptions in hand, and with further assumptions made about daily usage, Ammar and Chaiyut conclude that about 12 metric tons of opium, 25 metric tons of heroin, and 70 metric tons of dried cannabis leaf are consumed annually in Thailand.[112]

Thailand, contrary to many other principal producer or transiting countries, consumes significantly more illicit drugs than it produces. Ammar and Chaiyut estimate that more than 538 metric tons of opium are imported from Burma and converted to heroin in Thailand. More than 220 metric tons of dried cannabis leaf are either imported from Laos or produced in Thailand. Illicit drugs not consumed in Thailand are reexported.

For Myanmar/Burma, assessing consumption is as difficult as determining opium-production levels. The accuracy of available data is the most problematic of all the countries studied because of political turbulence and Myanmar/Burma's semiclosed borders. Yet, despite strong Buddhist injunctions against taking intoxicating or psychoactive drugs, considerable consumption appears to occur, and it is probably increasing, especially in the cities, where heroin use is spreading.

But not just heroin use is increasing in Myanmar/Burma. Since the mid 1970s, secondary school students have used cannabis widely, and the rich are beginning to consume cocaine.[113] Users of all drugs have defied jail, registration, fines, and reprisals as they continue their habits. The question is, why? Since serious political upheavals in 1988, Myanmar/Burma has been faced with "a large idle class of youth who are willing to try different types of narcotics."[114] Concomitantly, heroin seems to be increasingly available, which has driven prices down and contributed to luring unprecedented numbers of people into a consumption market. Ronald Renard notes:

> Former drug dependents returned to using heroin, while many urban youth then started trying heroin for the first time in unprecedented numbers. Drug dealers began marketing heroin through traditional outlets, like "betel shops" (where betel nut, a traditional mild stimulant was sold with a variety of other sundry goods) but also through new outlets. Reports of surprisingly high rates of students at secondary and tertiary educational institutions trying heroin have been heard. By some estimates, this confirmed by international officials familiar with the drug situation in Burma, 50 percent of the Rangoon University students have tried heroin. Other idle or frustrated urban youth throughout the country have taken to a variety of drugs from codeine to cannabis to heroin.[115]

In Laos, by local estimates, addiction to opium and heroin was a troubling condition before 1975, with the country having perhaps as many as 50,000 addicts.[116] After 1975, with the advent of the People's Democratic Republic, heroin addiction dramatically declined throughout the country, particularly in the cities. Known heroin addicts were placed in cold-turkey rehabilitation centers and subjected to rigorous manual labor. Those not picked up by law-enforcement officials either drastically reduced their consumption or went underground.

Fear and intimidation efforts notwithstanding, in areas where family and community have broken down in more recent years, opium and heroin consumption has spilled over to involve young adults and even children and may touch as much as 10 percent of the population.[117] The Lao government has admitted to an increasing problem of substance abuse among lowland Lao and Lao Soung ethnic groups[118] as well as a continuing problem of endemic addiction among some other hill tribes. Indeed, the Lao National Commission for Drug Control and Supervision estimates that 2 to 4 percent of villagers in the hill provinces of Vientiane and Xieng Khouang are addicted.[119]

Daniel Henning argues a supply-side consumption hypothesis to account for much of the addiction, finding that drug production in Laos has flourished in regions where economic conditions are inadequate to sustain an acceptable standard of living: "Such conditions push people to look for alternative income sources. Once illegal drugs emerge as a pursuit of choice, cultivation, processing, trafficking and drug abuse increase. Addiction rates are highly correlated with access to opium production and trafficking areas."[120] This finding appears to contrast with findings in Mexico, Peru, and Bolivia, where addiction rates are not so easily correlated with supply conditions.

Among Hmong Lao tested for their admissibility as immigrants into the United States (most refugees were not tested), an addiction rate of 4.5 percent was discovered (this among the ethnic group apparently most adverse to opium usage except among the elderly and for medicinal purposes). Among less socially resistant groups, impressionistic evidence points to an addiction rate of around 10 percent.[121]

In Pakistan, cannabis has been used widely since precolonial days, mostly being marketed locally or between neighboring provinces. Opium usage originated with Great Britain's organization of the international opium trade. Thereafter, as in Burma, Laos, and Thailand, opium production was maintained for government revenue. By 1980–1981, heroin had entered the Pakistani market on a large scale, although it had been widely available in outlying provinces (e.g., Baluchistan) for many years. Heroin was cheap in Pakistan and soon available everywhere, spilling over from the trade routes from the Northwest Frontier Province to Karachi or through Baluchistan to the Iranian border. Depots along the way quickly and inexpensively serviced the needs or desires of travelers and thereafter of the general population.[122] Pakistan's National Survey on Drug Abuse estimated that the 5,000 heroin users in 1980 swelled to over 650,000 in 1986,[123] with no end in sight to increased consumption. Some sources estimate Pakistan now has more than a million chronic users or addicts, with no region of the country, however remote, being free from the influence of a highly efficient and integrated but illicit distribution network that services national and international markets.

Aside from supply-driven addiction, it is thought that political anxiety and uncertainty in Pakistan in the 1980s contributed to the epidemic, which involved high-level white-collar professionals as well as ordinary citizens.[124] Drug pushers in all areas marketed heroin by giving free samples or by creating artificial scarcities in the cannabis market, thereby encouraging cannabis users to try heroin.[125]

As the international demand for heroin grew, Pakistan quickly developed the means to supply much of it. Diffusion into local economies and societies has materially contributed to the country's significant heroin-addiction problem. Indeed, Doris Buddenberg argues that increasing drug consumption in Pakistan from independence through 1992 can be described in three successive, partially overlapping phases—(1) traditional drug use, (2) the heroin epidemic, and (3) prescription-drug misuse—which serve to chronicle Pakistan's continuing slide into multiple drug addictions.[126] Why such a pattern? Buddenberg suggests that an "important reason for the surge in heroin consumption . . . lies in its cultural acceptability. In the Subcontinent, in general, drugs that calm down, quieten, and bring about 'peace of mind' are the drugs of choice, from cannabis to tranquilizers to heroin. In drugstores and pharmacies, tranquilizers are freely available."[127]

Although the country-study report for Kentucky, U.S. did not mention local illicit-drug consumption, large amounts of marijuana are produced in the state, and cocaine has found a haven there both in terms of consumption and transshipment to other states. As both a consuming and producing state, Kentucky has experienced a regional phenomenon not unlike that seen in the countries reported on here.

About 1.19 percent of the U.S. population 12 years old or older accounts for almost 60 percent of the marijuana consumed, or nearly 1,000 out of 1,600 metric tons.[128] This relative percentage may hold for Kentucky, although the country report did not give specific estimates. In the United States as a whole, around 20 percent of the population age 12–26 has tried marijuana, perhaps half that has tried cocaine, and a negligible number have experimented with heroin. Cocaine addiction, including crack, has been a serious public-policy concern.

Contrary to the experience of other countries studied here, illicit-drug use appears to be declining in the United States, although an apparent rise in drug use by younger teenagers may ultimately counter the trend.[129]

Summary and Conclusions

Production figures reported here or anywhere else should be understood only as estimates based on criteria ranging from seat-of-the-pants guesses to high-tech analyses. From whatever methodology, the results incorporate numerous assumptions and conditions that bear heavily on their potential accuracy. The statement that there are no accurate illicit-drug data is truer to the mark than its opposite.

Clearly, however, informed guesses are better than no guesses; at a minimum they point to qualitative circumstances that likely show production trends and suggest future prospects. In this chapter I have tried to weigh data offered by country-study authors and others to suggest gross estimates of illicit-drug production that *may* be somewhat reflective of reality. However, the qualitative descriptions found in each author's country study and briefly developed in this book may be more important than any set of quantitative figures advanced here or elsewhere. Readers are urged to consult the country-study reports of their interest to gain a more ample appreciation of this assertion.

Production declines are noted in some countries, increases in others. On the whole, the aggregate amount of illicit drugs coursing the world's markets appears to be higher now than several years ago. Traffickers have opened new production centers and new markets. Aggregate consumption also appears to have increased in recent years.

Determining consumption statistics of illicit drugs is as difficult as calculating production tonnages. Some countries run sophisticated surveys (e.g., the United States and Mexico), but the methodological pitfalls are legion. Other countries have hardly any systematic methods or data at all (e.g., Myanmar/Burma). Data gathering is complicated by political interests that work to have reports tailored to their liking.

Does the increasing supply of drugs translate into increased consumption—a supply-side theory of addiction? The data in the country studies support a mildly positive relationship in Latin America, but the trend is considerably weaker than one might at first blush suppose. In other words, the availability of drugs does not necessarily translate into increased usage. However, supply-side theories of addiction appear to be supported in Thailand, Myanmar/Burma, and especially Laos and Pakistan, where addiction has increased commensurate with illicit-drug availability. For all countries, more than one factor is certainly involved, and more than one type of policy approach is required to address social problems inherently connected to the illicit-drug trade.

Notes

1. More than 99 percent of the world's coca leaf is grown in those three countries, which also control most of the cocaine laboratories. Small amounts of cocaine—most likely less than 1 percent of the total—are produced in Brazil, Mexico, Chile, Ecuador, Paraguay, and Venezuela. According to the U.S. Department of State, (Bureau of International Narcotics Matters, *International Narcotics Control Strategy Report* [Washington, D.C.: The Bureau, 1993], 88, 96, 110, 116, 126; hereafter cited as *INCSR 1993*]), the following amounts of coca were produced in 1992: Argentina, 80 metric

tons; Bolivia, 80,300; Colombia, 29,600; Ecuador, 40 (1991); and Peru, 223,920. The same report for 1994 (hereafter cited as *INCSR 1994*) estimates the potential 1993 harvest for Bolivia to be 84,400 metric tons (p. 94); Colombia, 31,700 (p. 108); and Peru, 155,500 (p. 123).

2. James Painter, *Bolivia and Coca: A Study in Dependency* (Boulder, Colo.: Lynne Rienner Publishers, 1994), 35.

3. Ibid. Painter's source is José Antonio Quiroga, *Coca Cocaína: Una Visión Boliviana* (La Paz, Bolivia: AIPE-PROCOM/CEDLA/CID, 1990), 34.

4. For example, Anchalee Singhanetra-Renard, "Socioeconomic and Political Impact of Production, Trade and Use of Narcotic Drugs in Thailand," a study for UNRISD and UNU (draft of 23 April 1993), 7–8.

5. Elena Alvarez, "Illegal Export-Led Growth in the Andes: A Preliminary Economic and Socio-political Assessment for Peru," a study for UNRISD and UNU (draft of January 1993), 25.

6. Ibid., 26ff.

7. Ibid., Table 3, 31.

8. Painter, *Bolivia and Coca*, Table 1.1, 15.

9. Principal source on Bolivia is Painter, *Bolivia and Coca*.

10. Ibid., 5–42.

11. Ibid., 6.

12. Ibid., Table 3.1, 44.

13. *INCSR 1994*, 94.

14. Principal source on Peru is Alvarez, "Illegal Export-Led Growth in the Andes."

15. Ibid., 28.

16. Ibid., 27–28. The range is 129,000 to 380,000 hectares, the low figure coming from *INCSR 1993*, 126, the high figure from R. Peña, *Análisis Agroeconómico de la Producción de Coca en la Región del Alto Huallaga* (Lima: Project AD/PER/86/459–PNUD, 1987), cited by Alvarez, ibid., 27.

17. *INCSR 1993*, 126; *INCSR 1994*, 118–123. Although the 1993 tonnage for Peru shows a substantial decline from 1992, policymakers ought not take too much heart. Production has fallen in the Upper Huallaga Valley because of blight and the advanced age of the plants there. Plantings elsewhere in Peru have been accelerated, but leaf yields have not yet matured in the new areas. If growers can control blight and be successful in their new plantings, one should look for increased tonnage in years to come.

18. Alvarez, "Illegal Export-led Growth in the Andes," 26–28.

19. *INCSR 1993*, 126; *INCSR 1994*, 123.

20. See, for example, *INCSR 1991*, 122–123.

21. *INCSR 1993*, 126.

22. Alvarez, "Illegal Export-Led Growth in the Andes," 1.

23. Principal source on Colombia is Francisco Thoumi, *Political Economy and Illegal Drugs in Colombia* (Boulder, Colo.: Lynne Rienner Publishers, 1994).

24. *INCSR 1993*, 110.

25. The low figure comes from *INCSR 1993*, 110. See subsequent arguments in the text for rationale for the higher figure.

26. *INCSR 1993*, 110.

27. Thoumi, *Political Economy*, 179–183.

28. Ibid., Table 6.1, 304.

29. *INCSR 1991*, 101.

30. *INCSR 1994*, 108, lists 1992 yields at 1,650 metric tons and 1993 yields at 4,125 metric tons.

31. Thoumi, *Political Economy*, 185–187.

32. *INCSR 1993*, 101.

33. *INCSR 1994*, 108.

34. Principal source on Mexico is María Celia Toro, "Mexican Drug Control Policy: Origin, Purpose, Consequences," a study for UNRISD and UNU (revised draft of 9 June 1993). In press, Lynne Rienner Publishers, Boulder, Colo.

35. Ibid., 66, note 126.

36. *INCSR 1991*, 164.

37. Principal source on Thailand is Singhanetra-Renard, "Socioeconomic and Political Impact."

38. *INCSR 1994*, 299.

39. UNESCAP, "Proceedings of the Meeting of Senior Officials on Drug Abuse Issues in Asia and the Pacific," Bangkok, 1991.

40. *INCSR 1991*, 270 (46 tons revised to 40 tons in *INCSR 1993*, 307).

41. *INCSR 1994*, 299.

42. Singhanetra-Renard, "Socioeconomic and Political Impact," 5–6.

43. Ibid., 4, 149, 160.

44. *INCSR 1991*, 277; *INCSR 1993*, 307.

45. The principal source on Myanmar/Burma is Ronald Renard, "Socioeconomic and Political Impact of Production, Trade and Use of Narcotic Drugs in Burma," a study for UNRISD and UNU (revised draft of 3 November 1993).

46. *INCSR 1991*, 235.

47. *INCSR 1993*, 263.

48. *INCSR 1994*, 260.

49. Renard, "Socioeconomic and Political Impact," 24–25.

50. Ibid.

51. The principal source on Laos is Daniel Henning, "Production and Trafficking of Opium and Heroin in Laos," a study for UNRISD and UNU, revised draft of 26 May 1993.

52. Ibid., 4.

53. Ibid., 5.

54. Ibid.

55. Ibid., 19.

56. *INCSR 1991*, 257.

57. The U.S. Department of State argues for 230 metric tons. See *INCSR 1993*, 284.

58. *INCSR 1994*, 278, estimates 1993 production at 180 metric tons, down from 380 metric tons in 1989.

59. Henning, "Production and Trafficking," 20.

60. As cited in ibid., 20.

61. *INCSR 1991*, 252.

62. Ibid., 257.

63. *INCSR 1993*, 284.

64. *INCSR 1991*, 252.

65. Principal source on Pakistan is Doris Buddenberg, "Illicit Drug Issues in Pakistan," a study for UNRISD and UNU (draft of May 1993).

66. Ibid., 7.

67. Ibid., 3.

68. *INCSR 1993*, 247.

69. *INCSR 1994*, 246.

70. Buddenberg, "Illicit Drug Issues," 66.

71. Ibid., 55–61.

72. *INCSR 1991,* 226.

73. Ibid., 220.

74. *INCSR 1993,* 247.

75. Principal source on Kentucky is Richard Clayton and William Estep, "Marijuana Cultivation and Production in the United States, Appalachia, and Kentucky: The Context and Consequences," a study for UNRISD and UNU (draft of 25 January 1993).

76. See ibid., Chapters 3 and 5.

77. Two basic sources of statistics on cocaine use in the United States exist: a yearly report produced by the University of Michigan entitled *Illicit Drug Use, Smoking, and Drinking by America's High School Students, College Students, and Young Adults* and the National Institute of Drug Abuse's (NIDA) *National Household Survey on Drug Abuse.* Both follow the same approach, asking three different questions about proximity of drug use: Have you ever used? Have you used in the past year? Have you used in the past month? NIDA conducts a survey of households every two or three years to assess the extent of drug use in the United States. The survey methodology is essentially identical for all surveys conducted: "A national probability sample of households in the coterminous United States was selected from 100 primary sampling units. The household population includes more than 98 percent of the U.S. population. It excludes persons living in group quarters or institutions; such as military installations, college dormitories, hotels, hospitals, and jails; and transient populations such as the homeless. Alaska and Hawaii have not been included in the sample since the first National Household Survey because of logistic and cost considerations" (NIDA, *National Household Survey on Drug Abuse* [Rockville, Md.: NIDA, 1988]). Estimates are reported in three different age groups: 12–17, 18–25, and 26 and older. In 1985 and 1988, the 26 and older category was further broken down to include two different age groups: 26–35, and 36 and older. The results of the survey should be interpreted with caution. First, "the value of self-reports obviously depends upon the honesty and memory of sampled respondents. . . . Some under- or over-reporting may occur." Second, total U.S. population estimates may be biased as time from the last census increases, subsequently biasing the probability sample. Third, "the population surveyed is the non-institutionalized population living in households, and therefore does not include some segments of the U.S. population which may contain a substantial proportion of drug users, such as college students living in dormitories, transients and those incarcerated" (NIDA, *National Household Survey on Drug Abuse,* 1988).

78. *Presencia,* (19 June 1988), and U.S. Embassy (La Paz), unclassified memo 10 (no title), cited by Painter, *Bolivia and Coca,* 68–69.

79. Ibid., 69.

80. Ibid.

81. Ibid.

82. Ibid., 70.

83. Ibid.

84. Toro argues that the principal concern for Mexico is the United States's posturing and imposition of drug-control programs in Mexico to deal with consumption problems in the United States. The programs hurt Mexico ("Mexican Drug Control Policy," 1–58).

85. The surveys mentioned were made by María Elena Medina-Mora and María del Carmen Mariño, "Drug Abuse in Latin America," in Peter H. Smith, ed., *Drug Policy in the Americas* (Boulder, Colo.: Westview Press, 1992), 47–50, cited by Toro, "Mexican Drug Control Policy," 62.

86. Toro (ibid.) used the 1990 U.S. NIDA household survey for this comparison. Drugs included in the surveys are analgesics, tranquilizers, sedatives, stimulants, inhalants, marijuana, hallucinogens, cocaine, and heroin. For original sources on Mexico see Medina-Mora and Mariño, "Drug Abuse," 47.

87. See Medina-Mora and Mariño, "Drug Abuse," Table 3–1, 48; and Toro, "Mexican Drug Control Policy," 62–63.

88. See María Elena Medina-Mora, Roberto Tapia et al., "Encuesta Nacional de Adicciones," *Anales de la Quinta Reunión de Investigación del Instituto Mexicano de Psiquiatría*, 1990, 48–55; cited by Toro, "Mexican Drug Control Policy," 63.

89. Toro, "Mexican Drug Control Policy," 63.

90. Ibid.

91. Includes the states of Baja California, Baja California Sur, Sonora, and Sinaloa.

92. Medina-Mora and Mariño, "Drug Abuse," 50, cited by Toro, "Mexican Drug Control Policy," 64.

93. According to Medina-Mora and Mariño, "Drug Abuse," household surveys have been conducted in only six Latin American countries: Peru, Colombia, Costa Rica, Ecuador, Guatemala, and Mexico.

94. Toro, "Mexican Drug Control Policy," 64.

95. "Reunión de Evaluación y Perspectivas del Fenómeno de las Drogas en México," PGR Internal Seminar, held in Mexico City, 26–27 February 1992; cited by Toro, "Mexican Drug Control Policy," 66.

96. Medina-Mora and Mariño, "Drug Abuse," 53, cited by Toro, "Mexican Drug Control Policy," 66.

97. Toro, "Mexican Drug Control Policy," 66.

98. Ibid., 65.

99. Thoumi, *Political Economy*, 266.

100. Ibid., 446–447.

101. Ibid., 447–448.

102. Ibid., 270.

103. Ibid., 452.

104. Ibid., 453.

105. Alvarez, "Illegal Export-Led Growth in the Andes," 55.

106. Ibid.

107. Ibid., 55–56.

108. Singhanetra-Renard, "Socioeconomic and Political Impact," 162–163, citing Ammar and Chaiyut 1991, 18.

109. Dr. Vichai Poshyachinda observed in an in-house seminar when the findings were presented that because addicts do not always use narcotics every day, as assumed by Ammar and Chaiyut, even their lower estimates were high (Singhanetra-Renard, "Socioeconomic and Political Impact," 162).

110. Ibid.

111. Ibid., 163.

112. As cited in ibid., 165.

113. Renard, "Socioeconomic and Political Impact," 89.

114. Ibid., 123.
115. Ibid.
116. Henning, "Production and Trafficking," 38.
117. Ibid., 43.
118. Ibid., 42.
119. Ibid., 38.
120. Ibid., 41.
121. Ibid., 43.
122. Buddenberg, "Illicit Drug Issues," 83ff.
123. Ibid., 73.
124. Ibid., 81.
125. Ibid., 80.
126. Ibid., 66.
127. Ibid., 81.
128. Clayton and Estep, "Marijuana," 59.
129. Joseph B. Treaster, "Drug Use by Younger Teenagers Appears to Rise, Counter to Trend," *New York Times*, 13 April 1993, A1.

. . . 3 . . .

Drug Trafficking

In Chapter 1 we examined the pervasive role that drug traffickers play in drug-related criminality. These people, who may share only one common interest—money and power—link agricultural growers and petty producers with consumers in the illicit-drug chain. Their diversity has produced divergent drug-distribution and alliance patterns. These are associated with, first, traffickers' level of activity (wholesalers, middlemen, or retailers); second, their degree of organization (e.g., whether they develop payrolls or enforceable "personnel policies," establish specialized departments, have vertical integration, or struggle over regional or countrywide market shares); third, the type of drug marketed (e.g., cocaine, heroin, cannabis, designer drugs); fourth, the existence of trafficker-insurgent-terrorist alliances; and, fifth, competition for market share. Implications stemming from these patterns abound. For example, vertically integrated organizations with enforceable personnel policies tend to resort to extreme violence at all levels when seeking to increase shares in a competitive market.

Aside from the trafficking organizations that extend into or are based in principal consumer countries, evidence—both hard and soft—exists of substantial organized production and marketing networks in most of the producer and transiting countries.[1] In addition, sophisticated organizations either have existed or appear to be cropping up in countries peripheral to the drug trade. This chapter examines how trafficker organizations have operated in the countries under study.

The introduction to this chapter draws from LaMond Tullis, *Handbook of Research on the Illicit Drug Traffic* (Westport, Conn.: Greenwood Press, 1991), 49–54.

Colombia

During the 1980s, and perhaps even to the present day (the killing of Pablo Escobar on 2 December 1993 notwithstanding), Colombia has had the world's most efficient and expert illegal traffickers.[2] These traffickers are organized into several groups most often called "cartels" (but really just syndicates), the best known being Medellín and Cali.

Until perhaps 1990, the Colombian syndicates controlled 80 percent of the world's trade in cocaine, with the Medellín group in control of the bulk of that. Recently, however, the Medellín group has collapsed in shambles: Gonzalo Rodríguez Gacha and Pablo Escobar, two of its most notorious kingpins, are now dead, and many of their seconds-in-command have either surrendered to Colombian authorities or been killed by rivals in the drug trade. These events have seriously restricted the amount of cocaine that Medellín controls. However, the Cali group and growing organizations in Bolivia and Peru have readily picked up the slack.[3]

Despite traditional rivalries, Colombia's traffickers have tended to find common ground in six areas: (1) their repudiation of the country's legal system and formal institutions; (2) their criminal background—especially among the Medellín group; (3) their constellation of values regarding fate and providence that motivate them to be heavy risk takers; (4) their frenetic efforts to become assimilated politically and economically in Colombian society; (5) their making common cause with guerrilla organizations during the 1980s; and (6) their "insurance" collaborations with one another to protect shipments of cocaine.

Francisco Thoumi argues that Colombia's traffickers share with many other Colombians a belief in the illegitimacy of their nation's political and economic institutions.[4] However, checked by few if any traditional moral or behavioral restraints, they have become a particularly corrosive and violent element in Colombian society. They accept no reproach. Breaking the law—any law—is justified, and not just for the usual economic reasons that criminals favor. For traffickers, the law, law-enforcement officials, U.S. drug operatives, and drug-control organizations all represent the traditional elite, international imperialism, or other international competitive economic interests, none of which has any historical moral standing in their eyes. Therefore, moralistic arguments about restraining violent behavior do not capture these people's attention. The general feeling most Colombians have of their political and economic institutions—illegitimacy and profound inefficacy—allows traffickers to garner enthusiastic support in some areas.

Because they live by and apply their own laws, Colombia's traffickers are, by definition, criminals. But their criminality in almost every case preceded their involvement in the drug trade. They have long pursued wealth, power, and status using underground, illegal, and even violent means. Gonzalo Rodríguez Gacha, for example, trafficked in contraband emeralds and was an enthusiastic participant in the violence that characterized the trade.[5] Carlos Lehder stole cars and sold marijuana in New York[6] long before he became a chief among the Colombian narcos; he had a U.S. police record before he was extradited from Colombia to the United States on drug trafficking charges to serve a life sentence in a Florida prison.

Thoumi notes that Verónica Rivera, "who became known as the 'queen of cocaine,' began her career as a businesswoman in a 'San Andresito' [outdoor markets specializing in contraband], selling smuggled household appliances."[7] Pablo Escobar "began his criminal career in adolescence, stealing headstones from local graveyards, shaving off the inscriptions, and reselling the blank slabs to bereaved relatives at bargain prices."[8] So it is with every major Colombian drug trafficker on whom biographical information has been collected.

Aside from their disdain for Colombian institutions and their long criminal records, Colombian traffickers share other characteristics. They appear to be great believers in fate and providence and are therefore not reluctant to place themselves in harm's way. They seem unmoved by normal considerations of personal danger. It is a perspective unaltered by normal law-enforcement efforts and one that makes dealing with or trying to control them such a dangerous enterprise.

Disdain, criminality, fate, and providence aside, Colombian traffickers have an almost frantic desire to be assimilated into Colombia's society, polity, and economy. They see this as a way to protect and to legitimize their wealth and property, enabling them to repatriate most of it and to enjoy it as conspicuously as possible. They thus want economic status and social recognition comparable to that of other rich Colombians, and they expect to be able to participate in the political system and to have access to public office.

To pursue these ends, traffickers have established vast networks —both clandestine and aboveboard—involving normal politicians, financial institutions, members of professions, bankers, and others. The fact that most Colombians have a certain disdain for the state has served to facilitate traffickers' being admitted to a kind of full-fledged standing. Above all, the traffickers do not want to be extradited to the United States, and they have used all their networks to that end, using various forms of violence.

Thoumi illustrates that the "integration of illegal traffickers into the Colombian economy has been subtle, but pervasive."[9] They have penetrated the "last crevices of society, politics, the economy, and even cultural and sports activities."[10] One of the most visible investments for narco-traffickers is in professional soccer teams, a strategy that brings social support to the traffickers and political respect from the politicians. Also, altering gate receipts serves as an excellent method of laundering money gotten illegally from abroad.

In the process of seeking social assimilation, various illicit-drug groups have pursued different emphases, some working to legalize their assets, others trying to obtain political power and social status first, and others attempting simply to undermine traditional institutions through corruption or violence. In this process, all of them apparently have established close relationships with, and gained influence over, some parts of the political establishment.[11]

Political integration for the Medellín (but not the Cali) group was a particularly important goal before Medellín's apparent demise with the death, incarceration, or defection of its major chiefs. Most Medellín traffickers came from social outcast groups with few connections to the old and still highly influential traditional elite. To compensate, they created populist political movements and machines, which they maintained by economically favoring their followers (i.e., treating them as clients in a clientelistic system). In this process, both Carlos Lehder and Pablo Escobar became highly visible, and each had ample wealth to disburse. Other traffickers, taking a more low-key approach, simply sought to buy into the existing system with their remarkable wealth.

The Cali group has not pressed hard for social and political integration—its members are already well placed. The have eschewed indiscriminate violence in favor of discrete assassinations of their enemies. They have influenced the political establishment with economic and social favors rather than kidnappings and torture, as was customary in Medellín. The Cali group comprises "respectable criminals" who enjoy status accordingly. One might think of them as Colombia's "white collar" traffickers.

The Cali and Medellín groups have also differed as to their economic integration. Medellín, for example, concentrated on rural and urban real estate, Cali on urban enterprises and generalized contraband.

Colombia's narco-traffickers have formed their own paramilitary organizations and have, on occasion, allied themselves with guerrilla groups seeking the downfall of the Colombian state. The guerrillas and narco-traffickers have constituted an uncommon alliance, linked by their views of the illegitimacy of the existing government and political system but otherwise having quite opposite goals. The drug lords are unrestrained capitalists, whereas the guerrillas are equally unrestrained political ideologues who view capitalism as having been spawned by the devil himself.

But common practical concerns superseded contradictory ideals when the narco-guerrilla connection formed. Traffickers needed their clandestine drug-processing laboratories protected from government intervention, for which they paid guerrillas handsomely. Guerrillas needed funds for their political and terrorist activities, for which they happily performed drug-protection services. The relationship was synergistic and the benefits shared. The 1985 guerrilla takeover of the Supreme Court building was perhaps the epitome of cooperation. The guerrillas made their political statement but also conveniently destroyed nearly all the files containing cases against narco-traffickers.

All the benefits notwithstanding, the alliance of guerrillas and traffickers is temporary and fraught with conflict. For instance, Thoumi discusses how narco-traffickers' sponsorship of coca growing in guerrilla-controlled areas weakened guerrilla organizations by shifting peasant loyalty. Guerrillas attacked. Later, when the narco-traffickers themselves became large landowners in guerrilla-held territories, they resisted guerrilla-imposed taxation customarily applied to property owners. There was a general falling out between the two groups.

One of the outcomes of the initial guerrilla-trafficker cooperation and later fallout was the establishment by traffickers of self-defense capabilities—in the form of paramilitary squads—to protect their properties and persons. Another was traffickers' employment of young assassins for hire (*sicarios*) to settle scores with enemies; their victims included politicians, police, competitors, political ideologues, and unfortunate bystanders. Many of the sicarios had previously been trained by guerrilla organizations such as M-19.

Finally, Colombian traffickers, for all their differences, have frequently collaborated in making bulk cocaine shipments to markets in the United States and Europe. One bulk shipment might contain marked packages from twenty or more shippers. If that shipment happens to be interdicted by law-enforcement agents, each shipper is compensated on a prorated basis for his loss from an "insurance" pool funded by profits from shipments that make it through the interdiction net. This approach greatly reduces risks to individual shippers, especially to small shippers, who could be put out of business by an uncompensated loss. Losses to law-enforcement agents are therefore simply tallied up as a business expense.

With risks reduced, more and more people can be brought into the syndicate, with "small fry" paying a calculated premium to the larger, better-established traffickers. One of the consequences is that if large traffickers (e.g., the Pablo Escobars) are put out of business, the enterprise can nevertheless continue with experienced personnel. Someone is always there, ready to step in. This is a daunting challenge to law-enforcement agencies.

With a tenacity bordering on fanaticism, Colombia's politicians have created and held on to a political system that is widely viewed as illegitimate. Colombia's more nefarious citizens then entered the illicit-drug trade by offering the traffickers protection as long as they did not challenge the "integrity" of the state (as the Medellín traffickers did). Colombia's traffickers honed their skills in marijuana trafficking to and within the United States during the 1970s, so they needed only small organizational shifts to take advantage of the cocaine market when it emerged in the 1980s. Quickly becoming rather sophisticated, Colombian traffickers have been among the first to employ high technology to thwart interdiction on the high seas (e.g., air drops near U.S. coastlines packaged with electronic location beepers to aid pickup personnel traveling in speedboats). It is not surprising, then, that Colombia's traffickers are among the world's most experienced and successful.

Peru

Until recently, Peruvian cocaine entrepreneurs were completely subordinate to Colombian traffickers. They had few, if any, international marketing contacts. They lacked access to sufficient precursor chemicals to launch a viable value-added industry within Peru. They had trouble cooperating with each other to move large amounts of coca or cocaine products. Accordingly, Peruvian trafficking depended on Colombian representatives, who periodically approached Peruvian coca growers and middlemen with offers for their leaves and coca paste. Once purchased, the leaf crop was transported to clandestine or guerrilla-protected sites in Peru for reduction to coca paste. Virtually all the coca paste was thereafter picked up on remote airstrips for shipment to Colombia for refining.

Much of that has now changed. Colombian traffickers have been weakened by their mortal conflict with the Colombian state; Peruvians have become much more skilled in product technology, organization, and marketing; and Peruvian entrepreneurs now carry out considerable value-added production, which they feed into first-stage marketing networks from Peruvian soil. Peruvians' refinement of coca base is therefore now closely linked with coca cultivation; one can now legitimately speak of a value-added integrated Peruvian industry. Colombians are still involved, of course, but the balance has been tipping in favor of the Peruvians, who ship not only to Colombia but also to Brazil and Ecuador, where precursor chemicals are more readily available for final refinement.

Accordingly, the Peruvian illicit-drug industry involves increasingly sophisticated integrated organizations, beginning on the bottom end with thousands of coca farmers (some of whom are represented by the national labor federation) and moving thereafter to rural elites and their urban organizers and protectors. Because the organizational dynamics in Peru are still highly fluid and are complicated by internal civil strife, it is not possible at this time to be more specific.

We do know that in alliance with Sendero Luminoso the traffickers were until late 1993 a better than equal match for the combined efforts of the Peruvian military and international (mostly U.S.) drug-control efforts. Until late 1993 Sendero's power was only slightly diminished by the 1992 capture of its head, Amibael Guzmán. But the Peruvian state's successful elimination in 1993–1994 of much of Sendero's high command structure severely crippled the organization. Nevertheless, the traffickers and Sendero's remnants continue to force drug-control officers into "secure bases" in the Upper Huallaga Valley (e.g., Santa Lucía), from which they dare emerge only in armed air escort. The inability of the Peruvian state to exercise effective control over the Upper Huallaga Valley has left traffickers there and in other outlying areas free to operate virtually unimpeded. The U.S. Department of State opines that this lack of control has now been turned around as a consequence of the suspension of constitutional democracy by President Alberto Fujimori on 5 April 1992 and his dedication of significant military resources to the Upper Huallaga Valley.[12] Hardly anyone believes, however, that the turnabout will last over the long term unless Peru can settle its development/constitutional crisis.

More so than their Colombian counterparts, Peruvian traffickers—many still "petty" but clearly upwardly mobile in a growing industry—are driven by a desperate generalized poverty fueled by Peru's economic crisis and internal political disarray. Both the social psychology and perhaps even the social origins and background of Peruvian traffickers are likely, therefore, to be quite different from those of Cali Colombians.

Bolivia

Bolivia has been more akin to Peru than to Colombia in its historical association with the illicit-drug trade.[13] Until the early to mid-1980s Bolivians essentially grew coca, sometimes processed it into coca paste, and then turned the product over to the Colombians. Thus Bolivia, as Peru, historically provided the raw materials for others to ultimately refine and export. But, as in Peru, that is beginning to change as Bolivians move to integrate their industry and create a value-added product domestically.

At the production base, Bolivians are much more organized than are the Peruvians and have been for a long time. Five peasant federations account for all but a small portion of coca production,[14] with each of the federations sporting sophisticated organizational subdivisions (*centrales* and *sindicatos*) that actually function somewhat like local governments. For reasons attached to the coca industry, as well as to Bolivian history, in the 1980s these federations grew to become probably the most powerful political pressure group in the entire country, taking the place of the most militant miners' unions. They have brought considerable pressure to bear against outlawing coca production (in many places in Bolivia it is not illegal to grow coca). They have also fought crop eradication with unusual tenacity and effectiveness. Thousands of growers turn out on virtually a moment's notice to block roads, march in demonstrations, go on hunger strikes, and otherwise petition their legislators for redress against the DEA, the police, and the army. So far, at least, the pressure has been mostly nonviolent, although the same cannot be said for the state's response.[15]

These federations have historically taken a position in favor of coca but not necessarily in favor of cocaine. Only a portion of the coca grown in Bolivia can be used for traditional chewing and medicinal purposes, however, so most of it necessarily feeds to the international cocaine export industry, creating something of a voiced moral dilemma for some Bolivians.

From the peasant growers, represented by their powerful labor federations, the "surplus" coca usually goes into organizations run by traditional rural elites, particularly ranchers, who have controlled the country's manufacture and distribution of cocaine base.[16] Kevin Healy tells us that there are two principal groups of this economic elite:

> [The two groups] included owners of large cattle ranches and merchants (e.g., exporters of cattle, rubber and Brazil nuts) in the eastern department of the Beni, and the agro-business elite (whose wealth and income derived primarily from sugar cane, cotton, soybeans, cattle production, commerce and agro-industries such as sugar and rice mills) in the Santa Cruz region. Their multiple economic interests . . . extend into import houses, banks, automobile dealerships, retail stores and money exchange houses.[17]

Other observers have identified ex-cotton growers in the Santa Cruz area and transport entrepreneurs around San Javier, San Ramón, Santa Ana, and Paraparu in the Beni as part of this "value-added export elite." These groups appear to involve significant numbers of military personnel who received land concessions in the Beni in the 1970s. Indeed, some military officers continue to be directly involved in the trade, even following the ignominious collapse in 1981 of the "narco-government" of Gen. Luis García Meza and Col. Arce Gómez.

The most internationally famous of all Bolivia's traffickers appears to be Roberto Suárez Gómez, generally acknowledged as Bolivia's king of cocaine. A traditional landowner, well connected to political elites involved in the traffic, and possessing an insatiable desire to conspicuously display wealth, he was the first major Bolivian trafficker ever to be captured and incarcerated. Suárez and his associates appear to be more like Cali than Medellín Colombians—upper middle class, well educated, not as driven by anger or bent on vengeance as the Medellín group.

Painter tells us that "Jorge Roca Suárez, the nephew of Roberto Suárez Gómez and his apparent heir, is widely credited with initiating the process of both producing more cocaine within Bolivia and establishing Bolivian-controlled routes, particularly to the United States. By the mid-1980s Roca Suárez had clearly eclipsed his uncle, and the DEA and Bolivian antidrug officials identified him as the country's number one trafficker."[18] But others also gained considerable notoriety in the late 1980s: Bismark Barrientos, Gerardo "Yayo" Rodríguez, William "Pato" Pizarro, Hugo Rivero Villavicencio, Erwin Guzmán, Oscar Roca Vásquez, and Jorge Flores Moisés. All these worked hard to form a "cartel" based in Beni. These Beni traffickers enjoyed close links with the Medellín and Cali syndicates to which they supplied cocaine base and the final cocaine product.[19] U.S. Drug Enforcement Administration (DEA) officials described the Beni group as the "most aggressive traffickers, most interested in producing cocaine, rather than just . . . base for the Colombians, and the people most interested in expanding independent networks into Europe and the U.S."[20]

As in Peru, it is clear that in the early 1980s more and more cocaine processing was done in Bolivia by Bolivians. Painter notes:

> For as long as Bolivia remained primarily a cultivator of coca and an exporter of coca paste or base to Colombia, Bolivian drug trafficking merely supplemented the Colombian drug trade. In the early 1980s, however, Bolivians—and Colombians working in Bolivia—slowly started to manufacture more and more of the base into the

final product, cocaine HCL. U.S. drug officials estimate that by 1990 as much as one-third of Bolivian coca paste—or between 150 and 200 tons of cocaine—was being processed within Bolivia. U.S. officials were adamant that Bolivia had become the world's second-largest cocaine producer after Colombia, a world ranking the Bolivian government never accepted.[21]

These export efforts helped to consolidate between thirty and forty organizations working in the processing and marketing of cocaine. In the early 1990s Bolivia was able to pick up perhaps 25 percent of the U.S. cocaine market and also made a dent in the European market. Something of a cartel was created, with about forty buyers meeting twice a year in Cochabamba to set the price for coca and coca paste.[22]

The growth of a value-added industry notwithstanding, Painter emphasizes that the Bolivian trafficking organizations

were never capable of becoming truly independent of their Colombian masters and probably continued to sell the vast majority of their product—either base or HCL—to Colombian buyers for further sales to U.S. markets. Drug analysts say that the Bolivians' geographical isolation, their smaller financial capacity, and perhaps their lack of the necessary marketing aggression, meant that even when they could find new routes or bypass the Colombians, they usually did so with the tacit permission of the Colombians.[23]

Nevertheless, with the Medellín cartel in shambles and the Cali group not historically inclined to enforce trade dominance through self-initiated violence, it is to be expected that Bolivians will increasingly strike out on their own.

Mexico

Marijuana is the most important cash crop in Mexico.[24] It is grown in fields scattered all over the country, alone or in combination with legal crops, typically corn and beans. It is also grown under plantation conditions, frequently with the protection of local police forces.[25] But Mexico also markets heroin, and Colombians have found the country to be a good transit point for smuggling cocaine into the United States. Large-scale smugglers have appropriated the Colombians' penchant for high-tech devices to thwart interdiction efforts. Small-scale smugglers, most of them moving marijuana, abound; "mules" cross the border into the United States with small amounts of drugs every day.

Because Mexico has concentrated much of its drug-control effort on marijuana, and because marijuana is the most "democratic" of the illicit drugs (anyone can grow it anywhere), the main marijuana traffickers have had to develop supply bases on which they can rely. To this end, traffickers supply small-scale farmers with seeds, fertilizers, and money and sometimes use intimidation and coercion to get them to cooperate in growing the plant.[26] As for cocaine trafficking, Celia Toro tells us that although it

> continues to be basically a U.S.-Colombian enterprise, in the hands of highly organized trafficking rings, mostly Colombian-based, Mexico has become the most important transit point. Cocaine *capos*, in jail or at large, still find Colombia a better place from which to organize their activities. Whether this will continue to be true depends not only on what happens in Colombia but on the outcome of the ongoing joint U.S.-Mexican air interdiction program, which is pushing traffickers into following the land route more intensely or into completely reorganizing in Mexico. Over the last two years, Mexican and other traffickers have been pressing for a more active role in the smuggling of cocaine through Mexico, despite official Mexican efforts to avoid it: the Muñoz Talavera brothers, heads of the so-called "Juárez cartel"—which was based in Ciudad Juárez, Chihuahua—who smuggled enormous amounts of cocaine into the U.S. were arrested in 1992, as was the Colombian Pardo Cardona, believed to be a high-ranking member of the Medellín cartel.[27]

The most sophisticated of the smugglers operating on Mexican soil, the cocaine traffickers have successfully thwarted almost all combined interdiction efforts by Mexican and U.S. drug-control authorities.

In general, trafficking organizations in Mexico are called "families" and known by their leaders' names. For example, William Overend speaks of "seven major drug families of Mexico" who developed a partnership with Colombian syndicates to use Mexico as a transshipment point for cocaine bound for the United States and Canada.[28] Among the named organizations there is the Herrera family[29] and the Caro Quintero group (responsible for the torture murder of DEA agent Enrique Camarena), whose maximum leader was sentenced in 1990 to more than forty years in a Mexican jail. Ángel Félix Gallardo's group (he is in jail, too) is also placed among the highly active Mexican operations.[30] Not surprisingly, although the major families' maximum leaders are being held in jail, their operations continue.

Thailand

Thailand is no longer a major source for opium. However, it is the primary conduit for Golden Triangle heroin destined for the U.S. market.[31]

Thai illicit-drug trafficking is intimately tied to two major factors: the Communist defeat of Nationalist forces in China in 1949 and the continuing ethnic struggle in the Burmese/Thai/Laotian highlands (the Golden Triangle) against central political authority. Related to the former Kuomintang (KMT), Nationalist forces retreating from China entered Thailand and nearby countries, where some of them proceeded to set up opium and heroin production operations. As regards the latter, contemporary ethnic struggles against central political authority in Thailand, Myanmar/Burma, and Laos have contributed to the emergence of paramilitary groups who finance arms purchases and their maintenance by either taxing or actively participating in the lucrative opium/heroin trade.

Trafficking in Thailand is further aided by the country's well-developed transportation infrastructure, made possible by decades of relatively peaceful conditions. Although Thailand's aggressive eradication and crop-substitution programs have pushed growers and many refiners into neighboring Myanmar/Burma and Laos, heroin, compact and light relative to value, is easily hidden and moved through Thailand to world markets.

Whereas the Medellín traffickers in Colombia and many in Peru and Bolivia appear to be driven by class-based origins and politics, those in Thailand, Myanmar/Burma, and Laos are frequently driven by the need to finance ethnic warfare, some of which has spilled over into Thailand. Frequently the violence is directed against central political authority. Traffickers operating in remote areas and protected by private armies have so far been more than a match for authorities in Myanmar/Burma and Laos but not for the Thai government. Thus, traffickers' principal operations in Thailand are low-bulk, unobtrusive, and clandestine—moving heroin to the world's consumers.

Anchalee Singhanetra-Renard tells us that during the years following 1949, when the KMT was especially active in the opium business, production grew so substantially that irregular armies were formed to defend opium caravans, and insurgents took to trading in opium as a means of supporting their revolutions in the Burmese hills.

The most famous of such leaders were Lo Hsing-han from Kokang and Khun Sa from the Shan State of Loi Mwe, both of whom alternated between posing as ethnic heroes in the struggle against Ne Win's government, opium strongmen, and regional kingpins. Both formed their own personal armies and in a series of convoluted dealings with the Burmese army and each other variously fell in and out of favor with the rulers of that country. Lo Hsing-han's influence almost came to a complete stop when he made an offer in 1973 via two British journalists to sell most of his opium and that of

Shan rebel groups to the United States government. Subsequently lured into a Thai helicopter, he was flown to Bangkok where he was deported to Burma and there imprisoned for his links to ethnic insurgents (but not opium trafficking). From then on, Khun Sa became the dominant opium trafficker along the Thai-Burma border. As time passed, he established a fortified mountainside camp well inside Thailand at Ban Hin Taek in Chiang Rai Province from where he managed his operations.[32]

Because much of the operations' output was funneled through Thailand via its excellent transport connections to world markets, in due course a number of high-ranking Thai government and military officials became involved as facilitators and protectors of the trade.

Thus, Thailand has become a major trafficking nation for the international market, even though most of the drugs trafficked come from nearby Myanmar/Burma and Laos. Thai and Thai-Chinese marketing middlemen and financiers play a large role in the transit operations. It must be emphasized that because of the huge market for opium and heroin in Thailand, much of the trafficking is centered on meeting domestic demand.

Cannabis, unlike opium (which is grown mainly by individual hilltribe families in the northern Thai highlands), is produced by large organizations in the north, northeast, and south. In league with Western international traffickers, cannabis growers produce almost entirely for the export market.[33]

Laos

In the mid- to late 1980s Laos became a "spillover" country when Thailand and Myanmar/Burma began vigorously to pursue traffickers, perhaps not so much for their trafficking as for their status as ethnic separatists or revolutionaries.[34] The efforts drove some of the less risk-prone traffickers to other countries. Some of them went to Laos. Accordingly, since then and particularly since 1988, illicit opium and heroin production and the trafficking of both have increased significantly in Laos. Traffickers in the Golden Triangle, including Khun Sa, have shifted more and more of their activities to Laos.

Traffickers have found Laos to be hospitable to their operations. Provincial officials have been more or less cooperative, as has the Laotian military. For a time in the late 1980s the central government collected revenues from the drug trade and therefore did little to discourage it. Credible reports continue to surface that some Lao military and local government officials actively encourage and facilitate trafficking in opium and marijuana; some are also involved in the heroin trade. Efforts at concealment indicate that civilian authorities do not necessarily like this activity, but it is carried on nonetheless. Moreover, the country's vast remoteness impedes central government control even if vigorously attempted. The considerable provincial autonomy that is a product both of Laotian history and its lack of roads and communications enables traffickers to influence, if not control, farmers and officials alike.[35]

Given these conditions, can the extent of Laotian trafficking really be known? The cautionary note of the Laotian drug-control commission is instructive. The commission reminds us that Laos borders five other nations (Vietnam, Thailand, Myanmar/Burma, Cambodia, and China) and that

> control over these borders is very limited and illicit trafficking of drugs, timber logs, and other contraband constitutes a major problem. As in the case of processing of opium to heroin, it is not possible to determine the extent to which opium and heroin are transported from Laos to other countries or for which the Lao People's Democratic Republic serves as a transit country. Technical and financial resources are needed to improve control over its borders. Cooperation with neighboring countries will play an important role.[36]

Although more questions than answers exist regarding Laotian trafficking, some aspects are known. Lao lowlanders, reportedly including elements of the Lao military and local government officials or Chinese traffickers, purchase opium from farmers and convey it to major traffickers along the Thai border for further processing and distribution. The activity appears to be particularly noted in companies managed by the military, including the semi-autonomous Mountainous Areas Development Company (MADC), and in the Third Army Division.[37]

Trafficking routes through all of Laos's neighbors permit illicit narcotics to find markets and encourage continued production in Laos. Three major routes lead from central Laos to the Mekong River, the northern border by Myanmar/Burma, and the northern border by China (Yunnan Province). The Mekong River boundary is largely unpatrolled and provides a long unwatched stretch for traffickers' operations.

In recent years, in part because of the continuing antinarcotics efforts in Thailand, Laotian traffickers and their Burmese counterparts have opened up land routes through southern China to Hong Kong, Maçau, and Taiwan and from there to the world market. It may be of some significance that much—perhaps most—of the trafficking is done by people of Chinese origin,[38] which facilitates clandestine networking in southern China.

Laotian traffickers, like those in Myanmar/Burma and some in Thailand, Peru, and Colombia, are linked with insurgent and organized-crime movements (including Chinese crime syndicates). This combination has proved explosive in Laos and its neighboring countries. The insurgent groups have their own political agenda as well as their commercial illicit-drug expeditions. Some of the groups come armed from secure bases in the Thai hills to do their buying in Laos. Henning notes that this has

> led to the emergence of a situation of latent insecurity in certain poppy growing regions, particularly in the north of Vientiane Province and in Xieng Khouang Province. Given these conditions, it is currently not possible for the technical personnel assisting in the implementation of projects to travel to certain producing zones without armed protection. According to the authorities, the source of the change is not so much the Hmong villagers living in the mountains as the Hmong or other traffickers who come from outside the region. Relationships between the highlanders, particularly the Hmong, and the central political authorities have often been marked by difficulties and conflicts. The past and recent history of relations between the central authorities and the Hmong minorities has contributed to the creation of a climate of mutual distrust in many regions.[39]

Hilltribe people, generally disaffected from their respective central governments, do not tend to view illicit-drug traffickers as necessarily being criminals and are not inclined to turn them in. The traffickers treat locals better than the national government does, giving the locals considerable financial incentive to cooperate with drug runners. If this approach does not work, the criminal syndicates that control much of the networking from producer to market rapidly adjust their routes and methods, which include assassinations, terrorism, and paramilitary operations.

In addition to continually improving and adjusting trafficking technology, the drug traders have made high-tech, value-added improvements in production. They have developed a high quality "China White" heroin that drug agents say is up to 98 percent pure. Production of China White, which commands a premium in the market, has more than doubled in five years.[40]

Whether protecting narcotics sources, establishing trade routes, or improving product technology in the Golden Triangle of Laos, Myanmar/Burma, and Thailand, traffickers have been able to shift their operations without regard to political boundaries in search of areas least under control of a central government.

Myanmar/Burma

Myanmar/Burma's principal traffickers and trafficking organizations are virtually the same as those in Laos and Thailand.[41] They operate without regard to national boundaries. Khun Sa figures prominently among them, but Myanmar/Burma has produced its own native brand of trafficker, the most prominent apparently being a local warlord from Kokang named Lo Hsing-han (Luo Xinghan).[42] All trafficking has been intimately associated with ethnic divisions and ethnic warfare in Burma and with national political leaders' attempts to exercise control over the country's territory.

Groups forced out of power in Rangoon and, earlier, Chinese fleeing Mao Tse-tung gravitated to the opium and heroin trade to finance their insurgencies or lick their wounds. The Chinese Kuomintang (KMT) grew sufficiently strong to deny the ethnically Burmese-dominated government access to the northeastern Shan states, which left the KMT empowered to carry out the narcotics trade to its liking.[43] Thereafter, other ethnic groups took up the trade, including the fabled Khun Sa's group and the Burmese Communist Party. Khun Sa and the KMT ultimately battled for supremacy in the opium trade, with spillover effects into Thailand and Laos. Ronald Renard illustrates the consequences in a colorful narrative:

> Khun Sa chose to challenge the KMT for control of the opium trade. In 1967 he put together a 300-mule caravan carrying 16 tons of raw opium valued at $500,000 at its farm-gate price of $15 per kilogram. The profit he stood to make if he sold the opium in Laos, as he intended, would enable him to expand his army to about 3,000 troops, or equal to that of the KMT. Not surprisingly, the KMT rose to the challenge and pursued Khun Sa's caravan to Ban Khwan, at the point where the borders of Burma, Lao, and Thailand meet (and which later tour operators have dubbed the "Golden Triangle"). However, Khun Sa's efforts failed, when he so irritated Lao authorities that the Lao Air Force was used to drive off both Khun Sa and the KMT, forcing Khun Sa to leave most of his opium behind. The adverse publicity resulting from this "Opium War" made it clear to the world that the KMT had not retired from illegal activities which then led to the Thais severely restricting KMT movements."[44]

For his part, Lo Hsing-han made peace with the Shan state army, and the two cooperated in the international trade of opium.

In 1988 a quasi-military coup overthrew the Burmese government. The new leaders set up the State Law and Order Restoration Council (SLORC). Violently opposed to any separatist ethnic groups —such as the Karen, Kachin, and Shan—who might be financed in whole or in part by illicit-drug trade or anything else, SLORC has been unremitting in its suppression. Of course, SLORC's wide net also picks up ethnics who happen to be traffickers. This has impacted the trade somewhat, not much. The "not much" appears to be linked to compliance. If groups are compliant with SLORC, their drug-running operations are not called so much into question. Thus, whereas Khun Sa suffers strong attacks from Myanmar authorities, Lo Hsing-han (after a period of incarceration in Thailand and Burma) was welcomed back to Kokang in March 1989, set up seventeen new heroin refineries there, and opened an opium trade route through China to Hong Kong.[45] Renard describes the events:

> Kokang opium merchants have split into two groups. The Lo Hsing-han group, which includes the Pheung brothers, markets the *pitzu* [impure morphine base], which is easier to transport than raw opium because *pitzu* is several times lighter. *Pitzu* is also desired because it can be refined into No. 4 heroin. The second Kokang merchant group controls four refineries where, for the first time, No. 4 heroin is being produced on a large scale deep inside Shan State. This group then markets heroin across the border into China. There are also remnants of the Yang family still involved in Kokang's opium trade as are several other smaller groups.
> These groups are permitted to traffic in narcotics in exchange for fighting rebel groups, such as Khun Sa's forces, now known as the Muang Tai Army. Thus it was that the United Wa State Army of the Pheung family attacked Khun Sa, causing about 1,000 hurt or killed in 1990.[46]

Some of the opium and heroin trade routes lead west from Kokang to Mong Ko and thereafter into Yunnan Province in southern China before swinging northeastward on the old Burma Road. Heroin moves farther east to Hong Kong. Increasing amounts of the product are leaking into China from this trade route. Other routes lead into Thailand, and others link the northern Shan and Kachin states with India. Various forms of opium products leave Myanmar/Burma through all the export routes, including opium, *pitzu*, morphine base, impure heroin base, and No. 4 heroin.[47]

Pakistan

As in the Golden Triangle, opium production and trade in Pakistan have been a way of life for centuries.[48] From time to time one imperial power or another (e.g., the British, the Moguls) or a regional political authority has fostered it for tax revenues despite Muslim admonitions against drug abuse. Today, Pakistan is both a producer and an important transit country of opiates headed for the international market. Heroin production takes place in the remote Northwest Frontier Province (NWFP). More than a hundred heroin laboratories, most processing opium from Afghanistan, exist there within Pakistan's national borders. As in Burma, Thailand, and Laos, traffickers prefer remote areas under the control of ethnic or tribal authorities who are only occasionally beholden to national governments. The fierce regional independence in Pakistan works to the good of the traffickers.

As the entry into international trade developed in the 1980s, two main routes were established: the Great Trunk (GT) Road from Peshawar via Lahore to Karachi and a road due west lying between the GT Road and the Afghan border that courses the NWFP and Baluchistan Provinces. Trafficking routes from Pakistan, primarily out of NWFP, lead to India, Iran, Europe, and the United States. Traffickers in all areas push the drug domestically and develop connections to the international market. As a result, drug production and trafficking have taken on the trappings of big business—organizations are vertically integrated, and considerable value-added processing occurs on Pakistani soil. Doris Buddenberg describes the monetary consequences of big drug business even in out-of-the-way regional centers: "The big business aspect shows itself above all in the accompanying monetary flows. Suffice it to point out here that in Peshawar any currency of the world is acceptable, and traders and money dealers maintain accounts in all international banking centres, or . . . [with] tribals with branch offices in Hong Kong and Singapore, with foreign currency accounts in New York and Tokyo."[49]

Traffickers obtain on average about 165 tons of opium annually from Pakistani farmers, a sum augmented by imports from substantially higher production in Afghanistan. Pakistani and Afghan farmers are connected to the laboratories through operatives from Bajaur and Mohmand. They may be local shopkeepers, independent businessmen, higher-level merchants, or even representatives of heroin-conversion facilities. All are trusted both by growers in Pakistan and Afghanistan and by the processors. The trust is based on ethnic or family ties, with full knowledge of the "known swift sanction following any 'mismanagement.'"[50] Such trust and the threat of sanction produce high performance compliance. In fact, the local *hundi* dealers (a kind of banking-by-trust syndicate that can move money rapidly worldwide) cannot recall any trusts having been broken—ever.[51] The laboratories, at least those of the Khyber Agency of NWFP, are operated by either Shinwari or Afridi Pashtun tribesmen from Pakistan, although occasionally an Afghan Pashtun can be found operating a heroin laboratory in the tribal areas of Pakistan.

During the last half of 1982 the traffickers began to supplement shipments normally going through Iran by land or to the United Kingdom and the Netherlands by air from Karachi, routing them through Lahore and, finally, the Gulf states.[52] The principal motivation for using the Gulf states was to disguise shipments destined for the U.S. market.

Drug organizations in Pakistan are hierarchically organized and are frequently based on family ties. Millionaire businessmen intimately connected with senior politicians and government officials frequently become chief executive officers. They then bring in close relatives and other confidants to deal with second-tier operatives, who in turn organize cells on down the organizational ladder in order to protect chiefs from criminal investigation and prosecution.[53]

In sum, Pakistani traffickers operate in areas controlled by fiercely independent tribal authorities, who maintain armed protection squads if not paramilitary organizations to defend their operations. They have a long history of smuggling various kinds of goods across the Pakistan-Afghanistan border. In these areas no lab operators or owners have been arrested, and few labs have been raided. It is simply too dangerous for the Pakistani government to attempt to intervene. From these protected areas the traffickers and smugglers branch out into the world market.

Pakistan experienced a vast expansion of heroin production, beginning in 1979 with morphine processing and, later, with full-blown operations. During the initial stages of this expansion the laboratories could produce only heroin base, or what is known as smokeable heroin. Later technological developments permitted most laboratories to produce heroin hydrochloride, or injectable heroin. By 1980 a heroin epidemic was spreading rapidly throughout the country. The laboratories moved to meet domestic demand and situate themselves well for entry into the international market. Although considerable amounts of opiates remain in Pakistan to service the large number of Pakistani addicts, plenty is left over for international trade.

Summary and Conclusions

Traffickers as a class are alive and well throughout the nine countries reported on in this study as well as elsewhere. This condition exists despite concerted international efforts to curb trafficker activities and, in some cases, to incarcerate or kill their major representatives. New traffickers appear to surface as soon as old ones are moved aside.

Some traffickers wish above all to be integrated into their countries' societies in a peaceful and accepting way (e.g., in Colombia). Others are able to use national labor federations to their advantage (e.g., in Bolivia). Some want to bring down the national governments where they operate (e.g., in Peru). Still others accept or fight national governments depending on whether they are impeded or facilitated in their illicit-drug work (e.g., in Laos, Myanmar/Burma).

Traffickers are able to shift their production enterprises and their trade routes to wherever national governments are least in control, without regard to political boundaries. Thus, in the Golden Triangle, for example, border operations concentrate at the point of least resistance and are fluid from year to year. Ironically, Thailand's well-developed internal communication infrastructure has facilitated traffickers' work. Thai soil is used mostly for value-added processing and transiting because these activities are less visible and less subject to discovery than large-scale poppy or cannabis cultivation. On the whole, well-developed infrastructure and illegal-crop growing do not go hand in hand unless the territory is controlled by insurgent groups who protect growers from the wrath of national governments and their militaries (e.g., in Peru).

Traffickers have pursued product improvements with abandon, principally to reduce the detectibility and weight-to-price ratio of their products, which make for easier smuggling. Such processes also concentrate alkaloids and frequently heighten the addiction rate among local populations (e.g., in Pakistan).

Some traffickers create a vertically integrated industry by working with peasant growers from the beginning stages of crop planting to harvesting (e.g., in the Golden Triangle and Pakistan). Others just show up from time to time to buy farmers' illicit-drug crops, creating vast boom-and-bust cycles in local economies (e.g., in Peru and Bolivia). Many traffickers simply use countries as transit points to develop and to expand their international marketing networks (e.g., in Mexico). In recent years, large, vertically integrated, multinational organizations have developed that specialize in smuggling illegal narcotic drugs to principal consumer markets in North America, Europe, and, increasingly, the republics of the former Soviet Union. Countries such as Pakistan also have large internal markets that traffickers service.

Aside from their impressive smuggling abilities—sometimes the product of generations of informal and practical education in their areas—traffickers have found two phenomena to aid them greatly: first, the poor national governments and communication infrastructures in remote areas of the countries in which they operate; and second, the class- or ethnic-based insurrections that allow traffickers a cover for their operations, usually in those same areas. Thus, national governments that have not been able to control insurgency have likewise had little ability to control the illicit-drug trade.

Traffickers as a class seem analogous to the plethora of viruses that cause everything from the common cold to painful and fatal diseases. They are concentrated and active in certain countries—particularly those under study—but they exist elsewhere at various levels of dormancy or activity. Social, political, or economic change can call them forth with rapidity. And just as medical science has long and doggedly hunted viruses with inconsistent results, so have international legal and political authorities sought to find and curb trafficker activities. They may fight the symptoms, the source, or the "patient" and have even incarcerated or killed major kingpins. However, successes seem to little avail, for new traffickers (as new virus strains) appear when the old ones are removed from action as long as there is an available host.

Notes

1. For identification and bibliographical references, refer to LaMond Tullis, *Handbook of Research on the Illicit Drug Traffic* (Westport, Conn.: Greenwood Press, 1991), 51–52.

2. Principal reference for Colombia is Francisco Thoumi, *Political Economy and Illegal Drugs in Colombia* (Boulder, Colo.: Lynne Rienner Publishers, 1994).

3. Recent discussions about the killing of Escobar and the fortunes of Colombia's drug traffickers are contained in Robert D. McFadden, "Head of Medellín Cocaine Cartel Is Killed by Troops in Colombia," *New York Times*, 3 December 1993, A1; and James Brooke, "One Victory, a Long War," *New York Times*, 3 December 1993, A7.

4. Thoumi, *Political Economy and Illegal Drugs*, 154–163 passim.

5. Fabio Castillo, *La Coca Nostra* (Bogotá: Editorial Documentos Periodísticos, 1991), 13, cited by Thoumi, *Political Economy and Illegal Drugs*, 153.

6. Jorge Eliécer Orozco, *Lehder . . . el Hombre* (Bogotá: Plaza & Janes, 1987), cited by Thoumi, *Political Economy and Illegal Drugs*, 154.

7. Thoumi, *Political Economy and Illegal Drugs*, 154.

8. Guy Gugliotta and Jeff Leen, *Kings of Cocaine: An Astonishing True Story of Murder, Money and International Corruption* (New York: Simon and Schuster, 1989), 29, quoted by Thoumi, *Political Economy and Illegal Drugs*, 154.

9. Thoumi, *Political Economy and Illegal Drugs*, 156.

10. Ciro Krauthausen and Luis F. Sarmiento, *Cocaína and Co.: Un Mercado Ilegal por Dentro* (Bogotá: Tercer Mundo Editores, 1991), 17. Quoted as translated by Thoumi, *Political Economy and Illegal Drugs*, 156.

11. Thoumi, *Political Economy and Illegal Drugs*, 157–158.

12. United States, Department of State, Bureau of International Narcotics Matters, *International Narcotics Control Strategy Report* (Washington, D.C.: The Bureau, 1993), 121, hereafter cited as *INCSR, 1993*.

13. Principal source for Bolivia is James Painter, *Bolivia and Coca: A Study in Dependency* (Boulder, Colo.: Lynne Rienner Publishers, 1994).

14. Ibid., 23–24.

15. Ibid., 25.

16. Painter shows that peasant groups are trying to enter the first stage of value-added production in an effort to maintain income as coca prices fall. However, "there is yet to be one reported case of a major processing operation being found to be under peasant ownership" (ibid., 26).

17. Kevin Healy, "The Boom Within the Crisis: Some Recent Effects of Foreign Cocaine Markets on Bolivian Rural Society and Economy," in Deborah Pacini and Christine Franquemont, eds., *Coca and Cocaine, Effects on People and Policy in Latin America* (Boston: Cultural Survival, 1986), 104–105, quoted by Painter, *Bolivia and Coca*, 26.

18. Painter, *Bolivia and Coca*, 30.

19. Ibid., 31.

20. James Painter, "Bolivian Military Leader Questions DEA's Role in Drug Bust Gone Awry," *Christian Science Monitor*, 12 July 1991, 6. Painter advises that "it is worth noting that DEA officials often spoke of a marked difference between the period until the mid-1980s, when virtually all the major traffickers were ranchers or ex-ranchers. But it would seem that many of the younger traffickers to emerge in the 1980s were second-generation members of ranching or *latifundista* families who maintained their close links with each other" (Painter, *Bolivia and Coca*, 152–153, note 33).

21. Painter, *Bolivia and Coca*, 28.

22. Ibid., 29.

23. Ibid., 30.

24. Principal source on Mexico is María Celia Toro, "Mexican Drug Control Policy: Origin, Purpose, Consequences," a study for UNRISD and UNU (draft of 9 June 1993). In press at Lynne Rienner Publishers, Boulder, Colo.

25. Ibid., 49.

26. Ibid., 50.

27. Ibid., 57.

28. William Overend, "Cocaine Floods Southland via Colombia-Mexico Link," *Los Angeles Times*, 1987.

29. See Peter A. Lupsha, "Drug Trafficking: Mexico and Colombia in Comparative Perspective," *Journal of International Affairs* 35:1 (1981), 95–115.

30. See William Branigin, "Mexicans Arrest Prime Drug Suspect: Félix Gallardo Led DEA's Wanted List," *Washington Post Weekly*, 14–20 March 1989, 7; Brook Larmer, "Mexico's Corruption Clampdown: Arrest of Corrupt Officials Along with Drug Baron May Root out Graft," *Christian Science Monitor*, 13 April 1989, 1; and Larry Rohter, "Mexicans Arrest Top Drug Figure and 80 Policemen," *New York Times*, 11 April 1989, 1.

31. Principal source for Thailand is Anchalee Singhanetra-Renard, "Socioeconomic and Political Impact of Production, Trade and Use of Narcotic Drugs in Thailand," a study for UNRISD and UNU (draft of 23 April 1993).

32. Ibid., 69–70.

33. Ibid., 161.

34. The principal source on Laos is Daniel Henning, "Production and Trafficking of Opium and Heroin in Laos," a study for UNRISD and UNU (draft of 26 May 1993).

35. Ibid., 13.

36. Lao Peoples Democratic Republic, National Commission for Drug Control and Supervision (LNCDCS), *Drug Control in 1990* (Vientiane: LNCDCS, February 1990), 8, quoted by Henning, "Production and Trafficking," 30–31.

37. Henning, "Production and Trafficking," 33.

38. Ibid., 34.

39. Ibid., 35.

40. Ibid., 68.

41. Principal source on Myanmar/Burma is Ronald Renard, "Socioeconomic and Political Impact of Production, Trade and Use of Narcotic Drugs in Burma," a study for UNRISD and UNU (draft of 3 November 1993).

42. Ibid., 101.

43. Ibid., 93. Ironically, the U.S. support of the KMT in northeastern Burma contributed directly to the international narcotics trade because it protected the Nationalist Chinese in their autonomy from either Burmese, Laotian, or Thai governments. The impact of this decision was most vigorously felt in Burmese Shan states, where the majority of KMT operations were based. In retrospect, a U.S. political officer in Rangoon said, "We were suckers to back the KMT. . . . We never fooled the Burmese and were fools to think we could" (cited in Ibid., 54).

44. Ibid., 103.

45. Ibid., 115–116.

46. Ibid., 116–117.

47. *INCSR 1991,* 230.

48. Principal source on Pakistan is Doris Buddenberg, "Illicit Drug Issues in Pakistan," a study for UNRISD and UNU (draft of May 1993).

49. Ibid., 175.

50. Ibid., 155.

51. Ibid.

52. Ibid., 163.

53. Ibid., 178.

... *4* ...

Drug-Control Efforts
and Their Effectiveness

Given national and international decisions to illegalize cocaine, heroin, and marijuana and many of their semirefined and natural botanical precursors, it was only natural that national, bilateral, and multilateral efforts would be advanced to enforce the antidrug laws, decrees, treaties, and conventions. How effective have they been?

This chapter describes bilateral, multilateral, and national drug-control efforts in the nine countries under study. In addition, informed by a policy model presented in this chapter, I assess drug-control effectiveness. In Chapter 5, effects or consequences deriving from drug-control efforts other than goal attainment are discussed.

Drug-control efforts are advanced to curtail both consumption and production. By each country's own assessment and other anecdotal evidence, it can safely be asserted that most of the countries presented here (other than Pakistan and perhaps Thailand) appear to be more concerned about production than about consumption. However, real production concerns (as opposed to putative concerns in deference to multilateral agencies or the United States) sometimes have less to do with drug control than with anxieties about insurrectionist or counterstate groups working in drug-cropping areas. Still, most contemporary societies now demonstrate varying degrees of anxiety about illicit-drug consumption and have collaborated with international agencies in an effort to curtail consumption around the planet, especially of refined products such as heroin and cocaine/ crack.

The principal global strategy to control illicit drugs has been supply suppression, on the assumption that scarcity either will contribute to reduced consumption in the industrialized countries or will deprive counterstate groups of an income source. Thus, my principal interest in this chapter is to describe and analyze production-control initiatives inasmuch as they are the most extensive if not important initiatives undertaken so far in the "war on drugs." The logic and implications are made clear later in the chapter.

As for multilateral and bilateral drug-control efforts, the prelude to a modern international production-control strategy began more than eighty years ago (1909) when thirteen nations brought opium under international jurisdiction at the first international conference on narcotic drugs. The resulting Opium Commission eventually produced the first international drug-control treaty—the International Opium Convention—signed by the constituent countries in 1912 and ratified by their respective parliaments in 1915. The assigned task was simply to monitor global opium production.

The League of Nations later followed with committee discussions after 1920 and produced conventions in 1925, 1931, and 1936. The resulting international agreements were designed to limit drug production to amounts needed for medical and other licit use and to severely punish illicit-drug traffickers. Subsequently, the United Nations worked for cooperative agreements that would in effect expand signatories' criminal jurisdiction (by convention and treaty) and encourage national policies aimed at reducing both supply of and demand for illicit drugs.

Since the League of Nations's 1936 Convention for the Suppression of the Illicit Traffic in Dangerous Drugs, the United Nations, through conventions, protocols, and the work of its various subagencies that carry out drug-related agenda,[1] has attempted to facilitate law-enforcement efforts and other cooperation across national boundaries. The most frequently cited UN initiatives are the 1961 Single Convention on Narcotic Drugs, which consolidated most of the earlier international instruments, and the 1972 Protocol Amending the Single Convention, which strengthened provisions for suppressing production and distribution of drugs but also called for rehabilitation and social reintegration policies for drug offenders as possible alternatives to imprisonment.

Other milestones in UN-orchestrated agreements are the 1971 Convention on Psychotropic Substances, the 1981 International Drug Abuse Control Strategy, the 1984 Declaration on the Control of Drug Trafficking and Drug Abuse, a 1987 Draft Convention Against Illicit Traffic in Narcotic Drugs and Psychotropic Substances, and a 1987 International Conference on Drug Abuse and Illicit Trafficking—the first-ever meeting of UN member states to discuss and assess both the supply and demand sides of the drug-abuse chain. A practical handbook of recommended steps for governmental and nongovernmental organizations to use in combating drug abuse emerged from the conference.

In 1990 the UN General Assembly held high-level special sessions to expand the scope and effectiveness of current antidrug efforts, declaring the 1990s the "UN Decade Against Drug Abuse." The sessions dealt with tightening legal and practical cooperation among member states. The urgency was highlighted by Colombia's mortal struggle with its drug barons. Significantly, net consuming nations were obligated to take more vigorous measures to reduce their demand for illicit drugs. A consensus thus emerged that all affected countries, whether net consumers or net producers, collectively shared in the blame for the traffic's existence and must mutually direct their attention to all facets of the trade—consumption, trafficking, and production. At the same time, a new urgency arose about deleterious socioeconomic consequences of illicit-drug production, trade, and consumption.[2]

Rhetoric aside, forcing net consuming nations to look at their own consumption appears not to have significantly altered their attention to production. For example, a draft policy proposal circulated within the U.S. Department of Defense (28 October 1993) states, "The Department of Defense has issued new policy guidance redirecting its counterdrug program to emphasize support to nations battling cocaine cultivation."[3]

Aside from the many multilateral arrangements developed in response to drug trafficking, bilateral agreements—or at least working promises—are in force, too. Most appear to be between the United States and principal illicit-drug source countries; the chief focus is on reducing production. The first agreement was with Turkey,[4] followed by countries such as Pakistan, Peru, Bolivia, Colombia, Mexico,[5] and Italy.[6] The intent, through provision of money and matériel, is to suppress the drug traffic at its origin. The Andean Strategy in the Western Hemisphere is a most recent illustration.[7]

Net consuming and producing nations have responded in varying ways to the social and economic overhead of production, consumption, and control of illicit drugs. To reduce illicit consumption, countries combine both negative and positive sanctions. They have moved against users as well as traffickers, supporting, for example, drug testing in the workplace. At the same time, they have supported educational efforts in the schools, civic action in communities, and mass-media appeals to their populations. Countries are also turning more and more to strategies involving treatment and rehabilitation. To control production, which globally has been the principal goal, countries make both invasive and persuasive efforts. In the former they eradicate crops and seize precursor chemicals needed in laboratory refining. They interdict drug products in transit and destroy them. As for persuasion, they offer crop-substitution and rural-development programs.

To suppress illicit trafficking, countries attempt to disrupt major transit networks by imprisoning or killing principal traffickers or by depriving them of their income through various asset-forfeiture programs; by working to have them tried in countries with strict sentencing (e.g., by extradition to the United States); by launching sophisticated surveillance of land, water, and air approaches to principal consuming countries; and by exercising some control over ships and aircraft in international space through various kinds of interdiction programs.[8]

In the nine countries under study, all of the above have been implemented in one form or another. But the principal effort continues to be on reducing production. The theoretical justification for this bias will be outlined in the context of assessing the effectiveness of drug-control efforts. But first specific countries and regions are examined.

Colombia

Since the illicit-drug industry began to develop in Colombia, successive governments have "followed ambivalent, inconsistent, and conflicting policies towards it."[9] Much of the ambivalence derives from Colombia's cultural predisposition toward violence, but additional factors come into play, including: an already crowded policy agenda in the mid-1970s; the government's recognition that it was, to some extent, impotent in the face of the traffickers; the nationalist/sovereignty issues that played out as the United States attempted to force control efforts on Colombia; the Colombian government's need for and desire not to interfere with its foreign-exchange earnings; the general growth of an underground economy in Colombia; the prevailing view in the 1970s that drugs were a U.S. problem; and the fact that the conspicuously spending traffickers evoked a certain covetous respect in Colombian popular society.

With ambivalence the norm, in the mid-1970s Colombia had drug-control legislation but no active policy implementation. Thus, the illicit-drug industry grew almost unimpeded, to become a formidable foe before the Colombian state made any serious efforts to rein it in. Both laws and policies developed in piecemeal fashion, frequently at the behest of the United States or in response to an immediate crisis or social discomfiture at home, including assassinations of high-level government officials.

Initial government attention appears to have been sparked by traffickers' conspicuous consumption of luxury goods and by their efforts to make themselves economically legitimate and perhaps even socially acceptable. In the later half of the 1970s the central bank took note of substantial increases in the supply of foreign exchange, which reached unprecedented amounts by the late 1970s. Social unknowns—the "emerging class"—began making major investments that frightened existing entrepreneurs. Almost every businessman concluded that the monied newcomers were "drug tainted" and feared their social and economic competition. These social and economic preferences were reinforced when the central bank declared that the influx of money complicated macroeconomic management and distorted resource use.

The growth of tainted foreign exchange, which apparently came initially from the booming marijuana industry, sparked a national debate about what, if anything, should be done. This included a free-for-all battle over legalization of the marijuana industry,[10] a proffered solution that met widespread opposition. The United States entered the debate, increasing its international pressure on Colombia to attack the industry, a response made doubly difficult because marijuana influence had apparently infiltrated the highest levels of the Colombian government. The United States argued for herbicidal eradication of the crop, a policy that most Colombians vigorously opposed. As a sop, the Julio César Ayala Turbay administration began "Operation Fulminant," engaging 10,000 army personnel in manual marijuana eradication in the Guajira and Sierra Nevada de Santa Marta.[11] Because the military opposed its own involvement, the operation was short-lived.

But the Turbay government then enacted the National Security Statute, "which enhanced government and military powers to arrest and take action both against the drug industry and guerrilla organizations."[12] Self-defense groups were formed. The government also signed an extradition treaty with the United States, but it was not uniformly applied because the costs came too high. Traffickers insisted on the treaty's abrogation, a point they prosecuted with a campaign of terror against the government. A certain state indecisiveness resulted.

While the government was struggling over the extradition treaty, cocaine prices increased dramatically, thereby adding a new dimension to the problem. Increased prices signaled rising consumption and therefore a new market. Colombian suppliers readily geared up to meet new demand. Some of the traffickers were already seasoned from their involvement in the marijuana trade. Perplexed and perhaps even frightened, the Colombian government began active collaboration with the United States in anti-money-laundering and interdiction activities to try to control the traffickers' growing political and economic power. On money laundering, hardly anything was accomplished; interdiction efforts showed a better return. For example, the authorities located a sophisticated laboratory in "Tranquilandia" and destroyed it on 10 March 1984, the largest antidrug accomplishment of the time. The drug industry responded by assassinating Rodrigo Lara Bonilla, the justice minister. This escalated drug-control efforts to an all-time high, not so much over drugs per se as over the drug barons' threat to the state.

Five extraditions of jailed drug dealers were authorized. The government declared martial law, sent all drug-related crimes to the military penal justice system (less inclined to be influenced by threats and bribes), and launched a strong military campaign against the traffickers.[13] A general roundup and mass jailing followed. In further response, the government overcame its sensitivities about aerial spraying and launched a massive spraying program on all known marijuana fields. The armed forces were used in large numbers in this general response to Lara Bonilla's assassination. Traffickers fled to Panama and elsewhere and began to sue for peace.[14] The government refused. Violence escalated.

As the cycle of violence and reactive violence progressed, the government's antidrug efforts faced some legal setbacks. Francisco Thoumi catalogs them:

> On 12 December the Supreme Court had declared invalid the law that had approved the extradition treaty, and on 5 March 1987 it declared unconstitutional the decree that had expanded the jurisdiction of the military justice system. These Supreme Court decisions seriously constrained the government's chosen policies, which were delivered an even worse blow on 25 June 1987, when the Supreme Court found the extradition treaty invalid because its elaboration and ratification had not followed the required legal procedures. Until that moment fourteen Colombians had been extradited to the United States.[15]

The legal setbacks notwithstanding, the Virgilio Barco Vargas regime searched for other ways to counter the drug lobby and its accompanying violence and threat to the state. The administration sought every legal precedent (including nineteenth-century treaties) and renewed chemical eradication programs begun during the Belisario Betancur Cuartas administration. In the view of the United States, none of it was sufficient; the Department of State applied visa restrictions on Colombian travelers. Moreover, U.S. customs became obstructionist in dealing with Colombian imports.

The Barco administration enlisted more help from the military and moved again to make extradition a cornerstone of its antidrug policy, largely because it could not envision that anything else would work. Violence increased, with indiscriminate bombings in Bogotá and Medellín. Several presidential candidates for the 1990–1994 administration were killed, among them Luis Carlos Galán, the odds-on favorite to win the election. Like the assassination of Justice Minister Bonilla, the murder of Galán steeled the government's nerves. The Barco administration again declared all-out war on the traffickers, announcing new extradition decrees; arbitrary confiscation of drug-syndicate members' properties; criminalization of shadow ownership of illicit-drug-obtained properties; and a major military campaign, with U.S. support, to trap the traffickers.[16] Some were caught; the biggest were not. The Medellín syndicate responded with acts of terrorism, including the 6 December 1989 destruction of the twelve-story headquarters of the National Security Forces in Bogotá, which killed seventy-two people and injured hundreds.[17]

At the end of 1990, in the wake of an inability to reduce terrorist acts, the new César Gaviria administration sought to open a dialogue with the traffickers by offering to reduce sentences for those who turned themselves in voluntarily. Three brothers from the Ochoa Medellín syndicate family walked into jail because the new administration also appeared to be ready to ban extradition, something they feared worse. In 1991, Pablo Escobar also surrendered (but later escaped, eventually to be killed by security forces on 2 December 1993).

A new constitution was accepted, and new congressional elections were set for October 1991, which resulted in a majority win for the Liberal Party, a surprise to those who had thought radical political change would be forthcoming. But an accommodation of sorts was reached. Violence declined, and traffickers went back to business. After a short hiatus during which drug production declined in the wake of the "drug wars," cocaine production returned to normal and probably increased. Drug control in Colombia has apparently not reduced supplies at all. Moreover, coca and cannabis harvests have been almost stable for half a decade.[18] Worse, opium and heroin production have begun, showing dramatic increases after 1991.

Peru

Control policies in Peru have moved from ethical or moralistic approaches through the whole gamut of law-enforcement control measures—from military intervention to suppress production to long-term economic development to give growers income alternatives.[19] Whereas in Colombia the control measures have been directed mostly against traffickers, in Peru they are targeted toward growers as much as traffickers. Mostly, the Peruvian government has been agitated about the link between Sendero Luminoso and the illicit-drug industry. Given that until recently Peru had few traffickers but was (and continues to be) the world's largest producer of coca, this approach was quite logical. Only recently has the specter of local consumption begun to haunt the authorities sufficiently to cause them to seriously entertain control policies to reduce it.

In its drug-control efforts, Peru has taken most of its cues from the United States, whose support has been accompanied by moral persuasion, economic sanctions, and development aid,[20] all designed to suppress illicit-drug production. An oft-cited version of this moral position and its policy implications outline the resulting rights and duties of principal consuming and producing countries within the context of "co-responsibility:" "In the first place, it is necessary to determine the rights and obligations of each group of countries. It is obvious that it is the right of consuming countries not to have illegal drugs getting to them, and it is the duty of producing countries to undertake every possible effort to control production if not eliminate it."[21]

Rights and duties notwithstanding, Peru has never had the wherewithal to implement on its own a full-fledged supply-reduction program. The United States has therefore stepped in under the "shared responsibility" doctrine to supply logistics, personnel training, and sometimes even staffing to carry out major drug-suppression strategies—mainly crop-eradication and interdiction programs in the Upper Huallaga Valley, the biggest coca-production region in the world. According to Elena Alvarez, the ensuing supply-control efforts to solve the coca problem may be classified into five categories: (1) the "blackmail" approach (practiced by various U.S. administrations); (2) the "magic solution" (advocated by the U.S. Department of State); (3) input control (or control of precursors); (4) control through substitution (advocated by USAID); and (5) military intervention (promoted by the U.S. government but not necessarily its military).[22]

"Blackmail" entails reducing coca production in exchange for something—usually foreign aid of one kind or another, with the threat that aid will be cut off if specific crop-reduction targets are not achieved. Peruvian animosity to this conditionality is widely known. Regardless, when U.S. interests have been judged to be significantly at stake in other than drug-control areas, aid as a leverage of one kind or another has been forthcoming. This type of persuasion has made hardly anyone happy.

The "magic solution" refers to the search for a way to destroy coca plants. Herbicides and a much touted coca-eating moth have been advanced.[23] Herbicides, which do not work as nicely on coca as they do on cannabis plants, have been tried experimentally in Peru.[24] Widespread concerns over damage to the environment (shades of Agent Orange in Vietnam) and the possible unleashing of a biological pest that could destroy more than coca leaves have impeded implementation.

Input control refers to precursor chemicals required to process coca into cocaine hydrochloride. Authorities have even proposed putting kerosene on Peru's control list. Although kerosene is used in coca-paste production in the Upper Huallaga Valley, it is also the most commonly used household fuel for cooking. Thus, given the legitimate household use of kerosene, enforcement of this particular prohibition does not seem very practical.[25] Other banned precursor chemicals are slipped across border areas with little trouble.

USAID has implemented control through substitution in Peru. Coca growers receive funds to induce them to replace coca with other crops. This approach is accompanied by threats of eradication to raise the perceived risks and reduce the profit margins of coca cultivation to the point where growing substitute crops will be economically attractive. So far, the actual result of this approach has been to displace the cultivation of coca leaf from project control areas to other areas—not to reduce, let alone abolish, aggregate coca growing. Alvarez chronicles the details:

> In 1981, the Peruvian government subscribed to several joint venture projects with the U.S. government for the purpose of using the control/substitution approach in order to eradicate coca leaf in the UHV.[26]
>
> The three targeted projects were part of a single strategy whose major objectives were: (1) the voluntary and compulsory eradication of coca (CORAH); (2) the supply of technical and financial support for cultivation of coca substitutes or legal crops (PEAH); and (3) the enforcement of drug laws (UMOPAR).[27] However, the results of these projects have been rather poor. In 1986, of the estimated 60,000 ha of coca planted in the valley, about 12,000 were eradicated. These 12,000 ha become even less in terms of changes in cultivated areas when one considers that peasants started production of coca leaf in other areas of more difficult geographical access within the same valley. Moreover, in 1987, CORAH fulfilled only 5 percent of its projected area reduction goal for that year, and PEAH's financial resources (5.3 million US dollars) were so limited it could not compete with the cocaine trade.[28]
>
> The programs therefore were not successful in reducing the number of hectares under cultivation. Indeed, some observers argue that the program contributed to the "displacement" of coca to other parts of the country (as mentioned above) and to triggering the alliance between coca growers and the guerrillas.[29] Given the high price of coca leaf at the time when this program was

implemented, the programs had little chance of success. The Shining Path guerrilla group has literally immobilized the programs by threatening the lives of the people involved.[30]

With all these considerations of inadequacy or failure in mind, the U.S. government has advocated the fifth strategy mentioned above—a military solution to the problem of illegal crop production. Peru has signed agreements with the U.S. government endorsing this solution.[31] The result has been an active contingent of U.S. advisers, military hardware, and Vietnam-like "secure bases," such as Santa Lucía in the Upper Huallaga Valley. The U.S. or Peruvian military protects eradication teams and attempts to undermine the regional authority of insurgent groups such as the Sendero Luminoso. Since late 1993 the military has gained the upper hand.

Through late 1993 the guerrillas successfully fought this control initiative to a standstill in the Upper Huallaga Valley. For a time there was concern that the military approach would reduce coca supplies much less than it would enhance peasant opposition to the government, making a second Sendero Luminoso experience likely. The government has offered nothing but destruction to the growers, so many of them understandably sided with the Sendero Luminoso for protection. Now that Sendero Luminoso is in disarray and the government more in charge, production has declined. However, hardly any knowledgeable observers are taking much heart over this. Production declines appear to be due less to the government's success than to aging plants and a destructive fungus that has attacked Peruvian coca. Growers have moved to other locations and planted new crops, which can be expected to come on stream by 1997. If the fungus does not follow the new plantings, look for Peruvian coca production to increase.

Blackmail, magic, crop substitution, precursor chemical control, and military intervention apparently have made little long-term progress in aggregate crop suppression, so the experts are turning to a more widespread application of economic principles—general economic development. Advocates of this approach view coca control as an economic-development problem requiring a long-term approach. One version, focusing on the truly desperate economic conditions afflicting 50 percent or more of the Peruvian population, pushes a strategy of foreign aid. Another version advocates strengthening legal markets with an "alternative development strategy." Both versions are spelled out in specific proposals and have to a greater or lesser extent been implemented in Peru.[32]

In general, the efforts to strengthen the legal market focus on integrating Peru's vast informal (but not necessarily illegal) economy into the officially recognized one, thereby reducing growers' economic incentives to stay in the illegal economy. The alternative development strategy was endorsed by the Fujimori administration in May 1991 in an accord with the U.S. government.[33] The agreement provides for both macro and microeconomic adjustments. At the micro level, which is more likely to affect coca growers immediately, the accord provides for structural transformations to give growers easier access to property security (titles), credit, external trade, and price negotiations.[34] Moreover, it proposes to set up an Autonomous Alternative Development Authority (AADA) to coordinate applied projects. The UNDCP and USAID-Peru are the largest contributors to this strategy; the international financial transfers indicate considerable international enthusiasm with the prospects.

Nothing else has worked satisfactorily, so development, alternative development, market strategies, macro and microstructural adjustments, and so on are being tried. It is too early to tell if these approaches will be any more beneficial to Peru's supply-reduction goals than earlier efforts have been. But suppose they prove to be successful? Given the ready translocation experiences already noted, one might suppose that production would simply migrate elsewhere, perhaps to Bolivia, Ecuador, or southern Colombia. Thus, the problem may call for regional development strategies, which some people would consider a laudable moral position regardless of efficacy. Production mobility is a major concern for any supply-control program. In the meantime, Peru has enough coca and cocaine to continue flooding the world market. From 1988 through 1992 the net amount of land dedicated to coca growing in Peru probably increased by more than 5 percent, resulting in increased tonnage as well.[35] Some people believe that land dedicated to coca production declined by about 15 percent in the 1993 crop year.[36] I suspect that when new plantings are accounted for, the figures will show a rebound.

Bolivia

Like Peru, Bolivia has experimented with the full range of drug-control efforts to suppress supplies, ranging from fights with especially well-organized and aggressive coca-growers' unions over basic legislation to interdiction, eradication, military options, and alternative development.[37]

Regarding legislation, the political ramifications are best understood by reflecting on Bolivia's economic dependence on the coca/cocaine industry for export earnings and domestic employment. The extent of this dependence is generally acknowledged as being huge;

the industry accounts for as much as 20 percent of the country's GNP. Any effective disruption of the trade would therefore cause considerable economic dislocation and widespread unrest, both of which have obvious political ramifications. These considerations account for the government's reluctance to become aggressive despite clear indications that recent regimes, in contrast to at least one earlier one, have not been in favor of the illegal-drug trade and have actually thought of doing something about it. Nevertheless, inaction has been the norm.

Major departures from the norm of basic inaction have come as a result of international pressure. These departures include the use of U.S. troops in 1986 on search-and-destroy missions, the establishment of annual eradication targets (with nominal efforts to meet them), and, beginning in 1991, the militarization of the drug war through forced eradication programs and Operation Safe Haven. James Painter notes that "there have been important differences of emphasis in the drug policy of the UDP (Unión Democrática y Popular) government (1982–1985), the MNR government (1985–1989) and the Acuerdo Patriótico (1989–1993), but all three followed a tripartite strategy of more efficient interdiction against traffickers, faster eradication of coca bushes, and more effective economic alternatives for coca farmers."[38] These policies notwithstanding, each government has virtually surrendered supply-reduction enforcement to the U.S. DEA, pursuing eradication only where it has been politically possible and giving little effective support to alternative development programs.

Accordingly, drug-control programs that could produce considerable political resistance—mainly eradication and interdiction—have not been a success. Painter estimates that less than 2 percent of total coca products (paste, base, and cocaine) made in the country are seized. Bolivia today produces more of all three than ever before, coca yields are probably increasing, and eradication programs have failed every year except 1990 to produce a net reduction. This condition prevailed even when, because of significant one-time financial incentives, peasants queued up to have their coca chopped down under the supervision of DIRECO (Dirección de Reconversión Agrícola).[39] A solid legal framework notwithstanding,[40] negative economic considerations and a nationalistic political specter in response to U.S. pressure have seriously undermined supply-suppression efforts.

SUBDESAL (Subsecretaría de Desarrollo Alternativo) is responsible for coca substitution and alternative development. A 1,000-person police unit, UMOPAR (Unidad Móvil de Patrullaje Rural), is responsible for interdiction, which includes destroying coca-processing pits and laboratories, seizing paste, base, and cocaine, intercepting the flow of precursor chemicals, and arresting traffickers. In practice, however, the United States controls Bolivia's interdiction efforts and sets the bounds of its alternative development programs, a matter that has caused considerable political friction within Bolivia as well as poor coordination among antidrug units such as UMOPAR and the DEA.[41]

Fearing the kind of drug-induced violence seen in Colombia and Peru, in July 1991 the Paz Zamora government reduced prison time for traffickers in its custody and others who would turn themselves in within 120 days. Moreover, the government promised not to extradite to the United States any who did. All the traffickers had to do was confess their crimes and "make an efficient contribution" to the capture of other traffickers. To the substantial chagrin of DEA officials, eight top traffickers complied and were given light sentences. Violence *a la Colombia* may have been preempted by these measures, but coca production has continued largely unabated.

With forced eradication (no compensation to farmers) starting in earnest in 1991, mainly as a result of fierce pressure from the U.S. government, grower resistance to even nominal control efforts stiffened. Coca union leaders formed self-defense groups, announcing that they would protect themselves by force from DIRECO eradication teams, who by now had to be accompanied by armed UMOPAR guards for their personal safety. A truce was called, and DIRECO agreed to pull back.[42] Results? A downplaying of violence, to be sure. But in a five-year period from 1987 to 1991, although farmers voluntarily eradicated more than 18,000 hectares of coca (in exchange for financial incentives), they planted more than 26,000 new hectares in other locations. Coca planting therefore far outstripped coca eradication.[43] Some people concluded that the U.S. $2,000-per-hectare incentive to voluntarily eradicate was misguided, particularly in light of a 2,000-hectare increase in cultivation in 1993 over 1992.[44]

With basic political inaction the norm except when contravened by aggressive U.S. pressure, attention moved to employing the military in drug-control efforts. On this, Painter makes a trenchant observation:

Despite the low eradication figures and the poor interdiction efforts of UMOPAR, and given the desire for supply-side solutions from U.S. policymakers, it is surprising in hindsight that the use of U.S. troops and even Bolivian troops in antidrug operations was restricted to just two occasions throughout the 1980s. The first occurred in August 1984 when 500 Bolivian troops were sent by the Siles Zuazo government to destroy labs and arrest drug traffickers in the Chapare.[45] The other, widely publicized exception was in July 1986, when in an operation known as Blast Furnace 160 U.S. troops and six helicopters conducted a four-month campaign against trafficking operations in the Beni.[46]

Such moderation would change as a result of the increasing perception in U.S. policymaking circles at the end of the 1980s that the drug war was now more important than the Cold War in Latin America and that more manpower was necessary to improve interdiction results. Throughout 1989, a major new U.S. drug policy known as the Andean Strategy was developed by the U.S. Office of National Drug Control Policy (ONDCP) under the leadership of the then drug czar, William Bennett.[47] A major objective of the initiative was to reduce the flow of cocaine to the United States by 60 percent over a ten-year period by improving crop eradication, interdiction and enforcement in the Andean source countries.[48] While the initiative in many ways merely escalated past supply-side efforts, its major break with the past was the proposed incorporation of Andean countries' armed forces in the drug war, large increases in U.S. military assistance, and an expanded role for U.S. military forces in antinarcotic operations overseas.[49]

This decision to militarize the drug war met with decided and vociferous opposition in Bolivia from many who already distrusted the military. A fivefold increase in U.S. aid to Bolivia's military—which amounted to a 40 percent enhancement of its budget—was viewed by others only slightly more charitably. The consistent fears were (1) that the hand of the army could be dangerously strengthened in a historically weak democracy; (2) that this funding influx could lead to a "Colombianization" of the war by creating more situations where violence could occur and human rights be abused; and (3) that coca growers in the Chapare, in the absence of real economic alternatives, would take up arms against the army and the government.[50] Bolivians had fought a bloody civil war within the memory of many still living, and hardly anyone wanted a repeat of that experience. Beyond all this, internal struggles began immediately between UMOPAR and the army over role definitions and functions and, of course, over how the money would be spent and who would benefit from the spending. This wrangling added a certain cynicism to the proceedings, particularly because many supposed that the money would lend itself more to bureaucratic corruption than to reductions in the drug trade.

Despite the protests, U.S. advisers arrived in mid-1990 to start a ten-week training course for 500 members of the Manchego battalion in Montero, 30 miles north of Santa Cruz, as part of an operation code-named "White Spear."[51] Their arrival had the effect of galvanizing the coca growers into stepping up their protests. In November 1990, 10,000 growers held a raucous demonstration in Chimore in the Chapare and threatened to march on La Paz if the government went ahead with its plans to send a U.S.-trained and -equipped army to destroy their crops.[52] The national peasant union Confederación Sindical Unica de Trabajadores Campesinos de Bolivia (CSUTCB) called a two-day nationwide road and rail blockade, and thereafter demonstrations expanded. The government responded by signing an agreement that the army would operate only against traffickers, not growers, and that it would implement new alternative development programs.[53]

After the military made brief but inauspicious forays into the Santa Cruz and Beni departments, the political opposition got the upper hand, and the army's contributions to the drug war declined in word as well as in deed. The U.S. pulled back in frustration at not being able to mobilize the army. Violence was averted, but analysts believed that heavy damage was done to the government's image. Hardly any government assurances thereafter had credibility. The impact may well have been considerable, as Painter points out:

> The Paz Zamora government was, in essence, caught between the desire to maintain the goodwill of its major benefactor and to keep the lid on political opposition to the policy. But the government's handling of the issue was a sorry sequence of denials, then admissions, contradictions, and evasions, and then changes in its reasoning, which undoubtedly increased opposition to the policy. It also probably increased anti–United States sentiment as the government struggled not to appear to be bowing to U.S. pressure in implementing an unpopular measure. But perhaps the lasting legacy was the undermining of the government's sensible attempts to portray Bolivia's coca-cocaine problem as essentially economic, which required large infusions of economic aid, new markets, and new crops to wean the country from its economic dependence on the coca-cocaine industry. It was difficult to argue that alternative development was still the government's priority when it had accepted significant amounts of military aid in the face of concerted opposition from virtually every political force in the country.[54]

With failure of a "risk-raising" policy to suppress supplies, the Bolivian government, with financial and technical assistance from the United Nations and the United States, has launched economic development programs in the Chapare and elsewhere in an effort to give coca growers an alternative income source. The government hopes to wean growers from coca and accustom them to planting alternative, economically productive crops or seeking other gainful employment.[55]

It is too early to weigh how well such alternative development efforts have achieved their intended goal. Early indications are that regional dents are being made in coca production but that aggregate Bolivian production remains unaffected.

Despite drug-control efforts, traffickers and growers continue their operations in Bolivia with minor inconveniences from the authorities. The aggregate amount of coca grown has increased,[56] and processing by Bolivians in Bolivia has probably accelerated in response to the temporary discomfort and preoccupation of Colombian traffickers as they fought their own national government over who would control portions of the national territory.

Mexico

As in the other Latin American countries studied, government drug-control efforts in Mexico have been less motivated by concerns over U.S. drug consumption (or even by domestic consumption), which a supply-suppression strategy is supposed to address, than by concerns over traffickers' threats to the integrity of the state.[57] U.S. pressure has been widely felt in Mexico, of course, in part because of proximity but also because of large drug shipments transiting through Mexico from South America. Mexican political concerns and U.S. pressure have combined to elicit mutual cooperation in herbicidal spraying programs and interdiction efforts on Mexican soil.

Mexico's traditionally moderate concerns about traffickers had intensified by 1975, when Mexico became the main supplier of both heroin and marijuana to the U.S. market.[58] Successful eradication programs in Turkey and the elimination of the French Connection in the early 1970s had resulted in the opening of new production sites elsewhere in the world, including in Mexico. Thus, the government had to confront an unprecedented growth in illegal agricultural production, product processing, and smuggling. All this activity posed regional challenges to the state's authority and capacity to enforce law and to guarantee order. It even threatened to disrupt the political dominance of Mexico's established institutions, including the PRI (Partido Revolucionario Institucional), which had governed the country since the revolutions in the early part of the century.

In the mid-1970s the government tried eradication (e.g., Operation Condor), which resulted in little other than a proliferation of armed peasants and dealers rising to defend their interests.[59] As a consequence, Mexico sought bilateral support from the United States, quite happily given, to overwhelm the traffickers with modern technology—aerial photographic equipment useful in plotting fields, telecommunications, helicopters, specialized aircraft for herbicidal spraying, spare parts, training in the art of field spraying for Mexican pilots, and intelligence gathering.[60] In due course the Mexican government developed a three-pronged approach to the drug challenge:

eradication of marijuana and poppy fields; interdiction of narcotics in transit (including cocaine); and disruption of trafficker networks and organizations. The three states of Sinaloa, Durango, and Chihuahua in the north received the most attention.[61]

As for eradication, spraying statistics from 1975 to 1978 are impressive. Nearly 6,000 hectares of marijuana were destroyed each year, figures that even increased in later years. An average of more than 11,000 hectares of opium poppy were destroyed annually during the same period. Indeed, it can be said that Mexico's eradication programs, which date to at least the late 1930s, have been the most important Mexican policy instrument to counter traffickers in both the heroin and marijuana markets.[62]

Accompanied by a massive use of military force, seizures of heroin, cocaine, and marijuana rose dramatically. Some major drug-smuggling families' members were put out of business or incarcerated,[63] and marijuana and opium poppy production were largely brought under control. The Mexican government regained jurisdiction over its national territory, and many people basked in the peace of quietude and resolute victory. It did not last long. By 1983–1984 Mexico was once again experiencing high levels of production and smuggling, due in part to the cleverness of traffickers in reorganizing their activities and to the successful air interdiction program the United States had launched against Colombian cocaine being airdropped in Florida. The traffickers simply established overland routes, turning Mexico into a major transit country.[64]

The Miguel de la Madrid administration decided, as a result, to strengthen its eradication programs and more vigorously attempt to disrupt traffickers by giving a greater role to the military. U.S. financial contributions to this effort blossomed. However, this enterprise fell on hard times when the extent to which Mexican authorities had become involved in the drug trade became apparent to everyone. This has perhaps been the single most limiting factor in Mexico's antidrug efforts, one that has resulted in pain and suffering for many. Unsurprisingly, by the mid-1980s, "Mexico had not only recovered its standing as the main supplier of both marijuana and heroin for the U.S. market, but 30 percent of all cocaine available for U.S. consumers was believed to be crossing through Mexican territory."[65]

The torture murder of Enrique Camarena, a DEA operative in Mexico,[66] and the resumption of Mexico as chief supplier of cocaine headed for the U.S. market triggered a ferocious response from U.S. drug-control agencies. They demanded that Mexico purge its police and army of their more corrupt personnel. The Mexican government was not inclined to treat these demands frivolously. The resurgence of drug activity once again allowed traffickers to threaten state security and institutions through corruption and armed violence. In 1985 the government made several internal organizational adjustments that resulted in the Mexican police's seizure of ten times more cocaine than in 1984, a figure that had increased a hundredfold by 1990.[67] Part of this progress was made possible by the disbanding of the Dirección Federal de Seguridad in 1985 (because of corruption) and the eventual establishment in the Carlos Salinas government of a new drug-control post with an expanded budget in the attorney general's office. This new drug-control office has largely not been corrupted. But part of the success with cocaine, as well as allied improvements with marijuana and opium, was made possible by deploying 25,000 soldiers (approximately 25 percent of total armed forces on active duty) in almost year-round manual eradication efforts accompanied by massive air support for spraying.[68]

Aside from continued eradication and interdiction programs, the Salinas government's policies have focused more intensely on immobilizing large trafficking organizations. Several principals have been captured (e.g., Caro Quintero, Félix Gallardo), and increasing amounts of refined products, especially cocaine, have been seized, which appears to have weakened large-scale cocaine-smuggling organizations operating on Mexican soil.

The Salinas administration created the Northern Border Response Force, a rapid-response team of specialized federal judicial police agents who interdict airborne South American cocaine traffic. Correspondingly, the government carried out judicial and other reforms to help ensure that traffickers will serve time, that people involved in official corruption will be vigorously prosecuted, that police units involved in human rights violations will be reined in, and that specialized antidrug training programs for military personnel involved in eradication and interdiction will be launched. The government also set up a program to monitor precursor chemicals, and it aggressively began to target assets derived from narcotics-related transactions.[69]

Traffickers have not taken the spectacular successes at interdiction and eradication and the impressive policy developments under the Salinas regime lying down. They have responded with violence and intimidation that have cowed some people both in the government and among potential growers. Threats and money still easily corrupt many police and judges.[70] Moreover, growers have decentralized their fields into smaller sizes and planted in ravines and sharp valleys (both of which make aerial spraying more difficult). In defense of their crops, they have perfected a scattershot technique from multiple rifles that has intimidated pilots involved in spraying programs, bringing both aerial and manual eradication programs to a point of diminishing returns.

Cocaine traffickers, for their part, have become more sophisticated in their activities. Guatemala, El Salvador, and Belize have become important staging and storage sites from which cocaine is introduced into Mexico by air and land and thereafter into the United States. Also, air drops have increased in southern Mexico as a consequence of tighter controls in the north. Thus, despite the interdiction and eradication successes, illicit-drug production in Mexico and transit through its territory to the U.S. market have actually increased since the mid-1980s. Indeed, between 50 and 70 percent of total U.S. cocaine imports now transit through Mexico.[71] Celia Toro supplies a trenchant observation:

> The novelty . . . is not only the change in routes and means of transportation, but the speed of this change and the violence displayed by cocaine traffickers as they cross through Mexico and in their attempt to control smuggling in Mexico. In retrospect, Mexico was better off when hundreds of airplanes coming from South America carrying huge amounts of cocaine only stopped in Mexican territory to refuel and for repairs.[72]

Thailand

For 700 years, Thailand and its predecessor, the Kingdom of Siam, periodically banned opium use, although the application of the laws was carefully construed to implicitly permit medicinal use.[73] Cannabis was likewise proscribed, even though Thais hardly ever took it for its narcotic properties (it was used as an herb in curries and other foods and, since 1850, for hemp fiber among recently immigrated Hmong). The bans were generally not unpopular among most Thais, who had little patience with drug *abuse*, a sentiment fully justified by their understanding of Buddhist scripture.

King Rama I (reigned 1782–1811) called for an end to opium use and trade, imposing a substantial burden on convicted addicts: Their wives, children, and slaves became royal property.[74] In 1811 King Rama II added public whippings and forced labor (cutting "elephant grass") to family and slave confiscations for violators. These measure were not effective, which gave impetus to King Rama III's proscription efforts in 1839. He appealed to the religious conscience of all Buddhists. But the motivation for banning was more worldly: Opium was being imported from other countries, and Thailand was suffering a trade deficit. Moreover, the British had been pushing the opium trade in China, and Chinese coolies in Thailand were getting it through their ethnic networks and becoming addicted, creating social problems for the king and his government.[75]

The British continued to push opium on the Kingdom of Siam throughout King Rama III's reign (1824–1851) as part of their efforts to open up the country to trade. King Rama IV (King Mongkut) acquiesced and initiated a change in drug-control policy: The proscription laws would be relaxed, but any Thai smoking opium would be considered Chinese, have to wear a queue and bracelet (customs imposed on all resident Chinese), pay the triennial poll tax for Chinese, and suffer the inevitable contempt most Thais had for Chinese. Those willing to endure these conditions could buy and sell opium legally.

More important, opium could be taxed, and the king needed funds. He introduced what has come to be known as "tax farming"— putting opium-tax collection in the hands of the highest bidder. The king's money collections increased quite substantially,[76] reaching about 10 percent of the government's total revenues by fiscal year 1905/06.[77] But consumption among ordinary Thais rose accordingly, all the social disgrace provisions of the drug-control policy notwithstanding. Nevertheless, the largest consumers continued to be Chinese coolies.

Eventually, the government took over the tax farms and administered the drug policies itself through the newly formed (1906) Opium Department. There was a schizoid conflict in this policy development: The department collected the tax but also worked to reduce opium consumption. The contradictory signals undermined both the credibility and the outcome of the consumption-reduction efforts, particularly because the government continued to restrict opium-den licenses to operators who sold the most opium.[78] From the early 1900s to 1950 the conflicting impulses to sell more opium for tax revenues but reduce consumption to mitigate social ills dominated drug-control discussions in Thailand, greatly complicating the work of various agencies set up both to facilitate taxation and to deal with the social costs of narcotics consumption.

The second world war changed many things for Thailand, as it did for other countries in Southeast Asia. Burma became independent, and the ensuing political and economic instability encouraged opium production, which caused large spillover effects in Thailand. China exterminated many opium addicts and traffickers and drove most of the rest into the Burmese and Thai hills, where they, along with remnants of the defeated Chinese Nationalist Army (KMT), almost immediately went into the opium business. Thereafter, Thailand began to function as a chief producer and transit country for international markets.

The government felt threatened by these events and moved into the hill country to try to control supplies. However, drug-control agents soon became corrupted and actually facilitated opium imports into Thailand,[79] thereby defeating the government's aims. Thereafter, the government turned its attention once again to consumption. On 3 August 1955 it reimposed opium prohibition, but a later administration actually joined the smugglers. That regime was overturned when fears arose that communists in northern Thailand and in the hills of Burma and Laos were using proceeds from the opium trade to undermine national security. Like the governments of Colombia and Mexico, when security became an issue the Thai government acted decisively against the drug trade. Production, trade, sale, and consumption were once again prohibited. Anchalee Singhanetra-Renard describes the ensuing events:

> At midnight on 1 January 1959, government officials took over the opium dens, confiscating opium and opium derivatives and materials and equipment, such as pipes, used to take opium that were still on the premises. All of this, including 43,445 pipes, was destroyed at the Phramen Grounds, near the Royal Palace on 1 July 1959.
>
> Later, in an effort to keep people in the Thai military from maintaining their contacts with traffickers in Burma, Sarit issued an edict banning such contacts.[80] The effect of this effort cannot be measured although it does indicate that Sarit appeared determined to reduce the trade of opium in this country.
>
> According to the leading authority on Sarit, Thak, opium was banned in an effort to distance the new government from the old regime. Furthermore, says Thak,[81] Sarit was building his image as a *phokhun*, a morally superior and benevolent father figure. The connection Sarit makes between modernity and the elimination of opium as well as his distancing himself from Communism in his proclamation support this contention.[82]

The government set up a Central Tribal Welfare Committee to work with hill tribes to wean them from opium production. The government established controls on precursor chemicals (e.g., acetyl chloride, acetic anhydride) needed to produce heroin and repromulgated sanctions for consumption. Thus, a tripodal effort was launched—one on agricultural production, one on refining, another on consumption. The government also moved to rehabilitate narcotics addicts. These measures had immediate effects: Opium use continued in the hills but declined in the cities. Soon, however— whether or not by a communist plot, as rumored—heroin appeared in the larger cities. Police uncovered a heroin refinery in the center of Bangkok, a short distance from Chulalongkorn University. In response, and in deference to the United Nations Single Convention on Narcotic Drugs, adopted in 1961, the government took harsh action, which included executions of traffickers. By 1963 heroin use had declined.

The success was short-lived. By 1968 not only was opium still in wide use, a resurgence of heroin consumption was widely recognized, this time involving Thailand's students and urban youth.[83] All the control efforts notwithstanding, heroin had finally spread into the mainstream of Thai society. No longer was it mostly an "ethnic problem" among the hill tribes. In response to new markets in Thai cities, heroin trafficking in the northern hills increased dramatically. Irregular armies were formed to defend opium and heroin caravans, and insurgents used income from the trade to finance their wars against the government. A hard-line response from the government failed to eliminate the problem. Khun Sa became openly defiant, and heroin consumption in the larger cities continued to increase.

The unsettled conditions allowed the expansion of cannabis cultivation in the northeast. Plantations emerged despite drug-control laws. The increased prevalence of cannabis introduced more students to narcotics, serving as a "gateway" to heroin.[84] There followed a massive importation of psychotropic drugs subsequent to their popularization during the 1960s in the West.

By 1976 the government, by now quite desperate, passed the Narcotics Control Act, which brought the country's legal position more in line with the UN Single Convention than had previous antinarcotics acts. Now the police could search dwellings, vehicles, and business establishments for illegal narcotics.[85] Bureaus were established in the prime minister's office (e.g., Narcotics Control Board [ONCB]) to oversee the tightening of loopholes everywhere, including control over precursor chemicals. The board moved to pay rewards for seizures, coordinate government and private-agency efforts to prevent drug abuse, gather intelligence, establish rehabilitation centers, and do research. It maintained a law-enforcement section for the usual activities. These efforts have been maintained to the present day, albeit under increasing cooperation with international agencies.

Meanwhile, the government's recognition of its failure to control production in the hills prompted it to experiment with new approaches. The most impressive one attempts to create alternatives to opium cultivation in the northern Thai hills through crop substitution and integrated economic development programs. These programs, supported by international agencies such as the UNDCP, have posted impressive gains in weaning growers from opium production.[86]

All the efforts at drug-control notwithstanding, consumption of heroin and psychotropics has continued to increase in Thailand. Singhanetra-Renard attributes this less to the real failure of the drug-control programs than to other factors operating in Thai society: rapid urban growth in Bangkok; breakdown in family cohesiveness;

and cultural shifts that have given unprecedented individual freedom to Thais.[87]

Moreover, although the impressive crop-substitution and economic development programs have reduced production in the Thai hills, "geographic substitution" has taken place. Production has moved to Myanmar/Burma and Laos, countries that now provide feedstock and refining sites for illicit drugs smuggled back into Thailand and abused by increasing numbers of Thai youth. These conditions resulted in the ONCB's stating in its 1988 annual report that even though cultivation was down "to only a small amount of the total . . . of the Golden Triangle," the seriousness of narcotics problems for Thailand "seemed to be more aggravating."[88]

Laos

Laos is a major producer of illicit drugs in part because of regional isolation. Large areas are only nominally under the control of the central government.[89] Other reasons are associated with desperate economic conditions for some of the hill tribes and overall political instability. Moreover, for a period of time during the 1980s the Lao government was apparently deriving a significant amount of its revenues from taxes on the illicit-drug trade. Thus, the government's policies have been ambiguous in practice, if not in print. Nevertheless, the government has made nominal public efforts to control production and consumption.

The current Lao government professes a commitment to elimination of poppy cultivation if alternative income sources for growers can be made available. The potential economic desperation caused by destroying opium income would, the government fears, lead to additional political unrest in areas already vulnerable to insurgencies. Eradication programs or military involvement are thus not desirable options, but funds are lacking for economic development approaches. The government has looked to foreign sources for development project financing, and the United States and the United Nations have obliged in several areas.[90] The resulting projects, focusing on crop substitution, attempt to progressively eliminate opium cultivation by creating alternative income sources for the Hmong and other hill tribes and by providing roads as well as social, health, sanitation, and education services.[91]

Financial and tax considerations notwithstanding, the Lao government has two reasons to give attention to illicit drugs. The first is the knowledge that poppy cultivation and the refining and trafficking that accompany it are fueling insurgencies and other political disturbances in the poppy-growing regions. For reasons of national security, then, the government is interested in reducing production. The motivation derives more from fear of insurgency than from moral or practical compunctions about production, traffic, or consumption of narcotics. The Lao government therefore finds itself in a difficult position: Aggressive eradication of poppy production may fire insurgency, but failure to stop opium trafficking may ensure the eventual triumph of the government's foes.

The second factor motivating government attention is the conditionality imposed on foreign aid, principally by the United States. Conditional funding now involves millions of dollars that a developing country such as Laos cannot afford to pass up lightly. Many observers believe Laos pays lip service to U.S. development interests solely for purposes of acquiring bilateral funds, some of which are targeted toward suppressing insurgency in the hill country.[92] Thus, narcotics control is driven as a residual rather than prime interest of the government.

The government is involved in policies and practices affecting the environment that also may have an impact on poppy cultivation. Population growth (presently about 2.6 percent annually on a national level) has been substantially higher in the Lao hills, where opium poppy is cultivated. The slash-and-burn agriculture traditionally practiced to raise food for the increasing population is denuding the area and causing considerable environmental damage through topsoil loss and river silting. The government has tried forced and voluntary resettlement programs to lowland areas, which, if successful, could reduce poppy cultivation. However, both culture and politics have conspired to thwart the government's efforts.[93]

International agencies have funded several development projects in an effort to foster crop-substitution programs. Although sponsors give the highland development projects good marks, the impact these efforts may have on total Lao production is unclear. Giving the projects the benefit of the doubt, additional development efforts may be called for. Nevertheless, the uncertainties are highlighted by some of Daniel Henning's interviewees:

> These cash commitments, while considerable, are small compared to drug trafficking profits. Furthermore, apparent success of these projects may exaggerate their effectiveness. One interviewee indicated that Houaphanh Province is not a large exporter of opium and that it was selected by Houaphanh members of the Vientiane leadership who are trying to do something for the poor economic conditions of their home province. Another interviewee indicated that arrangements were underway for the growing of a licit drug, tobacco, as one of the alternate crops.[94]

Laos has been receptive to UN efforts to develop a subregional control policy to reduce the geographic mobility of cultivation and production. The approach involves creation of joint activities for the common hill-country border areas of Laos, Thailand, and Myanmar/Burma. It is unclear, however, whether Laos's receptivity to UN initiatives has had any impact on cultivation or processing on Lao soil.

It is quite significant, perhaps tellingly so, that Laos does not have a law prohibiting opium cultivation (although the government has passed a decree against marijuana growing and has undertaken large-scale eradication of commercial marijuana plantations).[95] Similarly, Laos has paid lip service to policies to reduce consumption. The best that can be said is that the Lao government does not believe consumption to be much of a problem. Nevertheless, a new penal code provides six-month to ten-year prison terms for possessing or selling narcotics.

What else can be said of drug-control efforts? Lao authorities have eradicated commercial marijuana plantations. They have seized limited amounts of marijuana in transit. But marijuana production has probably increased near the Thai border because Thai drug-control efforts have pushed numerous traffickers into Laos. Here, crackdowns on trafficking have generally been ineffective;[96] about 20 percent of total heroin entering Thailand is considered to have been produced in Laos.[97] Nevertheless, in 1990 the U.S. consulate certified Laos ("with explanation") as a cooperative country,[98] mostly, it appears, because Lao officials happily participated in U.S.-sponsored seminars on how to control illicit drugs.

Much talk and little action is the best summary of Lao drug-control efforts. The reasons are multiple: leadership inclinations, isolation, social fragmentation, budgetary considerations, political restlessness among the hill tribes, and indifference. Illicit drugs appear to be largely uncontrolled, although the U.S. State Department argued that there has been a slight temporal decline during the half-decade preceding 1992 (despite a slight rebound in the 1993 crop year).[99] Laos's drug-control policies appear not to have significantly affected opium production or consumption, so what of the future? Most drug-control policies in Laos are indeed "future"—they are "planned," or "will be carried out," or "are in the process of deployment." However, the government's commitment and initiative to bring closure to any of these is seriously questioned.

Myanmar/Burma

Burma's long experience with narcotic drugs, like Thailand's and Laos's, began in precolonial times.[100] The opium poppy was grown widely, but its product was used mainly for medicinal purposes. Because Burma was heavily influenced by Buddhist religious and cultural thought, abuse prevention consisted mostly of Buddhist and royal pronouncements, much as in Thailand. However, as they did elsewhere, the British entered Burma, removed the king and Buddhist hierarchy from political power, and opened up trade—including opium, which they pushed vigorously. Narcotics abuse soared. Coterminously, if not as a consequence, civil disorder grew. Beginning in 1782 a regional British commander responded by implementing a multitude of narcotics laws and regulations prohibiting the Burmese from producing, selling, and consuming alcoholic drinks, opium, and other intoxicants. The policies were not effective. Opium addiction increased.

The British soon abandoned prohibition for the same reason the Kingdom of Siam did: Although drug consumption was discovered to produce highly undesirable social outcomes, prohibition appeared to have little impact on demand reduction. So why not tax and control? An opium tax was highly beneficial to the colonial administration's revenue needs, so much so that in 1826 the military government instituted opium-tax farming in Tenasserim, a system that became institutionalized across Burma in 1866. The replacement of the tax-farm system in 1871 in favor of fixed duties on consumers and a shop-license fee on retailers only highlighted Britain's public-policy primacy of revenue enhancement over demand reduction.

None of this pleased traditional Burmese authorities. They were more inclined to make opium consumption a capital offense, something that King Bodawpaya had promulgated as early as 1826 and that royal sanctions in Upper Burma had continued to do throughout the nineteenth century.[101] The conflicting policies of the colonial government (which fostered consumption through tax farming and drug-den licensing) and traditional Burmese authorities (who prescribed use reduction in accordance with Buddhist strictures) produced a stalemate. There was no effective control over either consumption or production.

With post–World War II Burmese independence, traditional Buddhist views replaced previous British sentiments about narcotics in the new government. Severe penalties were imposed for drug abuse. From 1974 until SLORC came to power in 1988, the Burmese government increased penalties for production, possession, and abuse on at least three occasions. This trend coincided with the Burmese state's tendency to become more and more authoritarian. Although penalties (e.g., executions) were not as severe as in Malaysia, by Western standards they were nevertheless draconian.

The present government, SLORC, contends that it wants to eliminate narcotics problems. Opinions vary as to SLORC's political will.

Skeptics note that the government terminated its poppy-eradication program in 1989; optimists answer that the government renewed its efforts in 1990. The detractors counter that resumed programs were at a lower level than before and seemed a response not to opium production but to unfavorable international press. All is complicated by a general world dissatisfaction with Burma's authoritarian government and its civil rights record. Most countries have terminated their aid programs, thereby contributing to the catastrophic economic conditions that SLORC contends are the principal reason it cannot carry out an effective antinarcotics program. Whatever the cause, the circle seems continually to close on one conclusion—ineffective drug control.

Part of the reason for this ineffectiveness is that the government is not in control of the northeastern part of the country, where most of the opium is grown. Burmese laws, however weakly applied, have scant impact in the area. Government authorities make nominal efforts in areas under their control to enforce their laws, relying on seizures and apprehension of users in the act of consuming (there is no urine or blood testing or other types of detection for any narcotic).[102] In the insurgent areas, drug-control policy is subordinate to national security interests. Anything that would alienate growers is avoided; traffickers/insurgents are pursued not because they are drug traffickers but because they are insurgents.

With a reclusive and distasteful government to work with, many international drug-control efforts once operating in Myanmar/Burma have now been abandoned. Extant efforts are mostly associated with subregional planning (involving Laos, Thailand, and China) sponsored by the United Nations, principally through its chief antinarcotics organ, UNDCP. Myanmar/Burma has cooperated in this planning but will not submit to the jurisdiction of the World Court or permit extradition of its citizens. This exclusion notwithstanding, the general agreements to which Myanmar/Burma has subscribed seem reasonable enough: (1) reduce trafficking in narcotic drugs and chemicals used in refining heroin; (2) eliminate opium poppy cultivation in border areas through economic and social development programs linked to phased eradication; and (3) reduce the demand for and local consumption of narcotic drugs in the border areas.

Bilateral agreements between Myanmar/Burma and Thailand call for exchanging information on heroin production and trafficking along their common boundary and for cooperation in border development programs in Myanmar/Burma (e.g., integrated rural development in Tachilek, Mongphyak [Mong Hpayak], and Mong Yawng townships of Kengtung).[103] Similar bilateral agreements between Myanmar/Burma and China call for like development efforts in East Kengtung as well as in Kunlong, Kone Giang, and Guse in

Kokang. The Thai village development model is to be used. As Renard sees it, "key villages were to be identified, infrastructure such as health services, water supply, electrification, education, and feeder roads, were to be provided. Subsistence and cash crops as well as livestock development were to be promoted."[104] It is unclear where any of these development efforts have proceeded. Detractors continue to note that Myanmar/Burma's apparent motivation for entering into the agreements, and perhaps in actually making some effort to carry them out, had less to do with controlling drugs than with trying to calm insurgents in territory that SLORC is trying to control.

Myanmar/Burma remains a closed country. Anecdotal evidence speaks to increased production and consumption of opium and heroin there. If lower production and consumption rates represent a measure of drug-control success, the country's laws and drug-control policies can only be judged a failure. Insofar as anything is being done, perhaps one might attribute it to pressure from China, Myanmar/Burma's only remaining ally in the world of nations and a country that is responding vigorously to increased trafficking and consumption in border areas.[105] China is clearly unhappy about narcotics in Myanmar/Burma.

Pakistan

As the British did after them, the Moguls (1600–1750) controlled opium production for tax revenues, the principal difference between the Moguls and the British being that the latter greatly expanded opium acreage in order to generate increased revenue.[106] Under the Moguls, cannabis was not as widely used as opium and was marketed mostly locally, but the empire also licensed and taxed it. Under the British, both opium and cannabis flourished. Licensing and taxing produced black markets. All three—licensing, taxing, and black markets—exacerbated drug abuse.

When the Moguls fell at the hands of the British in the mid-eighteenth century, the British East India Company created an opium monopoly and extended incentives to greatly expand both production and consumption. In this way, the alarming consumption problems developing both at home and in the colonies notwithstanding, opium revenues and their management became part of British fiscal policy. The British organized and expanded the opium trade with abandon, their only major resistance coming from the Chinese. For this intransigence, the British launched the humiliating Opium War of 1839–1842, which effectively cowed the Chinese, thereby leaving the field wide open for British expansion in opium and other tradables. Whenever required, the British used military means to enforce their drug-distribution monopoly.

As the nineteenth century wore on, the British finally succumbed to anti-opium crusades at home and in the United States. Britain thereafter undertook efforts to undo the drug pushing that had consumed much of its colonial experience in Asia. Accordingly, with the Moguls gone, the British repentant, and new international moods developing prior to and following the post–World War II independence movements in British India and elsewhere, the time was right for domestic and international drug-control efforts to be launched.

The new antidrug mood became quickly focused on Pakistan. In 1947 Pakistan became independent and began to license opium production just as had the British. Revenue was a motivator; the British had taught their subjects well. Production and consumption expanded. Now, however, the British joined in the international pressure to turn Pakistan around. Under this pressure, Pakistan joined several drug-control conventions, among them the 1961 Single Convention on Narcotic Drugs (1964), but the country did not take immediate measures to implement its obligations. Nevertheless, in 1974 Pakistan began a modicum of compliance by establishing the Pakistan Narcotics Control Board (PNCP). In the meantime, however, opium poppy cultivation had exploded in the Northwest Frontier Province and in Baluchistan.

The civil war that soon unfolded in neighboring Afghanistan complicated Pakistan's drug-control efforts. As Soviet forces moved into Afghanistan, almost all the heroin laboratories in the region moved to Pakistan. Although poppy-eradication programs were underway in Pakistan, Afghan opium production increased in direct proportion and was shipped to the new laboratories in Pakistan for processing. Trafficking continued with abandon, ultimately producing a Pakistani heroin epidemic in the 1980s that continues to the present. By 1991 opium production had begun to increase again in Pakistan, making the country almost self-sufficient for its greatly expanded laboratory facilities.

From the late 1970s to the present, the Pakistani government has sought assistance from international and bilateral agencies to implement development projects in major opium-growing areas. By its own, probably correct, estimation, the country cannot adhere to international conventions to reduce production without offering alternative income sources for growers. The Buner Pilot Project for crop substitution was thus begun under auspices of the Pakistani federal government and financed by United Nations Fund for Drug Abuse Control (UNFDAC)/USAID and has been followed by numerous other development projects. Unfortunately, insofar as these projects have been successful in reducing regional opium cultivation,[107] any reduction has been fully compensated for by opium imports from Afghanistan. Thus, there is not now, nor has there ever been, a shortage of opium for the Pakistani heroin laboratories.

Pakistani drug-control institutions have been slow to adapt to the alarming increase in consumption and the changes in production and processing. The Pakistan Narcotics Control Board has been shifted from ministry to ministry (e.g., from the Ministry of Planning to the Ministry of the Interior in 1975) but has gradually been able to develop specialized arms for planning and development, enforcement, and intelligence. Although it has placed agents in all the major trafficking centers (e.g., Quetta in Baluchistan, Karachi in Sind, Lahore in Punjab, Peshawar in the NWFP, and Gilgit in the Northern Areas),[108] the PNCP has always been a "board," not an operational force. Moreover, it has found its work undercut by institutional rivalry, corruption, and lack of governmental political will.

With a change in government in 1988 leading to Benazir Bhutto's becoming prime minister, a rival Division for Narcotics Control (NCD) was established in 1989 within the Ministry of Interior to coordinate all law-enforcement antidrug activities. When Nawaz Sharif became prime minister, a full Ministry for Narcotics Control was established. These later agencies have been increasingly concerned about widespread heroin consumption in Pakistan and have at least given nominal support to supply-reduction efforts that international agencies have so vigorously pursued. In October 1993 the Pakistani electorate returned Benazir Bhutto's political party to power, and she was reinstated as prime minister. She has continued to reaffirm the need to focus attention on narcotics problems.

International agencies and NGOs are now permanently stationed in Pakistan. UNDCP has a field adviser, USAID supervises and coordinates all U.S.-funded activities, the DEA has seventeen officers in strategic locations, and the Commission of the European Communities (CEC) has drug liaison officers stationed in several embassies. Most of these represent a law-enforcement presence from their respective countries.[109] Their main purpose is to reduce supplies and trafficking and to assist where they can in reducing domestic consumption.

As far as most Pakistanis appear to be concerned, the principal drug issue is domestic heroin consumption. The government has therefore garnered support for its demand-reduction initiatives. For example, it has prohibited consumption as well as poppy cultivation (e.g., Prohibition Order of 1979, which brought existing law into conformity with Islamic injunctions set out in the Quran and Sunnah).

The punishment provisions of the Prohibition Order called for a minimum of two years and a maximum of life imprisonment for (1) trafficking, financing and possessing more than 10 grams of heroin or cocaine or more than 1 kilogram of raw opium or coca leaf, and (2) importing, exporting, or transshipping any illegal manufactured drugs, including opium derivatives.[110] To this order have been added extradition and forfeiture-of-asset laws. But an inefficient judicial system has complicated application of the laws even when the police make appropriate arrests.

How effective have these measures been? Buddenberg shows that they have failed to make Pakistan poppy free, although cultivation was reduced for a time. Regardless, Afghan poppies have taken up the slack, and the authorities have been unable to do anything about it. More telling, the drug-control policies have failed to reduce the number of heroin abusers, and the policies do not have a highly credible record with respect to seizures, arrests, and convictions of traffickers, nor have they reduced the impact of corruption on law-enforcement efforts. It is not surprising, therefore, that for these and related reasons one of the world's twelve most important drug kingpins is a Pakistani.[111] He appears to operate with impunity. Buddenberg sums up the state of affairs:

Taking the criteria into account, the drug control policy has failed so far in Pakistan. Though from a high opium production in 1979/80, the production figures dropped, Pakistan was never a poppy-free area. Indications point to a resumed increase of production in all traditional opium growing areas for the harvesting season 1992, but already for 1991, an increase was debated. Farmgate prices range between 2,000 and 2,800 Rs [rupees], but once harvesting starts are estimated to fall to 1,600 Rs per kg. Farmers are still gaining with these prices, and estimates for an overall production in Pakistan as collected through independent sources (NGOs, journalists, farmers, UN officials, government officials) go beyond 300 metric tons of opium, taking a conservative estimate average. Thus, the country is gaining self-sufficiency for its domestic consumption. Despite the crop substitution projects in Buner, Dir, Bajaur, Malakand, Kala Dhaka, Gadoon Amazai, and the inputs of millions of dollars, the output has either increased since the mid-80s, or has reached a plateau of approximately 200 metric tons annual production, or is increasing even beyond this plateau level. Individual crop substitution projects have certainly had successful components implemented. However, even in these cases, factors responsible for success have not been clearly isolated.

Whether the prevalence of drug users has increased or decreased is difficult to ascertain. Since a somewhat haphazard survey in 1988, which resulted in a one million heroin abuser count, no new survey has been conducted. A new survey was planned for 1992 with the support of INM, but is now planned for 1993. Street prices for heroin reached an all-time low in early 1992, availability was an established fact for all major cities, small towns and, above all, the rural areas and its villages.

No significant arrests have been made, nor can an increase in arrests be shown, though seizures reached a high, particularly with the activities of the FC (Baluchistan) and the record seizures of 2,000 and more kgs of heroin apart from other drugs (cannabis).[112]

According to the U.S. State Department, the 1992 opium poppy plantings were about 40 percent greater than in 1989, the 1993 plantings about 7 percent.[113] Unless the 1993 crop year heralds something other than an ephemeral decline, these are not good statistics for drug-control efforts. Regardless, in Pakistan's case the critical variable is not opium plantings (because opium is readily imported from Afghanistan) but heroin production, of which there appears to be a great deal.

Kentucky, U.S.

As in the other countries and regions studied, supply-reduction is the principal control initiative in Kentucky, U.S.[114] In this case it consists of manual eradication of individual marijuana plants. Agencies involved represent U.S. federal, state, and local law-enforcement systems, including the National Guard, a citizen-soldier organization attached to the United States's overall military and emergency defense systems.

Kentucky growers have a fast learning curve in dealing with eradication teams. Knowing that the teams count their success in numbers of plants destroyed, the growers sow lesser-grade plants in highly accessible areas where they will be easily found, thereby making eradication a simple matter. Satisfied with their "success," law-enforcement agents may then be less determined to find the relatively remote and more dangerous areas where the "real" marijuana growing occurs. The growers, having moved their crops further into remote areas (or having sprinkled them throughout corn crops or located them clandestinely indoors), pay little attention to their "losses." The growers' "protected" sinsemilla plants tend to have the highest THC content, which has been increasing in recent years. The THC content of 1991 sinsemilla, for example, was 37 percent greater than in 1986.[115] From fewer plants the growers therefore reap a higher reward. Needing to plant less marijuana for the same or better economic return would also appear to reduce risk by lowering detection probabilities.

Nationwide, from 1988 through 1991 a relatively stable number of cultivated marijuana plants were eradicated in the United States—about five million per year, except for 1990, when over seven million were eradicated.[116] In 1991 Kentucky ranked first among states for cultivated plants eradicated—a total of 2,254,919, or 48.6 percent of all plants eradicated in the United States.[117] Of these, 728,339 were sinsemilla plants, the most coveted, expensive, and potent cultivated variety around.[118] However, the eradication efforts appear not to have materially affected the price of marijuana in the United States at a time when the numbers of marijuana users have declined. Perhaps eradication has been just sufficient to keep the marijuana market from crashing as fewer people consume the product. Law-enforcement officials claim to destroy annually about half of the marijuana crop,[119] but the number of users has also been cut by about half. Thus, it would appear that declining use must be attributed to factors other than eradication.

Asset seizure is another vehicle used to suppress supplies by putting suppliers out of business, thereby keeping farmgate prices low and discouraging production. There has been a large increase in the number of traffickers' weapons seized—a 14 percent increase from 1988 to 1989, a 38 percent increase from 1989 to 1990, and a 31 percent increase from 1990 to 1991. Moreover, there have been substantial increases in other assets seized under the asset-forfeiture provisions of the federal law, up 32 percent from 1989 to 1990 and 37 percent from 1990 to 1991, yielding a return in 1991 of $53 million against a crop-suppression program budget of only $13.7 million. This suppression program brought in almost $4 in assets seized for every $1 invested by the DEA.[120] Does this herald success? Only if it materially affects supplies. It is unclear that such a linkage exists in Kentucky or anywhere else in the United States.

One reason asset forfeitures may not be consequential in dealing with marijuana production and trafficking, as opposed to heroin or cocaine trafficking, is that each grower, on the average, has only 250 plants. Moreover, marijuana growers tend to be their own traffickers. Putting one operator/trafficker out of business does not necessarily impact the market much or assure that other growers will fail to step in to take over. That appears to be the case, because marijuana supplies are holding steady with demand. On balance, therefore, successful forfeitures in terms of cost-benefit analysis (value of assets seized against costs of seizure) do not appear to have translated into a supply-suppression program sufficiently expansive to have independently affected the U.S. marijuana market.

Eradication is holding steady, as are prices, whereas numbers of users have been declining. Relatively speaking, this suggests that the absolute amount of marijuana may be subject to successful law-enforcement efforts. However, the best marijuana, with the highest THC content, is what the growers work most assiduously to protect. Thus, it is unclear whether the THC index (total amount of THC available on the market) has declined much, if at all, in the United States, particularly in Kentucky.

How Effective Have Drug-Control Efforts Been?

Effectiveness implies judgment, which in turn requires evidence. Both are informed by one's frame of reference. All three—frame of reference, evidence, and judgment—are not only subject to but also clearly governed by diverse points of view. Here a frame of reference is laid out showing the philosophical foundation of principal drug-control efforts. Evidence is then examined in its light. Perhaps that will help shed understanding on judgments that are not subject to precise measurement, an endemic problem in illicit-drug research.

Although the policy mix in the United States has now begun to change, drug-control efforts worldwide continue to assume a supply-driven consumption formula. That is, it is thought that consumption would decline if production could be curtailed. Accordingly, policies to reduce consumption have largely been indistinguishable from policies to reduce supplies. We may be on the verge of seeing this policy mix altered, but old ways change slowly.

Regarding drug-control policies, two lines of analysis and judgment are apparent, one for principal consuming countries and another for principal producing countries. For principal consuming countries, the analytic frame of reference can be characterized as follows: A suppression of supplies (which might derive from crop reduction at home or abroad, interdiction at home or abroad, or trafficker-network disruption) will create product scarcities, which, demand being constant or increasing, will drive up prices, which in turn will lower consumption as people consider the economic implications of their decisions. Moreover, greater difficulties in obtaining the products will deter all but the most dedicated people. The model is outlined in Figure 4.1. It was never thought that this model would necessarily work for addicts or heavy abusers. Clearly, however, observers thought it would deter first-time and recreational users and others who may be cost-conscious in their purchase decisions.

As for drug-control efforts in principal producing countries, the supply-driven hypothesis remains in vogue, mostly because principal consuming countries or multilateral agencies initiate, oversee, and finance most drug-control efforts in the principal producing areas.

Figure 4.1   Model of First-Round Policy Logic for Reducing Consumption in Principal
Consuming Countries

Thus, even though perceived complications with the straight-line formula noted in Figure 4.1 have dictated that other consumption-reduction efforts be tried, (as in Figure 4.2), principal consuming nations are still keen to reduce supplies abroad, particularly the amount of agricultural product grown. If the raw materials—coca leaves, opium poppies, and cannabis plants—and the initial refined products that derive therefrom can be materially reduced, the sequence of events shown in Figures 4.1 and 4.2 is thought to result. Simply put, reducing supplies will reduce consumption, a trend to be further aided by treatment, prevention, and user-penalty programs. But the principal trick is first to reduce supplies. From this assessment, policy initiatives have been concentrated in principal producing countries to suppress crops, as in Figure 4.3.

The intersecting lines of policy initiative in Figure 4.3 include the following: law enforcement, eradication, interdiction, trafficker disruption, crop substitution, foreign aid, and alternative development of a labor-absorbing kind. Each has its own logic. Eradication and product interdiction reduce the volume of drug crops and refined supplies. Interdiction also contributes to trafficker disruption, itself made more probable by law-enforcement agents' relentless pursuit of the traffickers themselves. This disruption ultimately depresses

Figure 4.2   Model of Second-Round Policy Logic for Reducing Consumption in
Principal Consuming Countries

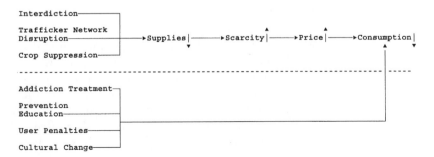

Figure 4.3   Model for Suppressing Drug-Crop Production in Principal Producing Countries

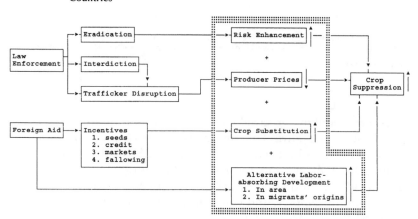

farmgate prices, as fewer traffickers with less money show up to make purchases, reducing growers' incentives to plant drug crops. Crop-substitution programs enable growers to switch to legal crops; a depressed market for drug crops reduces the differential between the value of those crops and regular crops and therefore improves the financial incentives to engage in legal cropping.

Both the agricultural technology for substitute crops and improved markets to facilitate their sale are made possible through foreign-aid incentives. Hence, a strong case for foreign aid is present in the model. In cases where farmgate prices cannot be driven down sufficiently through trafficker disruption and interdiction to make crop substitution economically attractive, alternative labor-absorbing development schemes are introduced either in the cropping areas or, in order to reduce migration to those regions, in principal migration-source areas to give people incentives to stay put rather than move to a drug-producing area. The logic is outlined in Figure 4.3. It must be noted that in this model no exogenous forces (e.g., guerrilla forces such as Sendero Luminoso) are accounted for, which illustrates one of the model's weaknesses.

The consumption-control model driven by a supply-reduction strategy can work only if most of its provisions hold in the real world. In the cases under study, do they? Consider the implications of Figure 4.1. Assuming consumption to be price-responsive (which does not hold in every circumstance), prices can be driven up only if true scarcities relative to demand are created. Supplies must be driven down to the point where such scarcities actually exist. This can happen only if interdiction, trafficker disruption, and crop suppression—

the three principal supply-control strategies—are sufficient to overcome strident grower and trafficker counterstrategies.

In fact, in most instances grower and trafficker counterstrategies have been more than sufficient to maintain ample supplies on the market. Thus, the stated goal of interdiction—to create scarcities in order to drive up prices—has failed in principal consuming countries, even though large tonnages of drugs are confiscated. One trafficker network dissolved appears to be the genesis of two new created. In the United States, for example, after strident campaigns to interdict and disrupt, drugs are as plentiful as ever and more affordable. All the law-enforcement instruments have been insufficient in this cause, including asset forfeitures that have brought tens of millions of dollars to law-enforcement agencies' operating budgets.

Given the failure of supply-control strategies at the borders of principal consuming countries, this model dictates only one remaining policy initiative—crop suppression. Thus, again and again, principal consumer countries' attention has moved to the third leg of the formula, suppressing crops abroad. Has that worked? In all the countries studied, pressure on growers simply stimulated them to move elsewhere as long as the provisions for producer-price suppression (as in Figure 4.3) were not met. Even when those conditions were met, Bolivian and Thai growers hedged their bets by staking out land in remote areas and planting drug crops—after just having received voluntary-crop-eradication payments for not planting those same crops elsewhere. The practice has become so widespread that both popular and academic wisdom concludes that voluntary eradication-for-payment programs are entirely counterproductive.

In Bolivia, Peru, Pakistan, Myanmar/Burma, and Laos, governments have not had the political will to move against growers without first having in hand an income-replacement program. Otherwise, the political fallout has been judged to be intolerable even for repressive regimes. But international funding agencies have been reluctant to provide alternative income sources (e.g., labor-absorbing alternative development programs) without first having indications that the governments are serious about supply suppression. But governments have frequently been more concerned about insurgency suppression than illegal-drug suppression (e.g., Colombia, Peru, Myanmar/Burma, Laos, Mexico).

In the cases under study, interdiction in the drugs' countries of origin has never been sufficient to affect prices much because traffickers have nearly always found ways to replace the losses. Although network disruption is effective for a time (e.g., the Turkish connection, the French Connection, the Medellín syndicate), traffickers either bounce back or find a hundred replacements vying for their territory. Crop suppression, as already noted, has not been much help in and of itself. More alarming, Peter Reuter has shown that even if crop suppression were sufficient to halve the amount of drugs grown, a dramatic impact on prices in net consuming countries would not necessarily result.[121] This conclusion basically invalidates the logic of the policy from the beginning.

In any event, crop suppression requires that a national government have not only a strong political will but also a strong sense of effective coordination and strong financial backing. Most governments have lacked one or more of these items; accordingly, aggregate crop figures have not been much affected. As Figure 4.3 shows, suppression of illegal crops requires that growers face heavy risks and that producer prices be depressed to the point where crop substitution or alternative development schemes become financially attractive. In fact, most of the time governments have not been able to depress prices for long periods of time. Their efforts to raise risks have been compromised through corruption of law-enforcement and judicial officers. Moreover, alternative income possibilities have rarely risen sufficiently to narrow the gap between drug-crop and regular-crop income and thereby to deter aggregate production. In some countries (e.g., Bolivia, Thailand) alternative development and crop-substitution programs have been marginally effective in discrete areas, but growers have sprung up elsewhere in the classic balloon effect to ply their trade in international and domestic markets. Mexico suppressed marijuana production; it sprang up in Colombia. Turkey suppressed opium production; Mexico picked up the slack. Mexico then suppressed the poppy, whereupon production migrated to Colombia and increased in Myanmar/Burma. Thailand reduced domestic opium and marijuana production, only to see producers move across the border to Myanmar/Burma and Laos, then return to Thailand to use its advanced transportation and communication infrastructure to reach world markets. The drugs still move. On the whole, the supply-suppression → consumption-reduction model has fallen on hard times. It has too many points that can unravel in practical applications. Usually, where it can unravel, it has unraveled.

Drug-control efforts to affect consumption directly include treatment for addiction, prevention education, enhancement of *user* penalties, and engineered cultural change (Figure 4.2). Treatment is thought to reduce the "contagion" effect of users who, by example and by recruiting clientele in order to finance their own drug habits, bring more people into the consuming market. Prevention education is thought to dissuade youngsters from experimenting with drugs. Enhancement of user penalties is thought to deter casual or first-time users who would have much to lose from an indiscretionary act. Cultural change, insofar as it can be engineered, is thought to contribute to the development of a new ethos that would eschew people's need for "crutches" such as psychoactive drugs.

None of these direct consumption-reduction initiatives has been applied systematically in principal producer countries where consumption problems have arisen (e.g., Pakistan). Their effectiveness is attested to by anecdotal evidence in some other areas. In principal consuming countries the evidence is contradictory, although in the United States it appears that drug consumption has declined markedly in the 1990s. Unverified claims are made as to the source of this decline.

Aside from whether direct drug-consumption strategies work, supply-reduction strategies to reduce consumption have not worked as intended and probably cannot be made to work. The remaining questions, therefore, aside from the implications of continuing a dysfunctional policy, focus on the unintended social, political, and economic effects or consequences of the policies and what, if anything, can be done to ameliorate the negative ones. Moreover, we want to examine policies beyond supply suppression that may actually hold some promise. I turn to these subjects in Chapters 5 and 6.

Notes

1. Numerous UN agencies have had drug-abuse and illicit-trafficking agenda, the principal early ones being the Commission on Narcotic Drugs (CND), established in 1946 as one of the six functional commissions of the Economic and Social Council (ECOSOC). The CND, the United Nations' central policymaking body, has been charged with in-depth review of drug-abuse controls for which the UN assumes some purview. Through 1990, three Vienna-based units in the UN Secretariat also had drug-related mandates: the Division of Narcotic Drugs (DND), the United Nations Fund for Drug Abuse Control (UNFDAC), and the International Narcotics Control Board (INCB). DND carried out multiple supporting roles for member governments and specialized agencies dealing with treaty implementation, scientific research and technical information, supply and demand reduction, and information coordination. UNFDAC aided governments in practical ways in combating the production, trafficking, and use of illicit drugs (including carrying out activities in rural development). INCB supplemented statistical estimates and controls on illicit drugs as it worked to ensure that member governments were in compliance with treaty provisions (working to ensure the availability of drugs for medical and scientific purposes and providing statistical information to limit the cultivation, production, and manufacture of drugs beyond those needs). These agencies and others are described in United Nations, *The United Nations and Drug Abuse Control* (New York: UN, 1987). In late 1990 and continuing into June 1991 (following a mandate from the UN General Assembly), the above three organizations began the process of merging into a new superagency, the United Nations

Drug Control Program (UNDCP), also headquartered in Vienna. Since 1991 the UNDCP has become the UN's principal drug-control agency.

2. For example, following a General Assembly resolution (44/142) on 15 December 1989 regarding international action to combat drug abuse and illicit trafficking, the Secretary-General convened an intergovernmental expert group to study the economic and social consequences of the illicit traffic in drugs. The report was made available to member states on 18 December 1990 (A/C.3/45/8).

3. The draft memorandum is on letterhead of the Deputy Secretary of Defense, is prepared for secretaries of the military departments and fourteen other entities including the chairman of the Joint Chiefs of Staff, and is referenced as "Department of Defense Guidance for Implementation of National Drug Control Policy," 28 October 1993.

4. James W. Spain ("The United States, Turkey and the Poppy," *Middle East Journal* 29:3 [1975], 395–409) chronicles Turkey's early agreements with the United States.

5. The 1986 implementation of the agreements were the subject of a congressional hearing (U.S. Congress, House Committee on Foreign Affairs, Hearing, "The Role and Activities of the National Drug Enforcement Policy Board," Ninety-ninth Congress, Second Session [Washington, D.C.: U.S. Government Printing Office, 1986]), as was the case in 1987 (U.S. Congress, House Committee on Foreign Affairs, Hearing, "Review of Latin American Narcotics Control Issues," One Hundredth Congress, first session [Washington, D.C.: U.S. Government Printing Office, 1987]) and 1988 (U.S. Congress, House Committee on Foreign Affairs, Hearing, "Narcotics Review in South America," One Hundredth Congress, 2nd session [Washington, D.C.: U.S. Government Printing Office, 1988]). Mary Ellen Welch discusses the nature of the agreements in Colombia and Bolivia from the vantage of an "extraterritorial war" ("The Extraterritorial War on Cocaine: Perspectives from Bolivia and Colombia," *Suffolk Transnational Law Journal* 12 [1988], 39–81). Cynthia McClintock ("The War on Drugs: The Peruvian Case," *Journal of Inter-American Studies and World Affairs* 30:2–3 [Summer/Fall 1988], 127–142) analyzes the antidrug efforts undertaken by the United States and Peruvian governments under bilateral agreements; Richard B. Craig ("Illicit Drug Traffic and U.S.–Latin American Relations," *Washington Quarterly* 8 [Winter 1985], 105–134) examines the international relations implications of the agreements.

6. Roberta Louise Rubin, "International Agreements: Two Treaties Between the U.S. and Italy," *Harvard International Law Journal*, 26, 1985.

7. For its impact on Bolivia, see James Painter, *Bolivia and Coca: A Study in Dependency* (Boulder, Colo.: Lynne Rienner Publishers, 1994), 91.

8. See LaMond Tullis, *Handbook of Research on the Illicit Drug Traffic: Socioeconomic and Political Consequences* (Westport, Conn.: Greenwood Press, 1991), Chapter 5.

9. The principal source on Colombia is Francisco Thoumi, *Political Economy and Illegal Drugs in Colombia* (Boulder, Colo.: Lynne Rienner Publishers, 1994). For this quotation, see p. 335.

10. Ibid., 209. Thoumi's sources are Luis J. Orjuela, "Narcotráfico y Política en la Década de los Ochenta: Entre la Represión y el Diálogo," in Carlos G. Arrieta, et al., eds., *Narcotráfico en Colombia: Dimensiones Políticas, Económicas, Jurídicas e Internacionales* (Bogotá: Tercer Mundo Editores—Ediciones Uniandes, 1990), 216–219; and Juan G. Tokatlian, "La Política Exterior

de Colombia Hacia Estados Unidos, 1978–1990: El Asunto de las Drogas y su Lugar en las Relaciones entre Bogotá y Washington," in Carlos G. Arrieta, et al., eds., *Narcotráfico en Colombia*.

11. Thoumi, *Political Economy and Illegal Drugs*, 210.

12. Ibid., 349.

13. Ibid., 212–214. Generally, Thoumi's sources are Orjuela, "Narcotráfico y Política," 234; Tokatlian, "La Política Exterior," 318, 321; and Guy Gugliotta and Jeff Leen, *Kings of Cocaine: An Astonishing True Story of Murder, Money and International Corruption* (New York: Simon and Schuster, 1989), 286–287.

14. Thoumi, *Political Economy and Illegal Drugs*, 215.

15. Ibid., 218.

16. Ibid., 369.

17. Ibid., 373.

18. United States, Department of State, Bureau of International Narcotics Matters, *International Narcotics Control Strategy Report* (Washington, D.C.: The Bureau 1991, 1993), 101 (1991), 110 (1993). Hereinafter cited as *INCSR*.

19. Principal source on Peru is Elena Alvarez, "Illegal Export-Led Growth in the Andes: A Preliminary Economic and Socio-political Assessment for Peru," a study for UNRISD and UNU (draft of 25 January 1993).

20. See Elena Alvarez, who develops these categories, ibid., 60–69.

21. Asociación de Estudios Peruanos sobre la Paz (ADEP), *Cocaína: Problemas y Soluciones Andinos* translated by LaMond Tullis (Lima: ADEP, 1990), 273.

22. Alvarez, "Illegal Export-Led Growth," 68.

23. Ibid., 69.

24. A flurry of concern was raised in 1988–1989. See Mark Day, "Peru: Battle Intensifies over Renewed Drug Eradication Plan," *Latinamerica Press*, 7 September 1989, 1; Michael Isikoff, "Peruvian Coca Fields Sprayed in Test of Plan," *Washington Post*, 22 March 1989, A16; and McClintock, "The War on Drugs."

25. Alvarez, "Illegal Export-Led Growth," 69, note 33.

26. For details on the features of these projects, Alvarez cites D. Strug, "The Foreign Policy of Cocaine: Comments on a Plan to Eradicate the Coca Leaf in Peru," in Deborah Pacini and Christine Franquemont, eds., *Coca and Cocaine: Effects on People and Policy in Latin America* (Cambridge, Mass.: Cultural Survival, 1985), 73–88; Edmundo Morales, "Coca Culture: The White Cities of Peru," *Thesis* 1:1 (Fall 1986), 4–11 (CUNY, The Graduate School Magazine); and DESCO, "Coca: La Realidad que se Ignora," *Quehacer* 52 (May–June 1988), 44–50.

27. CORAH (Project for Reduction of the Coca Crop in the Upper Huallaga) is based in the Ministry of Agriculture; PEAH (Special Project in the Upper Huallaga) is based in the Office of the Prime Minister of Peru; and UMOPAR (Mobil Unit for Rural Patrolling) is affiliated with the Civil Guard.

28. Alvarez cites DESCO, "Coca," 46–47.

29. Alvarez's sources on the alliances included *Informe Final de la Evaluación del Proyecto AID No 527–0244, Desarrollo del Area del Alto Huallaga* (Lima: ECONSULT, 1986) and E. Bedoya, "Las Causas de la Deforestación en la Amazonia Peruana: Un Problema Estructural," Clark University Institute for Development Anthropology: Cooperative Agreement on Human Settlements and Natural Resource Systems Analysis, 1990.

30. Alvarez, "Illegal Export-led Growth," 72.

31. Ibid., 70. Alvarez reports that the U.S. Congress House Operations Committee was opposed to this aspect of former President George Bush's Andean Initiative because, from its view, the initiative jeopardized human-rights policy in drug-trafficking countries and could have triggered more political instability there. See U.S. Congress, Senate Committee on Government Operations, *United States Anti-Narcotics Activities in the Andean Region* (Washington, D.C.: U.S. Government Printing Office, 1990). See also *Los Tiempos* (Cochabamba, Bolivia), 19, 21, and 22 March 1991.

32. Alvarez, "Export-led Growth," 72–76.

33. Ibid., 67.

34. Ibid., 68.

35. *INCSR 1993*, 126.

36. *INCSR 1994*, 122.

37. The principal source on Bolivia is James Painter, *Bolivia and Coca.*

38. Ibid., 77–78.

39. Ibid., 86.

40. Ibid. Painter catalogs a series of decrees and legislative initiatives that would clearly put the legal framework above reproach.

41. Ibid., 80–85.

42. Ibid., 88.

43. Ibid., 88–89.

44. *INCSR 1994*, 94.

45. Painter's endnote number 40 (*Bolivia and Coca*) states that 20,000 people temporarily fled the area in the wake of the operation, that the price of coca temporarily dropped, that no traffickers were arrested, and that coca-paste production was temporarily moved to the Upper Cochabamba Valley.

46. Painter's endnote number 41 (*Bolivia and Coca*) states that no active laboratories were found, few arrests were made, and little cocaine was seized. Coca prices, dropping below production costs, soon rose again after the departure of the troops in November, although prices never reached their pre-operation levels. The use of U.S. troops provoked widespread protests against the Paz Estenssoro government. One of the more pertinent observations from José Antonio Quiroga (*Coca/Cocaína: Una Visión Boliviana* [La Paz: AIPE/PROCOM-CEDLA-CID, 1990], 64) was that the U.S. Congress only approved the use of troops in antidrug operations in the United States in 1988.

47. For discussions of domestic consequences of the Bush administration's war on drugs, see M. J. Blachman and K. E. Sharpe, "The War on Drugs: American Democracy Under Assault," *World Policy Journal* 7:1 (Winter 1989–1990), 135–163. The authors take the position that the strategy erodes basic liberties, contributes to official abuses of power, and undermines the U.S. tradition of keeping the military out of civilian and police affairs.

48. For a full analysis of the Andean Strategy, Painter turns our attention to the Washington Office on Latin America (WOLA), *Clear and Present Dangers: The U.S. Military and the War on Drugs in the Andes* (Washington, D.C.: WOLA, 1991).

49. Painter, *Bolivia and Coca*, 91.

50. Ibid., 94–97.

51. Ibid., 97.

52. Ibid., 99.

53. Ibid., 101–102.

54. Ibid., 103.

55. Ibid., Chapter 6, 105–138.

56. *INCSR 1993*, 98.

57. Principal source on Mexico is María Celia Toro, "Mexican Drug Control Policy: Origin, Purpose, Consequences," a study for UNRISD and UNU (draft of 9 June 1993). In press, Lynne Rienner Publishers, Boulder, Colo.

58. Ibid., 24.

59. See Richard B. Craig, "Operation Condor: Mexico's Anti-drug Campaign Enters a New Era," *Journal of Inter-American Studies and World Affairs* 22:3 (August 1980), 345–363; and Francisco Ortíz Pinchetti, Miguel Cabildo, Federico Campbell, and Ignacio Rodríguez, *La Operación Cóndor* (Mexico City: Proceso, 1981).

60. Ibid. 29. See also Richard B. Craig, "La Campaña Permanente: Mexico's Anti-drug Campaign," *Journal of Inter-American Studies and World Affairs* 20:2 (1978), 107–131.

61. Peter A. Lupsha ("Drug Trafficking: Mexico and Colombia in Comparative Perspective," *Journal of International Affairs* 35:1 [1981], 95–115) discusses the drug organizations that so commanded the government's attention in the area.

62. Toro, "Mexican Drug Control Policy," 47.

63. Ibid., 31.

64. Ibid., 34.

65. Ibid., 37.

66. Detailed descriptions appeared in John J. Fialka, "Death of US Agent in Mexico Drug Case Uncovers Grid of Graft," *Wall Street Journal*, 19 November 1986, 1; John J. Fialka, "How the Mexican Trail in Drug Agent's Death Yields Cache of 'Crack,'" *Wall Street Journal*, 20 November 1986, 1; and Larry Rohter, "Mexico Is Accusing a Slain U.S. Agent," *New York Times*, 16 January 1990, A7.

67. Toro, "Mexican Drug Control Policy," 39, with detailed data provided in Table 1.

68. Toro's source is Sergio García Ramírez, *El Narcotráfico: Un Punto de Vista Mexicano* (México: Miguel Angel Porrúa, 1989), 141.

69. *INCSR 1991*, 157–159.

70. Representative of the numerous observations are the following: Craig, "Operation Condor;" Fialka, "Death of US Agent in Mexico;" Michael Isikoff, "Informer Ties Top Mexican to Drug Deals; Allegations Revealed in DEA Affidavit," *Washington Post*, 4 June 1988, A3; Luis Méndez Asensio, *Caro Quintero al Trasluz* (Mexico City: Plaza and Janes, 1985); and U.S. Congress, House Committee on Foreign Affairs, Hearing, "Narcotics Review in South America," One Hundredth Congress, second session (Washington, D.C.: U.S. Government Printing Office, 1988).

71. Toro, "Mexican Drug Control Policy," 58.

72. Ibid.

73. The principal source on Thailand is Anchalee Singhanetra-Renard, "Socioeconomic and Political Impact of Production, Trade and Use of Narcotic Drugs in Thailand," a study for UNRISD and UNU (23 April 1993).

74. Ibid., 13. Singhanetra-Renard's source is Chaloemtiarana Thak, *Thailand: The Politics of Despotism* (Bangkok: Social Science Association, 1979), 196.

75. Singhanetra-Renard, "Socioeconomic and Political Impact," 15–16.

76. Rising to about 100,000 British pounds in 1874 and 136,000 pounds in 1891, at which time there were over 1,200 shops licensed to sell opium

(ibid., 21). Singhanetra-Renard's source is Suehiro Akira, *Capital Accumulation in Thailand: 1855–1985* (Tokyo: Centre for East Asian Cultural Studies, 1989), 79.

77. Singhanetra-Renard, "Socioeconomic and Political Impact," 21.

78. Ibid., 24, citing "Kanfin," (Opium Matters), *Samitsan* (Excise Department Journal) 1:2 (November 1941), 38.

79. Singhanetra-Renard, "Socioeconomic and Political Impact," 51, citing Saengkaeo Wichian, "Yaseptit Hai Thot Kap Khwammankhong Chat Bangkok," *Nitayasan Ratchataphirak* 18:3 (3 July 1976), 39–40 (Thesis, National Defense College) and Thak, *Thailand,* 197–198.

80. Wichian, "Yaseptit," 40–41.

81. Ibid., 197–198.

82. Singhanetra-Renard, "Socioeconomic and Political Impact," 56.

83. Ibid., 65, citing Thailand, Office of Narcotics Control Board (ONCB), *Thailand Narcotics Annual Report* (Bangkok: Office of the Prime Minister, 1988), 3–5.

84. Singhanetra-Renard, "Socioeconomic and Political Impact," 76–77, citing Poshyachinda Vichai, et al., *Epidemiologic Study of Drug Dependence Patients at the Buddhist Temple Treatment Center: Tam Kraborg* (Bangkok: Chulalongkorn University Institute of Health, 1977), Research Technical Report No. DD-1/77, 11–18.

85. Singhanetra-Renard, "Socioeconomic and Political Impact," 78.

86. Ibid., Chapter 3, entire.

87. Ibid., 81.

88. Thailand, ONCB, *Thailand Narcotics Annual Report,* 3, as cited by Singhanetra, 82.

89. Principal source on Laos is Daniel Henning, "Production and Trafficking of Opium and Heroin in Laos," a study for UNRISD and UNU (draft of 26 May 1993).

90. For example, the U.S. Houaphanh Project (ibid., 54) and the UNDCP projects in Vientiane and Xieng Khouang Provinces (ibid., 53–54).

91. Ibid., 54.

92. Ibid., 48.

93. Ibid., 51.

94. Ibid., 55.

95. Ibid., 77, citing Joseph Westermeyer, *Poppies, Pipes and People: Opium and Its Use in Laos* (Berkeley: University of California Press, 1982), 272–275; 301–304.

96. Henning, "Production and Trafficking," 81.

97. Ibid., 84.

98. Ibid., 82.

99. *INCSR 1993,* 284; *INCSR 1994,* 278.

100. Principal source for Myanmar/Burma is Ronald D. Renard, "Socioeconomic and Political Impact of Production, Trade and Use of Narcotic Drugs in Burma," a study for UNRISD and UNU (draft of November 1993).

101. Ibid., Appendix A.

102. Ibid., 161.

103. Ibid., 167.

104. Ibid.

105. Ibid., 205–206.

106. Principal source for Pakistan is Doris Buddenberg, "Illicit Drug Issues in Pakistan," a study for UNRISD and UNU (draft of May 1993).

107. Success criteria are discussed by Buddenberg, "Illicit Drug Issues," 104–112.

108. Ibid., 86.

109. Ibid., 92.

110. For an extensive discussion of the legal framework as an instrument of illicit-drug control, see Buddenberg, "Illicit Drug Issues," 92–104.

111. Joseph B. Treaster, "U.S. Altering Tactics in Drug War," *New York Times*, 17 September 1993, A7. Ten are Colombians and two are Asians. The other Asian operates in the mountains of Myanmar/Burma.

112. Ibid., 119–121.

113. *INCSR 1993*, 247; *INCSR 1994*, 246.

114. Principal source is Richard Clayton and William Estep, "Marijuana Cultivation and Production in the United States, Appalachia, and Kentucky: The Context and Consequences," a study for UNRISD and UNU (draft of 25 January 1993).

115. Delta-9 Tetrahydrocannabinol (THC) is the principal psychoactive ingredient of marijuana. Richard Clayton provides the information below (p. 47).

Year	Commercial THC Content	Sinsemilla THC Content
1986	3.34	8.43
1987	3.46	7.93
1988	3.82	7.62
1989	3.12	6.96
1990	3.63	10.15
1991	3.83	11.55

116. Ibid., Table 3.1, 30.

117. Ibid., Table 3.6.

118. The retail market in 1992 ranged from $800 to $3,000 per pound for commercial grade marijuana, and from $1,500 to $6,000 for sinsemilla. A mature cultivated plant yields up to 2.4 pounds of marketable product (ibid., 48, and Table 3.8, 49).

119. Ibid., 60.

120. Ibid., 35.

121. Peter Reuter and Mark A. R. Kleiman, "Risks and Prices: An Economic Analysis of Drug Enforcement," in Michael Tonry and Norval Morris, eds., *Crime and Justice: An Annual Review of Research*, vol. 7 (Chicago: University of Chicago Press, 1986), 289–340.

. . . 5 . . .

Unintended Socioeconomic and Political Effects

That people produce, trade, and consume psychoactive drugs is socially and politically interesting. That countries pass laws either to control or prohibit such activity adds a strong political interest. That production, trade, and consumption laws combine to create unintended socioeconomic and political consequences ought not to be surprising. The dimensions of the consequences, however, may be alarming.

Some of the socioeconomic and political effects of consumption, production, and trade—*and* the laws and policies intended to thwart all three—are unintended, others expected. Some consequences are helpful to development, some tolerable to society, some counterproductive to drug-control efforts, others helpful in that regard. But some are inadmissible on all counts by most reasonable standards of common-sense public-policy analysis.

Conceptual Considerations

Consumption

An extensive literature addresses the socioeconomic and political effects of consumption.[1] These effects can substantially harm individuals, families, communities, and whole societies (e.g., impaired fetuses; poor parent-child bonding; neurobiological collapses from overdose, with attendant hospital costs paid either by the public treasury or by insurance companies supported by premium-paying citizens; substandard classroom performance; abnormal psychological and emotional development of adolescents; social and economic overhead costs associated with welfare and other social services).

Regarding society's interests, acute or chronic drug consumption (e.g., several times a week or at intoxication levels at any frequency) clearly has the potential to do more harm than occasional consumption; the same holds for use by many as opposed to a few. The occasional drinking of a moderate amount of alcohol or smoking a like amount of cannabis might produce self-harm but little social harm. Sufficient consumption of either to produce intoxication may lead to disaster for others as well as for the consumers. With harder drugs—heroin, cocaine, crack cocaine—the public implications are potentially more severe but not necessarily so. One person snorting a line of cocaine will hardly create the kinds of public burdens that 5, 10, or 20 percent of a country's population could produce through chronic use. By the same token, large numbers of people might use a small amount of a psychotropic drug infrequently and produce little social harm, whereas a small number of people *abusing* the same drug could create levels of socioeconomic and political harm totally unacceptable to modern society.

In the countries or regions under study, Pakistan appears to be the most adversely affected by chronic and acute consumption, perhaps followed by Thailand, Kentucky, U.S., Myanmar/Burma, and Laos. This ranking, though highly subjective, roughly follows percentage-of-population impressions regarding drug abuse. The Latin American countries studied—Colombia, Peru, Bolivia, Mexico—are less affected because consumption levels there appear lower than those in the United States or the other countries cited. However, as seen in Chapter 2, increasing consumption of *bazuco* in Colombia and Peru has begun to worry public-health officials and political authorities.

Depending on the extent and frequency of illicit-drug use, consumption would appear to offer a society few benefits and a discussable array of liabilities. Thus, principal consuming countries justifiably have tried to reduce consumption, although their concentration on supply repression as a surrogate policy has not been effective.

Production and Trade

The socioeconomic and political effects of consuming illicit drugs are deleterious to a society, though not overwhelmingly so. The same cannot be said for the effects of producing and trading drugs. Especially under conditions of illegality, production and trade create both benefits and liabilities, frequently pronounced, especially for principal producing countries. Moreover, individual beneficiaries certainly abound—the traffickers, the growers (for whom alternative income pursuits may not exist), and hundreds of thousands of low- and middle-level functionaries, many of whom otherwise face less attractive alternative employment options.

The array of economic benefits from supplying an international market can be—indeed, has become—quite substantial in some areas. If the benefits originated in a legitimate economic development model, the world would herald them as a positive sign of progress and improvement in less developed regions. Indeed, although the income source is criticized, hundreds of thousands of people heretofore marginalized from their countries' national societies, economies, and polities have benefited. As a consequence, some of them have earned more money, experienced more social mobility, and exercised more power over their destiny and that of their children than perhaps at any time in this century.

Consider Pakistan. The country's hill tribes have imported chemists from Asia to teach them how to convert opium into heroin, given that opium itself is less desirable for illicit international trade. The tribes now produce enough heroin to make Pakistan one of the world's leading drug exporters[2] and a principal provider for the North American market. They also supply a rapidly growing domestic market. These groups operate a sufficiently good intelligence program to overcome their central government's unevenly applied but tough suppression measures, in part because they are successful in corrupting some of Pakistan's military officers assigned to drug duty.[3] It might seem hard to believe that the relatively isolated tribes could orchestrate all this on their own. They did need a link to international markets, a service provided by what Yev Yelin describes as the "International Narcotics Mafia."[4] The result? By anyone's standards, the incomes of tens of thousands of these people have become relatively substantial, made possible by the confluence of demand, supply, illegality, ready traffickers, and international drug-control policies. Moreover, there are economic multipliers in regional areas where new money is spent on a better mix of life's necessities (food, shelter, clothing) and even luxury goods (radios, music players, trucks, weapons). As locally produced products are purchased, cottage and service industries develop, and regional economies generally become more active.

In the Afghan hill country that borders Pakistan, opium poppies have proven to be a quick, reliable source of money for rural Afghans. Poppies are particularly attractive because of the relative absence of alternative income sources in the region.[5] The economic facts are quite simple. Peasants and isolated villagers can usually earn more cash income with an illicit-trafficker-serviced market than with any other cash crop they could plant or any other product they could produce. Similar economic considerations prevail in all the other countries studied.

Quite apart from the drug industry's being a substantial source of income, in several countries it has even developed a large popular and political base.[6] That base is already reflected in insurgent movements in Peru, Colombia, and Myanmar/Burma. Thus, absent multilateral agencies' addressing the situation head-on with development aid, it is often argued that the consequences of a successful crop-suppression program would imperil the industrialized world's security interests.[7]

International pressures aside, domestic governments are understandably reluctant to deprive their rural subjects of the income and employment provided by illicit-drug production unless alternative income sources are clearly available. Government officials and politicians do not miss the political implications described above. Thus, despite substantial help from the United States and the UNDCP, the Thai government has been reluctant to move against some of its more recalcitrant opium poppy growers, remembering that it was an earlier destruction of opium fields that allowed communist cadres to infiltrate and win over many hill tribesmen to an antigovernment cause.[8] The result continues to tax Thai authorities and to contribute to political stress within the country. By the same token, Myanmar/Burma, Laos, Bolivia, and Peru have little courage to move against growers—unless, of course, the growers become allied with an insurgency.

If the nexus of illicit-drug demand, supply, ready traffickers, and international drug-control policies has boosted rural incomes, the increased income itself has produced its own consequences. Among these are peasant and labor migration to open up frontier lands as well as social mobility for some rural families. Internal migration and social mobility have further enhanced some rural people's incomes and have begun to increase their political power (usually through their unionizing or joining insurrectionist groups). Peasant or grower federations in Bolivia provide a case in point. The logic of the process could lead eventually to a restructuring of the economic and political power bases in net producer countries in ways that open them for expanded leadership recruitment and greater involvement of their citizens in the use of productive resources. The process could occur benignly if income growth continues but could become violent if opportunities for income are suddenly withdrawn.[9]

If, both conceptually and practically, a list of benefits and beneficiaries emerges from illicit-drug production and trade, it is equally certain that both activities produce a substantial variety of liabilities and victims. Most of these are caused by traffickers as they and their money infiltrate bureaucracies, buy public decisions, make alliances with ideologues (sometimes insurrectionist groups), launch intimidating threats and violent attacks on ordinary citizens and public officials, and create, quite effectively, an antistate wholly outside the rule of law and central government control. Many observers argue that these ills far outweigh any commensurate benefits in income and supplemental employment—for the peasantry or anyone else.

More specifically, traffickers exploit, corrupt, foster illegal markets, help sustain a nontaxed underground or parallel economy, require the expenditure of hundreds of millions of dollars on law-enforcement, and undermine banking institutions. They assault the environment, shrink credit pools for legitimate lending, inflate values of land and property, hurt manufacturing, lower the quality of investments, undermine a nation's ability to compete internationally, build economic empires on terror and bribery, and finance businesses that compete with, weaken, and frequently destroy legitimate enterprises.

In the social sphere, traffickers corrupt a population by attracting new generations to the drug trade, glamorizing gangs, and glorifying role models of the conspicuously consuming new rich, thereby detracting from social values on which a legitimate state and its people may be built or maintained. They thereby contribute to social disorganization and to a certain amount of social and value anarchy. The children attracted to their trade become pitiably addicted, roaming as homeless street urchins, and the traffickers indiscriminately murder uninvolved bystanders. It is easy to see why traffickers pose the most serious threat to overall society in producing countries.

Drug-Control Laws

Consumption, production, and trade offer a wide array of socioeconomic and political impacts. So do drug-control laws. Most of the benefits and liabilities associated with production and trade of illegal drugs ultimately derive from illegality itself, a condition that prohibition laws, by definition, establish. Illegality provides what James Inciardi calls the "crime tax,"[10] the difference between what a product would cost in a legal market on the one hand and in an illegal one on the other. Cocaine selling for $100 a gram on the illegal market in Kansas City could probably be marketed for less than $5 a gram in a competitive legal one. The "tax" is reaped principally by traffickers, who pass a sufficient amount of it on to induce peasant growers and minor underlings to flock to the drug enterprise with abandon. Thus, illegality makes it almost impossible to devise a policy mix (risks and incentives) that would generally induce growers to abandon their crop.

Traffickers use the crime tax to accomplish their business ends, which produce the socioeconomic and political externalities described above. Thus, a careful empirical and introspective examination of the effectiveness of drug-control laws is warranted in every nation, because it is the drug-control laws and their application that create the conditions necessary for a crime tax to exist.

If production-control laws are ineffective in reducing consumption (as the evidence examined in Chapter 4 for the countries under study affirms), and if the ills that derive from illegality create, independent of consumption, a mix of benefits and liabilities that is judged to be deleterious to principal producing countries, then observers must seriously wonder if the benefits that growers and others derive from the drug trade could not be achieved in some alternative fashion (e.g., "alternative rural development" programs) in the interest of reducing a nation's crime-tax liabilities. The frequent response is to argue for abandoning drug-control laws against producers (but not necessarily consumers) and to create conditions wherein the general quality of life in principal producing countries can be improved.

Drug-control laws establish the bounds of illegality; they therefore contribute to the intended and unintended consequences that result. Inasmuch as laws attempting to suppress production have done little to reduce consumption, the negative consequences of supply-suppression laws would seem to be in the ascendancy. Indeed, the success of crop-substitution and alternative labor-absorbing development efforts set aside, drug-control initiatives have contributed indirectly to social dislocations, corruption, militarization, abuse of human rights, and a general disregard for human decency.

With these general conceptual considerations in mind, I now turn to the socioeconomic and political consequences in two of the countries under study. The vast array of externalities associated with these two cases illustrates the range of socioeconomic and political consequences encountered. The first country, Colombia, is representative of countries for which traffickers and their externalities are the principal concern. The second, Bolivia, illustrates the dilemmas of countries for which drug crops and their associated externalities are a major concern. Some countries (e.g., Mexico and Pakistan) both grow and traffic, a condition that compounds their dilemmas.

Colombia

Colombia has become the quintessential "impact country."[11] Many of the economic, social, and political/administrative considerations specifically raised for Colombia are also experienced in other countries. Nevertheless, to understand both the pervasive and perverse

impact the illicit drug trade has had on Colombia, one must mini-
mally understand Colombia.

At least since the end of World War II (if not before), Colombia,
once characterized as segmented, isolated, and backward, has progressively become integrated into the international economy. In the
process, its people have become more socially and economically mobilized and have progressively turned their political demands on national leaders. Among other things, many of Colombia's citizens want
their country to address what they believe to be an egregiously unfair
distribution of income, wealth, and property. Until a decade ago, ro-
tating elites (among conservatives and liberals) generally ran the
country to their benefit and to the general exclusion of the less powerful. People have responded angrily, sometimes violently. Thus,
even though mainstream economists never tire in pointing to Colombia's impressive aggregate economic indicators (e.g., growth in GNP),
the truth is that the social context has been deteriorating markedly in
the last several decades.[12]

Being slow to adapt, for a quarter-century or more Colombian
political and economic institutions have progressively lost their legitimacy. Regimes of income and wealth distribution—and, as a corol-
lary, of property rights—that the old political institutions sought to
retain unchanged could not be sustained in the face of the social and
economic trends that Colombians have experienced since World War
II. Rather than modernize politically, the old elite held on to power
through a generation of savage violence and bloodshed. Accordingly,
the recent history of Colombia is one of conflict between an old society and a newly forming one. The resulting caldron of violence, dis-
trust, greed, and manipulation has invited the illegal-drug industry to
step in and take advantage of an already deteriorating situation. Thus,
it can be said that the drug trade did not cause Colombia's problems
so much as it aggravated them by situational appropriation.

Having been invited in by social upheaval, by the archaic elite,
and by the progressively deteriorating legitimacy of economic and social institutions, the barons of cocaine have been able to operate
from a position of relative power, frequently with impunity. The current disarray among some of Colombia's traffickers will improbably
lead to a long-term change. Regardless, the havoc the barons have
rendered in all the categories outlined in the conceptual section of
this chapter has been substantial.

Economic Consequences

The illicit-drug industry appears to have the typical structure of
many agriculturally based industries. Operating under competitive

market conditions, a large number of farmers produce the basic raw materials. The number of participants declines at each stage of the refining or preparation process until, at the top, or wholesale, level, a few sellers control most of the industry. However, as the product moves to the final consumer, markets become more competitive, with a host of retail sellers becoming involved. One sees an "hourglass" phenomenon at work here.

Despite its similarities with other agriculturally based industries, the drug trade has important differences deriving from the illegality of production, distribution, and consumption. Illegality heightens risk. Risk avoidance includes selective (and sometimes indiscriminate) violence in order to protect value-added processes. In turn, profits received are not proportional to factor costs but rather are proportionally related to the risks and the degree of monopoly at each stage of production and marketing. All this adds to the retail value of the product. Absent this risk factor and assuming competitive markets, the value of cocaine would be on the order of one-twenty-fifth of 1990 street level prices in principal consuming countries.[13] Given that most profits are attributed to risk factors, growers who may be at low risk (e.g., some peasants in Bolivia who grow legal coca and who have, in any event, legal coca labor unions) get a small share of the final sale price. Thus, the industry has a tendency to concentrate wealth, thereby exacerbating one of the problems that has helped cause Colombia's political institutions to fall into enormous disrepute.

Any GNP, foreign exchange, or investment increases for the national economy that derive from the illegal-drug trade must be interpreted in light of their tendencies to concentrate income and wealth. How wealth concentration becomes socially important (through conspicuous consumption) or economically important (whether invested in productive industries or not) has enormous political implications for the country. This is so even if, in the short run, low-level growers view their income pittance to be a personal financial windfall.

Many of the illegal-drug industry's economic consequences for Colombia are attached to how illicit-drug money is integrated into the national economy. However, conceptual and methodological problems hinder an adequate understanding of this issue. It is extremely difficult to measure the illegal-drug industry's size, certainly a prerequisite if one desires to measure its economic impact. Thoumi is convincing in his argument that one would need estimates of income accruing to Colombians, of what they invest and spend in Colombia, of the size and composition of assets that traffickers have accumulated in and outside Colombia, and the distribution and concentration of assets among those involved in the illegal-drug business.[14] Neither the figures for size nor those for categories that lend themselves to considerable impact are or will be forthcoming.

Regardless, it is clear that considerable money is returning to Colombia. Francisco Thoumi's extensive review of the literature shows estimates ranging from U.S. $1.1 to $5.5 billion a year during 1988 and 1989,[15] figures that have likely held constant since then. The industry may have accumulated from $39 billion to $66 billion from 1975 to 1989, depending on assumptions about revenues and investment returns.[16] "Very large" is an appropriate term, particularly since Colombia's entire GNP for 1991 is listed as being only slightly above $48.5 billion.[17] Thoumi notes:

> The possibility that figures of such magnitude are real is very threatening to Colombia's power structure, as they suggest the illegal PSAD [psychoactive drug industry] businesses would have huge combined drug and capital incomes relative to the size of the country's economy. For instance, between 1976 and 1986 gross private fixed investment ranged from $1.6 to $3.7 billion and averaged $2.8 billion,[18] figures that clearly indicate that the illegal businessmen had the capacity to invest in Colombia an amount as large as what official data attribute to the country's whole private sector. These figures also indicate that Colombian policymakers must take into account a possibly large "illegal PSAD capital external overhang," made up of the amounts that could be brought into the country in the future. It should be pointed out that these are estimates of "tainted" capital and income, and not just those of the drug barons —since there has been some "spreading of the wealth" to lawyers, chemists, politicians, pilots, guards, and so on.[19]

With this massive amount of money, the Medellín group preferred (in its heyday, before its collapse began in 1992 because of internal feuding and an all-out war with Colombia's security forces) to buy large tracts of rural land, thereby driving up land prices (from about U.S. $500 to $2,000 per hectare),[20] restructuring the political base of local communities,[21] and highly disrupting the lives of thousands of normal citizens living in them. Of course, the syndicate's chosen method of relating to the Colombian state—indiscriminate violence in Medellín and Bogotá—took its own toll on individuals and families in urban settings. By contrast, the Cali group (stronger than before in the wake of Medellín's decline) has preferred to invest in urban enterprises (e.g., office buildings, shopping malls, auto dealerships, sport teams, recreational facilities), specialize in "normal" contraband imports, and hone to perfection a variety of money-laundering devices.

The traffickers' money has distorted many of Colombia's fiscal and monetary policies. During the 1970s and 1980s the government granted periodic tax amnesties in order to bring substantial illegal but nevertheless "clean" capital to sufficient visibility to be counted. This increased the government's revenues but also made it possible for "dirty" capital to be legalized.[22] Normal underground capital might well be absorbed in this way. However, with so much extraordinary capital from the drug trade riding piggyback on funds from the "normal" informal economy, drug money has introduced more macro distortions than the central bank has been prepared to handle. Macroeconomic impacts were felt on foreign-exchange flows, aggregate demand and inflation, policy formulation and implementation, and economic growth.[23] This greatly complicated the government's management of macroeconomic policies. Explains Thoumi:

> The growth of the illegal PSAD industry has made it more difficult to formulate and implement macroeconomic policies. One problem arises simply because as the underground economy grows, the quality of data used by the government to formulate policy declines.[24] For example, it has become increasingly difficult to determine the actual amount of goods and services exported and imported, and of capital flows in and out of the country. The level of measured unemployment tends to be overestimated as some of those who work in the underground economy are counted as unemployed. The increased use of dollars as currency as a result of the need to launder foreign exchange, regardless of the peso's soundness, makes monetary policy more complex. Another problem arises from the difficulty of taxing the informal economy, which penalizes legitimate economic activity and erodes the tax base. All these effects of a larger underground economy make it more difficult to formulate the right policies and to implement them.[25]

The periodic tax amnesties pulled in underground monies, thereby achieving their intended goal of attracting additional finances into the country. However, those in possession of both illegal clean and drug-tainted dirty capital learned just to await the next tax amnesty in order to have ill-gotten gains, from whatever source, legalized.

Separating illegal clean from illegal dirty money for purposes of tax amnesties may be of minor consequence when compared to dirty capital's impact on the flight of legitimate capital from the country. As Thoumi notes, "The illegal foreign exchange funds have also financed a significant amount of capital flight from the country. Thus, the 'dirty' capital inflows have not only been large relative to the size of the economy, but they have substituted for 'clean' capital that has flowed away, increasing the relative importance of the dirty capital to the economy."[26]

It is thought that a country's swapping clean for dirty capital would be economically if not socially deleterious, at least in the short term. First-generation traffickers likely spend heavily on unproductive conspicuous consumption. Colombia's productive capital base is therefore likely gradually impoverished as dirty capital moves in to supplant normal capital.

Real estate development is one area where drug money is most vividly seen. When marijuana reigned supreme in the 1970s, with a concentration of drug entrepreneurs in Barranquilla, the city prospered through a construction boom that lowered unemployment and enhanced incomes across the board. The same occurred in Medellín during the 1980s with the cocaine boom.[27] About specific impacts, Thoumi says that "in 1987 the real value of the construction finance supplied by the official constant value mortgage system (UPAC) declined by about 20 percent, while the total licensed construction area increased by 14.6 percent."[28] Drawing on their profits, drug-industry barons did not even have to go to the banks to solicit construction loans! Once construction drew to a close, however, both Barranquilla and Medellín suffered economic setbacks and high unemployment because so little alternative productive investment had been made.

Despite the earnings in foreign exchange and other income transfers to Colombia, Thoumi shows that the growth of the illicit-drug industry has contributed to a decline in Colombia's aggregate economic growth.[29] First, illegality led to investments that were less productive economically than advantageous for money laundering. At the same time, as the level of drug-related violence increased, legitimate enterprises liquidated their Colombian investments and sent their capital abroad. Thus, dirty capital not only replaces clean capital, it also operates less productively.

Second, the social-psychological characteristics of drug capitalists who have legitimated their money have not always been conducive to growth and, indeed, in some instances have clearly worked against it. Their rough-and-tumble personalities (especially of the Medellín drug lords), have not made them good modern entrepreneurs. The Cali group is an exception, but on the whole drug entrepreneurs are likely "to be less qualified to manage a modern business than the best managers the country has produced."[30]

Third, the drug industry has been a catalyst for regime delegitimation and, as such, has contributed to the rapid growth of some industries that probably contribute little to higher incomes (e.g., the boom in home and office security systems). Though increasing violence and lawlessness contribute to the growth of such industries, money is withdrawn from other, more important sectors to support them. Some require expensive imports of technology, draining the foreign-exchange accounts.

Fourth, the environment for direct foreign investment has greatly deteriorated because the weakening of the judicial system has made civil-dispute resolution increasingly difficult. Guerrilla kidnappings of foreign businessmen have heightened the unease about investing in Colombia.

Fifth, uncertainty about the future has promoted a shortsighted perspective regarding economic investments (quick, in and out, with high rates of return), with a focus on immediate profits as opposed to long-term growth.

Sixth, efforts to suppress drug trafficking and the violence it spawns have forced Colombia to increase its police and military budgets significantly. These are fundamentally "consumption" costs and do not contribute to economic growth.

Seventh, because the drug industry must rely on an underground economy, it ends up promoting it. A lower rate of economic growth ensues, in part because underground firms are limited in their expansion inasmuch as they cannot become conspicuous. Marketing significant quantities of their products through formal channels is burdensome.

Thoumi's significant analysis of the implications of all these economic impacts is sobering:

> It is no wonder that most Colombian economists argue the negative effects clearly outweigh the positive ones, and do not consider the illegal PSAD industry beneficial to the country's economy. Clearly, if the illegal PSAD industry were to disappear, Colombia would run a risk of having a recession for a couple of years.[31] However, it is likely that even a mild recession might be avoided. Since the illegal drug industry is likely to be responsible for promoting substantial "clean" capital flight, its elimination could actually be compensated for by "clean" capital repatriations. Since income from capital investments that the illegal drug entrepreneurs are likely to have outside the country may be as large as current cocaine profits, the elimination of the industry would allow for an easier repatriation and assimilation of that income. In conclusion, there is no question that Colombia's economy could do better without the illegal drug industry than with it.[32]

Social Consequences

The drug trade has exacerbated an endemic social institution in Colombia—violence. Violence is the most obvious symptom of Colombia's profound social crisis, a situation that has played into the hands of traffickers as they ply their business. The infamous period of what Colombians call *La Violencia*—which saw the extermination of between 200,000 and 300,000 of the country's 11.5 million citizens—

began in the late 1940s.[33] Today it is fueled to ever increasing heights by the drug trade and is marked by extreme cruelty and inhumanity. Francisco Thoumi provides the statistical parameters:

> While violence waned after la violencia, it did not cease. Although data about many variables that reflect the level of violence in Colombian life are sparse, data on homicides and intentional deaths are staggering. Losada and Vélez (1988 and 1989)[34] surveyed homicide rates from 1955 to 1988, and estimate that at the beginning of the National Front in 1958 they peaked at 51.5 per 100,000 inhabitants. The homicide rate fell continuously during the 1960s and early 1970s, bottoming out between 1973 to 1975 at about 16.8 per 100,000. However, in the late 1970s, the homicide rate increased rapidly, reaching 62.8 per 100,000 in 1988. Losada and Vélez also show that, according to United Nations data on 70 countries, between 1955 and 1969 Colombia's homicide rate was among the top five, while during the 1970 to 1978 period, which can be considered a peaceful one, Colombia ranked between sixth and tenth. After 1978 the homicide rate returned to the top five, reaching third in 1988, behind only El Salvador and Zimbabwe.[35]

Homicide in Colombia is the main cause of death for males aged 15–44. In 1987 about one in twelve deaths was a homicide. Outside the emerald- and banana-producing zones of Boyacá, Cundinamarca, and Urabá, this remarkable Colombian phenomenon is concentrated principally in areas of coca growing, drug-trafficker real estate investments, and guerrilla activity, where insurgents, traffickers, and locals are in high-level competition. These areas are the recently settled Middle Magdalena River Valley; the plains of north Antioquia; the Indian reserves in the north of Cauca and in some valleys there and in Nariño; parts of northwest Cundinamarca, southern Guajira (where new settlers are pressuring resident Indian populations and where contraband enters and exits Colombia in large quantities), the north of Valle, the adjacent area of Risaralda, and the newly settled basins of the Carare, Upía, and Cusiana Rivers and the plains of Arauca and Casanare; and San José del Guaviare.[36] Add to these broad areas the endemic violence in cities such as Medellín, and one sees illicit drugs compounding an already repugnant social institution.

Organized criminals, including narco-traffickers, target politicians and journalists, private individuals, state facilities and institutions, the police, and armed forces. The state responds with violence not only against traffickers and other criminals but also against innocent bystanders. Private individuals (organized and unorganized) respond by lashing out indiscriminately. Of particular concern is the development of the *sicario* industry in Colombia—teenage assassins, for whom the value of a human life is approximately $13 (the going rate to snuff one out). Traffickers employ them by the scores to carry out their grisly business. In 1989 it was reported there were some 2,000 contract killers in Colombia and that the drug traffickers had even established an "academy for killers."[37]

Aside from murders and assassinations, kidnapping has become a popular sport—by guerrilla groups looking to replenish their war chests, by drug traffickers pressuring government for a change in drug-control policy, and by common criminals taking advantage of political- and drug-related kidnappings for personal gain. Kidnapping in Colombia is a flourishing business. The data are shocking. Kidnappings occur daily; the monthly average from March 1988 to December 1989 was 59.1, a figure that jumped to 158 in January 1990.[38] Democracies probably cannot survive indefinitely an infestation of wholesale murder and kidnapping, even if, in the short run, they are able to mount sufficient police power to turn some of it around. Even the most casual and lightly interested observer must view the long-term social implications for developing a civic culture in this situation—thought to be a requisite for a functioning democracy—as staggering.

Explanations of Colombia's violence abound in the literature, ranging all the way from an undemocratic political system to high levels of poverty and income inequality. However, according to Thoumi, these are not strong predictors. The best explanation, he argues, is found in "uncertain property rights in newly settled areas, illegal mining and agriculture, and conflict generated by the drug traffickers' investments in areas where peasants and guerrilla groups have been fighting for land rights."[39] As for the sicarios in Medellín, their involvement is statistically related to "being unemployed, belonging to a gang, having a low education level, having been abandoned by one or both parents during childhood, and having a mother with a background of prostitution, alcoholism and drug-addiction."[40]

Even Colombia's drug-control laws contribute to violence, because in an informal economy it is through violence that "business contracts" are enforced or markets expanded. The increased violence, in turn, has a corrosive impact on society. Thus, through violence and very large externally derived incomes, the drug industry exerts a dramatic impact on Colombian society, an impact that has every prospect of increasing. Drug traffickers could easily become the dominant economic group in the country. Moreover, as Thoumi notes, "a portion of the illegally generated capital is today owned by individuals not easily identified with the illegal PSAD industry, so the true impact on the Colombian economy transcends that caused by those who can be identified as current or past drug traffickers."[41]

The astonishing upshot of all this is that, far from destabilizing the old social order that legitimated a highly skewed distribution of wealth and property, the drug trade has already reinforced it. The cocaine barons have become the new rich, simply replacing the old coffee oligarchy that evolved in the late nineteenth century.[42] This is most vividly seen in rural areas, as the Medellín traffickers preferred to take their illicit-drug money to remote, recently settled areas characterized by weak and questionable property rights and possibly significant guerrilla activity. In the Middle Magdalena Valley, where guerrillas reigned before cocaine, the traffickers actually pacified the countryside when they arrived, making investments more secure and reducing the incidence of cattle rustling. But even in areas that were targeted for land reform, the traffickers' wealth served to concentrate landownership, indicating that what Thoumi calls a "violent land counterreform" was taking place.[43]

As the new capitalists invested in their properties, they increased productivity by adding new technology but put people out of work by concentrating landownership and introducing labor-saving devices. The result in these areas has been technological progress with social decline, exacerbating regional violence as people struggle with each other over their "rights" and guerrillas and drug-industry paramilitaries jockey for position. From one moment to the next, rural peasants, caught in the middle of the struggle, do not know from whom to buy protection. As a result, industry groups can create a climate of fear from which they are able, quite handily, to enact their own laws.[44]

In the coca-growing areas of rural Colombia, the new agricultural pursuits completely changed regional social and political structures. New migrants were ready and willing to use violence to get themselves a stake. Old shopkeepers were put out of business as consumption mixes changed. Alcohol use and prostitution increased. The violence further weakened the capacity of the state to govern, and the political left lost its hold as people turned to the wild frenzy of making money, now that money could be made. But when coca prices fell in 1982 following a crackdown on traffickers, many peasants went bankrupt, a condition leading to further land concentration as people were forced into distress sales. In came the guerrilla organizations, obliging the peasants to produce foodstuffs and limiting coca production to a small percentage of land owned by each peasant. The state was powerless.

Another of the social consequences of the illicit-drug trade is its addiction spillover into the general population. A supply-side hypothesis is not inappropriate here. The data show that when Colombian marijuana was a growth industry during the 1970s, cannabis consumption increased dramatically. By the same token, when cocaine soared and marijuana declined, during the 1980s, bazuco use, in particular, increased alarmingly. It was reported that Medellín alone had 435 locations where bazuco was sold, an astonishing figure but one nevertheless exceeded by Bogotá, which had 513.[45] Although Colombia's new wave of drug takers have begun to ingest multiple drugs, bazuco continues to be seen as the main problem. It is highly addictive and is linked to violence, criminality, and a host of social problems, including those related to the sicario industry. Nevertheless, one must keep in mind, as shown in Chapter 2, that compared to countries such as Pakistan, Thailand, and the United States, Colombia still does not have a drug-consuming epidemic—unless one includes alcohol in the list.

Political/Administrative Consequences

The drug trade has exacerbated Colombia's institutional crisis, itself caused by the slow adaptation of the country's political apparatus to a relatively rapid transformation of Colombian society. Urbanization, changed labor relations, adjustments in the economic role of women, a consolidated national market, increased communications and travel among the regions, and a dramatic rise in educational levels have all put pressure on the political system. In the minds of many people, the slow "absorptive" response of the state has only enhanced perceptions of its political illegitimacy. Traffickers have played on this to great effect.

As an illustration of this dilemma, Colombia's administration of justice is in crisis. The regular justice system cannot withstand threats and bribes. Judges who resist under-the-table payments are frequently assassinated. Justices of all persuasions are vulnerable, including a majority of those on the Supreme Court, who were killed in a trafficker/police shoot-out.[46] Indeed, judges, policemen, and others in the judiciary and law-enforcement agencies are routinely assassinated, sometimes with family members. Small wonder that some policemen and some judges lack courage or may be amenable to a bribe.

As a consequence, separate courts with hooded judges and twenty-four-hour bodyguards have been set up to try drug traffickers. At least some judges function under the aegis of the military. The anonymous judges, more highly paid and therefore presumably less prone to being corrupted than their judicial counterparts, have become the envy of others in the judiciary,[47] producing considerable conflict.

One assassination provoked the Colombian government to take a harder stand against the illicit-drug industry. The episode also exemplifies how the Colombian political system became almost fatally compromised. During 1983 and 1984 a significant confrontation arose when Justice Minister Rodrigo Lara Bonilla argued that the illegal-drug industry's influence was corrupting congress, principally because some of the chief traffickers had managed to get themselves elected as "alternative congressmen." Bonilla pressed for the removal of Pablo Escobar and others like him so they could not operate their drug trade under the cloak of parliamentary immunity.

In an unusual smear campaign, the traffickers retaliated by charging the minister with having taken campaign contributions from one of them. Bonilla, generally considered an uncorrupted official with strong but uncomplicated antidrug sentiments, hotly denied the accusation. An ensuing acrid and aggressive debate forced Pablo Escobar out of congress. In apparent retribution for his antidrug stand and his public humiliation of a world-class trafficker, Bonilla was assassinated on 30 April 1984.[48]

In regimes of gross wealth and land inequality undergoing rapid social change, population and political pressures are sometimes relieved by migration. In Colombia's case, migration has been a safety valve for the government. Unable, or unwilling, to incorporate newly mobilized and urbanized people into the economy as people had hoped, the government has undeniably motivated many of its citizens to strike out for other places. For example, over the last forty years both the Caguán and Guaviare regions of Colombia have attracted many migrants. The first were displaced by La Violencia, others by bad economic conditions where they lived. However, these "expulsion factors" from home regions changed to "pull factors" when international demand for illegal drugs, especially cocaine, arose. Thousands migrated, perhaps thereby temporarily reducing pressures for political reform in the center. Successful coca growing in these two regions soon attracted a new migration wave, people in search not of land but of quick profits. They were more urban; some had experience in criminal smuggling gangs, and some had higher education. Some were chemists who came to work in drug laboratories, and others were educated, young, urban, unemployed, people in search of fortune.[49]

Migration to new areas in order to undertake illegal-crop production accentuates the problem of weak property rights facing the Colombian government. This is a problem to which the state has not responded adequately, in part because of its historical attachment to regimes of wealth and property inequality. The government's inability to respond with timely cadastral surveys and land-registration systems has contributed to the sense of governmental illegitimacy, leaving the door open for guerrillas and traffickers to settle disputes on their own terms. This lack of order further weakens the state and compromises the government.

In these isolated regions, "government" has been taken over by lawless elements—drug traders and guerrillas—thereby contributing to the high level of violence. Principal traffickers, not the government, have tried to reduce violence by building a "legitimate" political base. But this effort has simply "encouraged entrepreneurs to influence regional policy by bribing and intimidating politicians and law enforcement authorities, and to finance virtual private armies to protect their investments and attack industry enemies, real or imagined. This extensive influence has increased the level of corruption in the rest of society."[50]

Distribution of income from the drug trade is a function of risk taking. Most risks are associated with transportation and smuggling. Colombians, apparently more than people of any other single nation, transport and smuggle cocaine. Therefore, the largest portion of overall profits for Colombian residents comes from transporting and smuggling to the United States. This enterprise is amenable to economies of scale in order to reduce risk, and Colombian traffickers have excelled in cooperation and intelligence gathering. Pooling resources and knowledge, they are able to identify the least vulnerable routes or ones that can be made less vulnerable through bribes and payoffs. Spreading the risk by pooling shipments allows everyone to turn a profit even if some cocaine is seized.[51] The higher profits at this stage trigger more resource investment and more tenacity when the enterprise is thwarted. As a result, most of the time the traffickers have been in a standoff with the authorities, able to thwart both Colombia's and the United States's best law-enforcement efforts. Nevertheless, large state budgets continue to be approved to try to turn the situation around.

Concentration of wealth among traffickers has made them attractive targets for kidnappers and counterassassins. In response, the traffickers created MAS (Muerte a Secuestradores), a paramilitary group established to prevent kidnappings by attacking anyone who allegedly or actually dared do so—or dared to even think publicly about it.[52] The traffickers agreed not to pay any ransom, as such payments would only invite more kidnap attempts. They also agreed to create a mutual protection society by contributing cash, arms, and manpower to MAS. With these resources, MAS attacked M-19 guerrillas hard enough for the latter to sue for peace in 1987.[53] MAS has summarily executed a number of drive-by kidnappers. But, apparently, MAS now also takes on the random policeman and judge.

If the resulting violence were not enough, in 1987 the Medellín and Cali syndicates attacked one another, which further escalated drug-related violence.[54] This kind of systemic violence is extremely difficult for the government to try to stop because it feeds, in part, on the weak political foundations that over the years the government has sought to protect.

The police have been tempted simply to stand by and watch the drug syndicates self-destruct fighting one another. But the violence has spilled over to inflict harm on ordinary citizens. Stray bullets, mistargeted victims, and bungled rescue attempts have all taken their toll. Police and the military have fallen into even greater disrepute because of the negative publicity the violence has created and the continuing evidence that the authorities have been unable to do anything about it. Perhaps this perception helps to account for the exuberance among the security forces that killed Pablo Escobar (not to mention the fact that they would share in the multimillion-dollar bounty for his death).[55]

Particularly difficult for the government has been the narco-guerrilla connection and the formation of each group's paramilitary organization. The narco-guerrilla connection arose because of a common enemy—the government. Otherwise, traffickers and guerrillas have fundamentally opposite goals—unrestrained capitalism on the one hand, a fight against capitalism on the other.[56] This conflict is obviously irreconcilable, yet in the early 1980s the two groups struck up a working alliance. The guerrillas advanced themselves as a ready source of protection for drug manufacturing centers and shipments concentrated in sparsely settled areas, where guerrillas liked to operate anyway. The evidence of such linkages was found in the Amazon jungle at the Tranquilandia manufacturing complex that the government destroyed in 1984, in the words of trafficker Carlos Lehder, in apparent links between the Nicaraguan Sandinistas and the illicit-drug industry in Colombia, and in the M-19 guerrilla takeover of the Supreme Court building on 6 November 1985 in which the guerrillas destroyed files of pending cases against traffickers.[57]

Although the alliances have proved to be temporary and fraught with conflict because of trafficker encroachment on land and resources in guerrilla-controlled areas such as the Middle Magdalena Valley, the alliances and violence associated with periodic "fallouts" have further weakened the authority of the state in the country's hinterland. Policemen, political officers, and even the military are reluctant to show much of a presence in those areas. Public administration and political authority from the center are thereby weakened, which weakens the state in general.

Thoumi argues that the main effect of Colombia's illicit-drug industry has been to accelerate the delegitimation of the country's political and social institutions. It has done so by fueling the under-

ground economy, contributing to growing violence, having utter disregard for the legal system, intimidating members of the judicial
branch, corrupting state political and administrative functionaries,
and promoting expectations of extraordinarily high short-term profits (thereby encouraging speculative investments). The government's
inability to implement social and economic measures such as land
reform or anti-inflation policies has added to the process. "Each variable contributed to the gap between de jure and de facto socially accepted behaviors—accelerating regime delegitimation and weakening the State."[58]

Some have said that the drug crisis will do for Colombia what no
other political pressure can—force the political system to modernize.
The industry may force reforms toward democratization, but the industry itself is structured at the core to be one of the main obstacles
to democratization. Beyond this, the acquisition of democratically
dysfunctional social values in the wake of the cocaine era would
argue against structural reforms' being a panacea for anything. The
prognosis does not look good for Colombia.

Democratization would entail a certain redistribution of wealth
and land or, at least, a rethinking of income-stream beneficiaries.
The drug barons, with probably more money and capital hoarded or
invested abroad than Colombia's entire GNP for a single year, would
and could resist such tendencies. Colombia has waited too long to
hope that its political system can be modernized at the end of a
drug-industry branding iron. The "new oligarchies" favor raw capitalism, disregard laws, and have a high propensity for violence,
hardly an indication that they will contribute to the deepening of
democracy in Colombia.

Now overlaid with an illicit-drug industry, Colombia's historical
political economy serves to delegitimize a capitalist, democratic
economy and polity. Current drug-control efforts produce the unintended consequence of hastening the process through an increase in
violence, militarization, and compromised government. For its part,
the drug industry concentrates income and wealth, feeds the underground economy, opposes some socially progressive reforms, and
weakens the state.

The increased violence, corruption, underground economic activity, tax avoidance, economic instability, money laundering, and social crises associated with the illicit-drug trade can have—and, in
Colombia's case, appear to have—a corrosive effect on a society and
a polity. Most people consider that the illicit-drug trade has therefore
brought more sorrow than happiness to Colombia, more liabilities
and victims than benefits and beneficiaries.

Bolivia

Whatever socioeconomic impacts from the illicit-drug trade may be generally noted, for Bolivia they have the prospect of being more acutely felt.[59] Perhaps 20 percent of Bolivia's GNP is attached in some form to the illicit-drug trade. Ups and downs in the trade and the consequences for those it benefits and hurts are therefore more significant.

Although Bolivia has not experienced Colombia's level of violence either as a social norm or as attached to the illicit-drug trade, the potential certainly exists. Significant disruption to 20 percent of a nation's economy would probably trigger some violence. Bolivia is the second poorest country (after Haiti) in the Western Hemisphere and resembles sub-Saharan Africa in its social statistics (e.g., high infant mortality and morbidity, low educational levels, general economic deprivation). Income from the drug trade has mitigated some of the worst extremes of poverty. More important, however, the drug trade has accelerated people's ambitions about material rewards and the prospects of achieving them. A significant downturn in these prospects would not augur for social peace. Thus, the aggressive U.S. effort to eradicate peasant coca crops very well may turn Bolivia from a peaceful and "passive" country into a more violent one. Some people speak of the prospects as the "Colombianization of Bolivia."[60]

Significantly, two small, left-wing guerrilla groups—the Comisión Nestor Paz Zamora (CNPZ) and the Ejército Guerrillero Tupac Katari (EGTK)—emerged in 1990 and 1991 and have tried to drum up popular support against the government.[61] Although such groups come and go in Latin America, frequently without much impact, one ought not discount the possibility of their galvanizing genuine coca-grower discontent and inducing the peasantry to return to a conflict-resolution model popularized in the early 1950s in Bolivia—armed rebellion and civil war.

On the whole, Bolivians, or at least some of them, have benefited immensely from the illicit-drug trade, both directly and by collaborating with international agencies and the U.S. government in their efforts to suppress the trade. For example, peasants in the Chapare earn incomes by growing and selling coca leaves; others there and elsewhere earn money by cutting their coca bushes down and participating in alternative development programs funded from outside Bolivia. The combination of income from coca selling, coca destroying, and coca substituting may be unequaled by any other economic sector. Indeed, James Painter states that "in the late 1980s Bolivia may have been the country in the world with the highest degree of dependence on the revenue and jobs from the production and trafficking of a narcotic."[62]

Like individual Bolivians, the state has been both helped and hurt by the illicit-drug trade. Income from the coca/cocaine trade helped give the government enough of a cushion at least to bank against immediate failure of the economic-stabilization plan it initiated in 1985. Illicit-drug income gave the government more flexibility in exchange-rate and monetary policy and financed imports that otherwise would not have been possible. All this bought a period of social peace.[63]

There have been drawbacks from the trade, of course. Painter notes the major ones as being an overvalued exchange rate, "which weakened local industry and lowered the value of non-traditional exports,"[64] and a boom in financial speculation that severely impacted thousands of peasants who had invested in sure-to-go-broke savings and loan companies, which did, indeed, fail in the early 1990s.

The general weakness of the Bolivian economy and the relative importance to it of the coca/cocaine trade meant that Bolivia would become vulnerable to U.S. prescriptions for fighting illicit drugs, regardless of the initiatives' prejudiciality to Bolivia. Thus, Bolivia has become more dependent, if not subservient, than ever.

There are other costs, of course—addiction, ecological degradation, widespread corruption, abandoned families, corrosive social norms, incipient violence, militarization, and weakening of the state in the face of drug-industry advances. But all these problems have not yet been felt sufficiently grave to cause Bolivians to forgo their drug incomes.

Economic Consequences

As with Colombia, an estimate of the value of the coca/cocaine industry to Bolivia is not possible within normal expectations. A 1991 U.S. embassy internal document calculated the value of the trade to be between U.S. $375 and $550 million, of which $150 and $300 million stayed in the country. The embassy researchers thought that perhaps 97,000 to 100,000 people spent at least a quarter of their time in the industry, either as hired hands or as entrepreneurs.[65] Samuel Doria Medina, the government's chief economic adviser from 1989 to 1990 and a key negotiator with the United States over the U.S. contribution to Bolivia, estimated the total value of the industry at $1.5 billion, of which $600 million stayed in the country. He also judged that upwards of 300,000 people were productively engaged in some aspect of the coca/cocaine chain. Other estimates of the industry's size range from $300 million to $5.7 billion, generating employment for 120,000 to 500,000 people.[66]

These estimates have very wide margins of error. As in the Colombian case, in assessing their potential accuracy one must entertain not only the diversity of assumptions that underlie each set of figures but also the political ends the figures may be intended to serve. Regardless, as with Colombia, it is fair to say that, relative to Bolivia's overall GDP of $5.1 billion and a population of 7.5 million in 1992,[67] even the lowest estimates are very large, indeed.

In making the estimates, we have only one factor that is known with reasonable accuracy—the amount of land dedicated to coca production, a fact established by aerial photography. Observers take this fact, look at stages of coca and cocaine production, and then try to give a detailed breakdown of the value at each stage. However, aside from the hectarage itself, all else derives from assumptions regarding yield, alkaloid content, storage time, domestic consumption, legal industrial use, market prices, percentage of funds repatriated, and so forth,[68] as we saw in Chapter 2.

This process yields the following estimates with respect to grassroots employment in the drug industry. About 60,000 farmers grow coca, with thousands more involved in harvesting, transporting, and marketing the leaves, and processing and distributing the paste.[69] All told, recent estimates suggest that between 120,000 and 500,000 people are employed full- or part-time in the drug chain. The fluidity of the estimates hinges, in part, on assumptions about how many members of a given grower's family are involved. Some researchers have assumed two, others five, which obviously affects the result. Table 5.1 shows some of the sources and the ranges.

James Painter has attempted to estimate the value of the Bolivian coca/cocaine economy in 1990, compare it to the values posted in Colombia and Peru, and then derive a comparative estimate of the percentage of the economically active population (EAP) involved in the illicit-drug trade.[70] In Colombia, the drug industry involves 0.4 percent of the economically active population. In Peru it is between 2.4 and 4.5 percent. In Bolivia the figures range from 6.7 to 26.2 percent, depending on who is doing the estimating (Table 5.1). Most assuredly, a higher percentage of people depend on the trade in Bolivia than in Colombia or Peru, which nevertheless have large illicit-drug incomes. For this reason it has become somewhat popular to think of Bolivia as "narco-addicted."[71] Clearly, the industry is attractive for a country such as Bolivia, whose population is largely rural and unskilled:

Coca production . . . along with its initial (but not final) processing, is very labor-intensive; frequently uses lands unsuitable for any other agricultural purpose; is carried out in remote, not easily accessible areas; improves small-farmer incomes; and gives local economies a boost as regional per-capita income rises. Indeed, in this regard and at this level, the coca industry does almost all that

Table 5.1   Estimates of the Number of Workers Employed in the Bolivian
Coca/Cocaine Industry

Study	Year for Estimate	Number Employed	% EAP
Franks[a]	1989	207,000	12.0
Aguiló[b]	1987?	456,000	26.6
USAID[c]	1990	243,000	13.5
U.S. embassy[d]	1989	138,000–143,000	8.2
	1990	145,000–150,000	8.2
Bolivian government[e]	1990	300,000	16.7
De Franco and Godoy[f]	1990	120,000	6.7

Source: James Painter, Bolivia and Coca, 50.
Notes: EAP = Economically Active Population (1,718,000, 1989; 1,800,000, 1990).
   a. Jeffrey Franks, "La economía de la coca en Bolivia: ¿Plaga o salvación?" Informe Confidencial 64 (June 1991), 23 (Table 6) [La Paz: Muller Associates]. Franks's own figure for the percentage of EAP is 9.5 percent, as he includes the 207,000 employed in the coca/cocaine industry.
   b. Federico Aguiló, "Movilidad Espacial y Movilidad Social Generada por el Narcotráfico," in Efectos del Narcotrásfico (La Paz: ILDIS, 1988), 68. It is not clear from the study which year Aguiló is referring to. The Aguiló figure should more reasonably be taken as a percentage of the total Bolivian population (around seven million), which would give a percentage figure for EAP of 6.5 percent.
   c. USAID Update, "Estimates of Economic Impact of Coca and Derivatives in 1990," Mimeo 30 (April 1991), La Paz.
   d. U.S. Embassy, mimeo, La Paz, 1991.
   e. Presidencia de la República, Estrategia Nacional de Desarrollo Alternativo (La Paz: Presidencia de la República, 1990), 31.
   f. Mario De Franco and Ricardo Godoy, "The Economic Consequences of Cocaine Production in Bolivia: Historical, Local and Macroeconomic Perspectives," mimeo, Harvard Institute for International Development, 13.

the "current view" on rural and agricultural development in lesser-developed countries calls for: It is labor-intensive, decentralized, growth-pole oriented, cottage-industry promoting, and foreign exchange earning. If the coca industry were completely licit and high returns to the growers held, it could be the final answer to rural development in economically stagnating areas [of countries such as Bolivia and Peru].[72]

The economic impact of the cocaine trade not only has been substantial for individuals but also has had strong positive and negative institutional impacts. For example, many people have argued that the trade helped Bolivia carry out one of the most radical Latin American economic restructuring programs yet. Tens if not hundreds of thousands of people drew on earnings from the informal economy—including the illicit-drug trade—while the formal economy was undergoing considerable restructuring and constriction during the mid-1980s. Coca and cocaine therefore acted as a huge safety net, "absorbing labor from the collapsed mining and industrial sectors and replacing large portions of the dollars previously generated by minerals, gas, and other exports."[73] Moreover, many illicit-drug dollars entered the formal economy through the central bank's liberal purchasing procedures (no questions asked). Painter calculates that at its peak in the late 1980s as much as U.S. $20 million per month could have been entering the private banking system, "an amount sufficient to cause an economic collapse if the flow had been interrupted."[74]

Nevertheless, as in Colombia, the influx of coca dollars in Bolivia probably contributed to an overvaluation of the national currency, thereby suppressing exports by making them more costly on the international market. The influx made imports less costly, thereby damaging local industries, especially those in shoes and textiles, which had to face competition from cheap imports from Brazil and Chile. All these factors began to decrease employment just at the time when the new coca-export industry had begun to absorb people. Thus, dislocations must have been severe in some areas, but the coca/cocaine industry was apparently able to take up the slack. Thousands of unemployed or underemployed people migrated to the Chapare to try their hand at a different kind of export industry—coca/cocaine. Painter notes that "the only sector to increase its participation in GDP was agriculture, which grew from 18.4 percent in 1980 to 22.4 percent in 1988, despite the drought and flooding during the period. Coca cultivation was the main reason for the increase."[75]

Computer-simulation models have been run to try to assess the direct and indirect effects of the illicit-drug traffic on the Bolivian economy. A model developed by Mario de Franco and Ricardo Godoy estimates that a 10 percent increase in coca/cocaine production increases aggregate GNP by 2 percent and lowers unemployment by 6 percent. Real incomes increase for nearly all social groups as the multiplier effects of increased income are felt in commerce, construction, and service sectors.[76]

The model is for the whole of Bolivia. In the real world, regional effects are markedly felt where the coca/cocaine industry is concentrated—Cochabamba, the Chapare, the Yungas. Indeed, in the department of Cochabamba in 1987 coca production represented 63 percent of total agricultural production. Moreover, the good fortunes experienced by some of the major trading centers have been well documented.[77] As an example, industrial production of toilet paper has increased substantially in Bolivia, 60 percent of it destined for the Chapare, where it is employed in coca-paste/cocaine production as a filtering agent. This activity provides 2,000 jobs for people who transport and sell it.[78]

Although incomes from the coca/coca-paste economy have been widely enjoyed in Bolivia (despite representing a minuscule share of the total value of the illicit traffic), most of the proceeds deriving from the cocaine industry itself are probably not repatriated to Bolivia—except for what traffickers need in order to pay local expenses, make land investments, and competitively and conspicuously display their wealth. Contrary to the case in Colombia, this does not have much positive impact on Bolivia's total economy. Indeed, Painter notes that "there is little evidence of traffickers making large-scale investments in other, more productive sectors of the legal economy [outside small-scale investments in infrastructure, local television and radio stations, and other forms of entertainment]."[79]

Providing jobs that have even limited multiplier effects for an economy such as Bolivia's is generally viewed as a plus. However, the financial resources from the coca/cocaine trade also complicate life for the government and the normal economy. Two ways by which this complication occurs are through financial speculation and increased support for the informal economy. Speculation and informal economic activity during the 1980s and 1990s—in the form of contraband stalls at markets such as Miamicito in La Paz and La Cancha in Cochabamba, small-scale "building societies" (e.g., savings and loan institutions), high interest-bearing dollar deposits in Bolivian banks,[80] and so forth—have undoubtedly been fueled by cocaine dollars, although it is difficult to disaggregate illicit-drug and legitimate funds.

One form of speculation derives from the need to launder money. In Bolivia's case, expensive electrical goods are imported and sold at below cost in the Miamicito and La Cancha markets. This practice is a boon to consumers and has the added advantage of having a negligible impact on Bolivia's foreign-exchange accounts because the goods are purchased in places such as Panama with illicit-drug dollars that have never entered Bolivia. The goods are then shipped to Bolivia as regular imports. Moreover, because there is hardly any industrial base in the country, disruption of local markets through cheap imports appears to be limited mostly to cottage industries (e.g., shoes and textiles). Money laundering via cheap imports therefore appears to have a spotty negative impact on the economy.

The long-term impact of laundering money in this way could be substantial, however. The reason is based on the economic principle that industrialization is necessary to support a growing population. The surfeit of manufactured goods appearing in the underground markets at below cost (to facilitate immediate liquidity) impedes Bolivia's industrialization because hardly any legitimate entrepreneur, even one using a cheap labor force, can compete. Without industrialization, the growing population will have nowhere to go other than into the cocaine economy. When the cocaine economy crashes—inevitably it will, as drug-consumption fads change around the world—Bolivia will be thrown into one more export "boom and bust" tailspin, and the country's recovery will be seriously hampered by the lack of an existing industrial base and skilled labor force.

Speculation in small-scale building societies (savings and loan organizations) has had a more immediate impact, social as well as economic (the social impacts will be discussed later). By mid-1991, half a dozen societies, all based in Cochabamba, had attracted between U.S. $100 million and $120 million from about 40,000 depositors. Painter reports how the largest of these, Finsa (Firma Integral de Servicios Arévalo), started as a small-time radio-taxi company, began to expand in 1989 (after the Arévalo family received a $30,000 inheritance), and soon included not only the taxi service but also "a discotheque, a TV station, a hotel, a furniture factory, an air-taxi service, a travel agency, a construction company, and a financial interest in at least one major football [soccer] club."[81] When the police did a "narco-test" in February 1991 on two of the company's aircraft and found traces of cocaine, two of the Arévalo brothers failed to elude an arrest warrant and served short jail terms. Finsa closed down after authorities interdicted the cocaine and deposits, leaving 20,000 depositors with little chance of recovering the $56 million they had placed with the firm during the previous three years.

Remarkably, top police officers, politicians, and highly visible entertainment personalities had invested in Finsa, one to the tune of more than $500,000. It was assumed, but never proven, that the Arévalo brothers were linked to cocaine trafficking. Regardless, much of the financial foundation they built most assuredly rested on some major depositors' cocaine-related assets. But the real people hurt when Finsa closed were thousands of small depositors who had entrusted their life's savings of $100 to $1,000; some depositors had even borrowed from regular banks to deposit with Finsa because the interest differential actually gave them a net return on their borrowed money.[82]

Ripple effects that dipped into government and business were felt far and wide. The other building societies soon crashed, sending Cochabamba into an economic slump and giving opportunity for a few people to once more concentrate wealth.

Aside from employment and speculation issues and their economic implications for Bolivia, there is evidence (somewhat contradictory depending on who is interpreting the data) that the coca/cocaine economy also has an adverse effect on basic food production in Bolivia. Labor costs increase regionally as people dedicate their time to the coca/cocaine trade and land that might grow foodstuffs is dedicated to coca. The probable effect—increased commercial food and food-aid imports notwithstanding—has been a rise in the real cost of foodstuffs. As a consequence, people outside subsistence agriculture who are either unwilling or unable to integrate themselves into the cocaine economy become further impoverished as they spend more of their real incomes to try to stay abreast nutritionally.[83]

Some of the economic impacts from coca/cocaine production and trade that affect individuals and institutions have been examined. These have all derived from the creation and movement of illicit products. Other economic impacts derive from international efforts to stamp out the trade, including eradication and alternative development programs.

Coca eradication obviously affects farming families substantially if their crops are selected for destruction. Fortunately for the growers, there has been very little, if any, net reduction in coca hectarage due to eradication. Thus, eradication has had little national economic impact in Bolivia, although, to be sure, individual families and some areas have been severely affected. Alternative development programs, which in effect pay growers not to grow coca, have had a more substantial impact. Most of it has been positive for the thousands involved, although the underlying purpose of the projects—to reduce aggregate coca growing—has not been achieved. It is useful to deal with alternative development in some detail in order to see how various kinds of drug-control programs have affected Bolivia.

Alternative development. Alternative development in its many guises —e.g., crop substitution, socioeconomic development, integrated rural development—has been attempted most vigorously in Bolivia and Thailand. The attempt is to devise some way for peasants to earn attractive incomes other than by growing crops destined for the illegal-drug trade—opium poppies in the case of Thailand, coca bushes in the case of Bolivia. Alternative development is more acceptable politically than other means generally employed to reduce illicit-drug supplies—e.g., crop eradication, incarceration, institutional terrorism. Its attraction is that it promises a reward of new income opportunities within the context of socioeconomic development.

Hardly anyone doubts that continued crop eradication is required if alternative development is to work. Otherwise, it would be virtually impossible to close the income differentials between growing coca and other income opportunities. Thus, the combined strategy is to suppress the coca economy through destruction of coca bushes and trafficker networks and to elevate every other possible economy. This is a difficult feat, given that product scarcities tend to raise, not lower, prices. Thus, it is necessary to destroy the trafficker networks along with crops in order to depress the coca market. In Bolivia's case it is necessary to depress coca prices below about U.S. $30 per *carga* (approximately one hundred pounds) and to raise alternative incomes above that figure with similar factor inputs of land, labor, and capital.[84] This makes alternative development a world-class challenge; it requires technical assistance, markets, infrastructure, productive investment, and social services. Otherwise coca cultivation will be the preferred income activity.

In Bolivia the virtues of alternative development have been enshrined in elaborate legislation. The guiding assumption is that failure of rural development has caused the peasants to move into coca. Thus the policy mandate and expected consequence: Correct the rural-development failures and coca production will decline commensurately. The Bolivian government, the United Nations, and the U.S. government vigorously support alternative development for this purpose, at least in principle.

Practice tells another story. Painter shows that linking interdiction and development has biased policy application toward interdiction. Indeed, Bolivians speak of "repressive development," or *desarrollo interdictivo*.[85] Conditionality clauses insist on achieving eradication targets before alternative development funds are released. Contradictions abound. For instance, lime could help neutralize the Chapare's acidic soils so that something other than coca could grow. But lime is a precursor chemical for cocaine processing, and its importation into the Chapare is prohibited. Likewise, farm-to-market roads into the Chapare are needed so that agricultural products other than coca can be sold,[86] but USAID stopped funding road construction because it aided drug traffickers. The DEA even blew up highways in the Chapare essential for getting goods to market; small aircraft were apparently landing on the roads for drug pickups. Likewise, the United States squelched an electricity-distribution project that was needed to create off-farm employment in the Chapare for fear that the plant would help the illicit-drug trade.[87]

The dilemma is clear. Without agricultural inputs, farm-to-market transportation infrastructure, basic energy, and bedrock social services, alternative development cannot work. However, providing such factors in drug-growing areas may aid the traffickers. Drug-control administrators are truly in a difficult position. But there is a way out: In Bolivia, alternative development is emphasized *outside* the Chapare and other drug-growing regions as well as within them. The hope is that success elsewhere will deter migration into drug-growing regions, reduce the resident labor force, and therefore diminish coca production. Unfortunately, there is a caveat: Labor-force reductions in the Chapare sufficient to reduce coca production would likely cause the price of coca and labor to rise, giving workers in alternative development areas considerable incentive to go to coca-growing regions, where their labor would command the best return. Again, a key necessity in all these plans is the virtually complete destruction of trafficker networks so that a farmgate market for coca leaves dries up.

Clearly, with alternative development emphases being carried out in non-drug-growing areas as well as within them and with a potentially mobile labor force that can migrate, reverse migrate, and remigrate, it is not possible to do other than think of replacement incomes. Thus, alternative development in Bolivia is not geared to replace a hectare of coca with a hectare of something else but rather to provide competitive jobs and incomes for a mobile labor force, particularly in areas where transportation infrastructure is denied because it aids the traffickers. Thus, "social emergency funds" have been created to provide short-term employment for farmers who give up their coca. The United States has stepped in with balance-of-payments support to replace some of the foreign exchange lost and thereby to reduce the Bolivian government's anxiety. Foreign investors are also being courted to diversify the economy and provide jobs.[88]

Aid for alternative development comes from three main sources: USAID, the Bolivian government, and the UNDCP. In reality, the United States provides most of the money advanced by the Bolivian government. Most of UNDCP's funds come from European countries. Therefore, with overall funding mostly originating outside Bolivia, alternative development is likely a net economic improvement to the country—that is, if it is assumed that any external funds are better than no funds, and that some people benefiting is better than no one benefiting.

USAID money is channeled through the Chapare Regional Development Project (CRDP), established in 1983, the main recipients being IBTA-Chapare (agricultural research and extension centers at La Jota and Chipiriri), PDAC/PDAR (alternative development and regional alternative development programs for Cochabamba, including funding for the national road service), and the Associated High Valley (AHV) project.

In 1992, development aid from USAID was $31 million. Painter has desegregated this figure and others for previous years, concluding that "the actual amount of money spent on alternative development that directly aids or reaches coca producers since 1983 has been remarkably small; the amount spent in the Chapare even smaller; and the amount spent on concrete, productive, income-generating activities there even smaller still."[89] Some people have calculated the total 1991 productive investment capable of creating alternative income sources for coca growers in the Chapare to be a mere U.S. $667,000.[90] Unsurprisingly, coca growing goes on largely unabated by any USAID efforts. Net benefits do accrue to Bolivians even though the program's goals of reducing coca production go unmet.

USAID's funds to the IBTA-Chapare agricultural and extension research centers appear to be better spent from a technical point of view. The centers have identified crops that can be grown in the Chapare—macadamia nuts, coconut, peanuts, spices, black pepper, dyes, hearts of palm, and various tropical fruits such as maracuya, bananas, pineapples, and passion fruit—and they have developed agronomic systems to control weeds and pests and eliminate the need for large amounts of commercial fertilizers.[91] Remarkably, however, the research centers have paid little or no attention to marketing needs or prices. Hence, what can be grown is usually not grown because farm-to-market infrastructure is inadequate, prices are unattractive, inputs are too expensive, or sufficient credit on acceptable terms is unavailable. On the whole, coca growers continue to grow coca. According to Painter, "the failure to study and identify markets for alternative crops was one of the main reasons why it took eight years of IBTA experimentation before any alternative crop could be exported from the Chapare."[92] The long planting-to-harvest lead times of slow-growing crops such as macadamia—which requires ten years to mature—further complicate this whole matter, even if the science and the markets are right.

Only in 1991 did the first Chapare exports—turmeric, pineapples, and bananas—appear, bringing a gross return to growers of approximately $800,000, a net economic boost to probably fewer than 550 families in the Chapare.[93] The coca unions are critical of this paltry amount. The peasants keep growing coca.

With so many alternative-development implementation problems in the Chapare, attention turned to keeping people from migrating to the region by providing them jobs and income in their own villages or regions in the high valleys of Cochabamba. Resources were redirected away from the Chapare to the AHV project. The program was begun, but not in the areas contributing most migratory labor to the Chapare. Thus, there is considerable doubt that the main aim of the project—to stem migration—will be achieved.[94]

The UNDCP began its first alternative development project in the Yungas in 1985. Its objectives were twofold: reduce farmers' economic dependence on coca and thwart increased production in new colonization areas in the Yungas. The UN chose a package of services: new crops, new technologies, agroindustrial processing, soft credits, and farm-to-market infrastructure. To benefit, farmers had to sign up and agree not to expand their coca production.[95]

The principal alternative crop was a new variety of coffee. The yields were much higher than for old coffee varieties, and, despite a slump in world coffee prices and the Bolivian government's designation in 1988 of most of the Yungas as a "traditional coca-growing zone" whose inhabitants did not need to worry about their coca being eradicated, the results have nevertheless been quite positive for the 2,400 participating families. Their incomes have held steady while other farmers who chose not to participate saw theirs drop by 34 percent.[96] Social services and infrastructure have improved for participants, and there is less dependence on coca growing. It is not known whether the Yungas's contribution of migratory workers to the Chapare has in any way diminished.

One problem and one enigma remain. The problem: UNDCP's efforts were stoutly resisted by coca-growers' unions, and some violence ensued; generalizing UNDCP's program would surely generate even greater resistance. The enigma: Coca growing in "transitional" areas of the Yungas expanded in 1986 and 1987 to 8,900 hectares (but dropped in 1990 to 8,200).[97] Clearly, 2,400 families benefited from the program, but it is unclear if in the aggregate its goals were achieved. They probably were not.

With the tacit permission of USAID, the United Nations, through UNDCP's predecessor, UNFDAC, moved into the Chapare in 1988 with goals similar to those it had undertaken in the Yungas. It offered a package that would enhance income opportunities and diversify the local peasant economy, thereby reducing dependence on coca. Forty-five communities benefited from drinking-water improvements; 4,000 families enjoyed new or improved roads; an electrical generating grid was planned and work begun; six small agroindustrial plants were either built or improved; and dairy facilities were constructed at Ivirgarzama to process 50,000 liters of milk a day, giving some 3,000 families who provided the milk a new income source.

The militant coca unions were won over and agreed to participate, which UNDCP concluded was good evidence of their program's success.[98] Nevertheless, nothing UNDCP did was sufficient to reduce coca prices below U.S. $30 per carga or convincingly increase equivalent wages in alternative pursuits above that amount. People may have had a better life with better nutrition, infrastructure, income, and social amenities, but coca production was not changed much.

There are only three basic ways to pursue a supply-suppression strategy. The first is to eradicate and interdict; the second is to create alternative development opportunities; and the third is to employ a combination of eradication and development. The first brings no benefits to growers and has not proven successful in meeting crop-reduction goals. The second has brought considerable improvement in the quality of life of thousands of Bolivian growers but also has not brought about desired levels of crop reduction. It may be too early to tell if the third will be more productive.

The point is clear, however. On balance, the economic benefits of the illicit-drug trade to Bolivia derive from people's being engaged in the illicit market, from their being engaged *not* to be engaged in the illicit market, and from their being engaged in both at the same time. Thousands of individuals have benefited from the illicit-drug trade in Bolivia, and coca continues to flourish.

Social Consequences

One notable consequence of the drug industry for Bolivia is upward mobility. The illicit-drug trade makes it possible for thousands of families and tens of thousands of individuals to amass heretofore undreamed-of incomes, some of which they spend on education, health, and skill development. Some individuals reap not only short-term economic benefits but also enhanced prospects for future generations.

Income gains are complicated, however, by conspicuous consumption, which is more of a problem perhaps in Bolivia than in Colombia despite Colombians' grabbing the lion's share of illicit-drug profits. In Bolivia, the vast majority of the population is uniformly poor. There is no significant industrial elite. Commercial and landed elites tend to be of a "traditional kind" and have been tolerated as they reemerged from oblivion following the 1952 civil war. Thus, a "bright new economic burner"—usually a drug trafficker—is both readily noticed and readily emulated. The illicit-drug trade may provide the only opportunities for social and economic upward mobility available to many Bolivians. Thousands of Bolivians are drawn each year to savor the benefits. Talent—labor, management, social support, entrepreneurial—that might otherwise enter the formal economy finds its way into the informal one, principally in the illicit-drug trade.

If emulation of illicit activities is in any way prejudicial to the social well-being of a society, Bolivia is in trouble. But emulation that drains productive talent and investment from the formal economy may not be the most significant part of the social problem. The bedrock difficulty is emulation of an activity that must necessarily respond to new competition with violence. Because of the inherently oligopolistic nature of the greatest income-earning activities in the illicit-drug trade, the industry cannot spread its major benefits to all newcomers. Moreover, conflicts cannot be resolved in the legal system as could perhaps be done within the formal economy.

Thus, social emulation could lead to the "Colombianization" of the informal economy in Bolivia, with an increase in violence, a cheapening of life, radicalization of the military and police, and a general decay in an already low standard of living for most of the population. Moreover, when the drug economy eventually busts, the social result will likely be ruthless. This likelihood does not augur well for those trying to raise a new generation of Bolivian youth interested in legitimate development and the kinds of family and personal sacrifices required to achieve it. A lot of people therefore worry about social values in the wake of conspicuous consumption. As Bolivia attempts to incorporate more value-added activities within its borders, a concentration of wealth will continue to occur. If Colombia's experience is any guide, owners of that wealth will not make productive investments so much as they will conspicuously consume it or hide it in safe havens abroad.

Another principal social consequence in Bolivia, more so than in Colombia, is migration. Tens of thousands of peasants and low-income workers have migrated to the Chapare and other coca-growing regions, leaving ancestral homelands and, frequently, their families. Painter notes that what they find "is a sorry story of bad sanitation, bad hygiene, and insufficient housing as well as high infant mortality, severe malnutrition, and numerous dropouts from junior and senior schools."[99] But the same conditions generally exist in the migrants' ancestral villages, so surroundings and circumstances in the drug-growing regions do not impede migration. People are pushed from the highlands, by low opportunities, made annually worse by increasing demographic pressures, and pulled to the Chapare by economic opportunities despite the grimness of social amenities there.

In the short term these opportunities in new settlement areas—both promised and real—have provided a safety valve against general social upheaval. In the long term, the problems of emulation, speculation, and oligopolization will continue to present new rounds of social challenges for Bolivia.

Political Consequences

In Bolivia, the most obvious political consequence of the drug trade is public corruption. The Roberto Suárez family helped to finance the 1980 military coup of General Lucas García Meza.[100] The general and his confidants turned the country into an official haven for illicit-drug traffickers, the government itself being chief among them. Consequently, bribing police and government and judicial officials is now considered routine despite Bolivia's reentry into the community of respectable nations. The United States, which continues to give significant aid to Bolivia's military, nevertheless asserted in December 1989 that "all elements of the military are involved in drug trafficking to some extent and police, prosecutors and courts have been subject to corruption and intimidation."[101]

Almost everyone inside and outside Bolivia assumes that drug money has penetrated the highest reaches of everything. Part of the reason is economic. In 1990 a Bolivian soldier earned U.S. $50 a month, his commanding officer $300 a month, a member of congress $800 a month,[102] and members of the judiciary about the same. A trafficker may offer a judge $15,000 for a favorable decision; a commanding officer will receive that much or more if a drug shipment is in jeopardy. Few Bolivians appear to have the stomach to resist such enticements as a matter of principle.

Corruption is also evidenced by the fact that high-visibility murders remain unsolved (e.g., Bolivian scientist Noel Kempff Mercado, who stumbled onto a major cocaine factory in the Santa Cruz department while doing field research. The complex was apparently being protected by local police and politicians).[103] Top drug traffickers are also set free or allowed to escape. UMOPAR officials are caught facilitating the traffic they have a public trust to destroy. Political parties are compromised by drug money. Senior politicians are on the take.[104] Nevertheless, Bolivia does have ten years of "democracy" under its belt, and the optimists consider that a good sign.

Impact on the Environment

In Colombia, where coca growing is less prominent than cocaine manufacturing, the environmental impact of the industry is mostly felt in waterways polluted from discarded laboratory chemicals. However, the impact on countries such as Bolivia, where much slash-and-burn agriculture transpires, is more obvious and equally as damaging. Among the impacts are deforestation as new lands are cleared, attendant hillside erosion and river silting as freshly cleared lands meet the rainy season, pollution of rivers and waterways (as in Colombia) from discarded precursor chemicals, and chemical contamination of soil and water and ecological alterations through excessive use of pesticides (increasingly necessary as coca production becomes monoculture).[105] Some areas are hit worse than others. For example, the steep hillside cultivation in the Yungas undertaken by the few novice growers there has proven an environmental minidisaster. And the intense pesticidal applications in the Chapare are now even contaminating the groundwater.

One obvious impact is deforestation, which has spilled over even into national park reserves. Around 780,000 hectares have been cleared for coca cultivation in the Chapare alone.[106] However, the most damaging impact, as Painter sees it, is associated with the increasing processing that is now occurring on Bolivian soil. The lime, sodium carbonate, sulfuric acid, kerosene, acetone, and hydrochloric acid used in the processing range from being moderately toxic to extremely destructive of the environment. Around 30,000 tons of toxic chemicals are flushed down the waterways each year, and this does not count what the police confiscate and then characteristically discard in the country's waterways. Nor does it count the 200,000 tons of contaminated coca leaves thrown about annually and left to leach into the soil.

Summary and Conclusions

Socioeconomic and political effects of the illicit-drug industry derive from consumption, production, trade, and the drug-control laws themselves. In the countries under study in this chapter—Colombia and Bolivia—the principal effects are associated with production, trade, and drug-control laws, although consumption poses a great potential problem.

Production and trade create both short- and long-term benefits and liabilities. At an individual and family level, these activities offer new income sources that are much appreciated and coveted among people for whom grinding poverty is a generational way of life; among the few enriched traffickers, conspicuous consumption and despotic power are heady drugs. By the same token, traditional values are eroded as illegality permeates a society, violence becomes a way of life, and people become less inclined to accept norms on which consensual politics (including liberal democracy) rest.

At a societal level, production and trade shore up foreign-exchange earnings. They produce regional economic multipliers as new money is spent on more food, shelter, and clothing. They also create safety nets for large numbers of people who cannot sustain an existence in chaotic formal economies. But the industry also produces liabilities and victims for a society. Traffickers infiltrate bureaucracies, buy public decisions, make alliances with insurrectionist ideologues, and conduct business through violence and intimidation. They foster illegal markets and thereby disrupt the formal economy, create an anti-state wholly outside both the rule of law and central government control, inspire law-enforcement responses costing hundreds of millions of dollars, and introduce macroeconomic distortions that make it almost impossible for central banks to control anything.

Drug-control laws themselves are strong factors in this mix deriving from the illicit-drug industry because most of the benefits and liabilities associated with production and trade ultimately derive from illegality itself. Drug-control laws produce a "crime tax," the difference between prices in legal and illegal markets. That difference produces heavy profits in an illegal economy and draws hordes of risk-prone or desperate people to try to reap them. Most of the profits go to the traffickers. A relative pittance trickles down to producers, but, given their other options, it is enough to keep them heavily engaged in producing for the illicit market.

Unfortunately, although drug-control laws have contributed little to suppressing the illicit-drug trade, they *have* contributed much to social dislocations, corruption, militarization, abuse of human rights, and a general disregard for human decency. The most transparent of these is violence, which traffickers in Colombia have nurtured with abandon and which those in Bolivia could well be on the verge of figuring out how to create.

Colombia's economy could do better without the illicit-drug industry, Bolivia's probably not. In Bolivia, grassroots populations earn money from being in the illicit-drug industry and from being paid by international entities to stay out of the industry (e.g., through alternative development projects); they profit by playing the industry and its antagonists off against each other. Some observers have estimated that up to a quarter of Bolivia's economically active population makes a significant portion of its income from the illicit-drug trade or the many ancillary economic opportunities that it creates. No economic activity on the horizon appears capable of absorbing the hundreds of thousands of people thus employed into a legal, formal economy. This fact presents difficult policy options for Bolivia.

At the social level, the drug trade has exacerbated endemic violence in Colombia and threatens to do the same in Bolivia. Both the reality and the threat severely weaken each country's efforts to create modern democratic institutions. In Colombia's case, the exacerbation is brought about by the illegal-drug trade's tendency to concentrate wealth and produce oligopolies in the informal economy. In Bolivia's case, the prospects are created by the sheer desperation people feel at the prospect that the government's antidrug efforts will destroy an activity that allows them to subsist.

In both Colombia and Bolivia, the drug trade has helped to relieve population pressures by encouraging migration to new areas for colonization and settlement. This trend may have had the unfortunate consequence of prolonging each government's inability to modernize to match the needs of rapidly changing societies.

At a political level, both governments are hard pressed to retain jurisdiction over the countryside and prevent their own collapse from internal corruption and bureaucratic rot. In Colombia, the illicit-drug industry has accelerated the delegitimation of the country's political and social institutions. It has done so by spurring the underground economy, contributing to growing violence, undermining the legal system, intimidating judges, corrupting state political and administrative functionaries, and promoting expectations of high extraordinary short-term profits, thereby encouraging, speculative investments. The government's inability to implement social and economic measures such as land reform or anti-inflation policies has made matters worse.

Aside from socioeconomic and political effects of the illicit-drug trade, Bolivia, in particular, presents evidence of the trade's impact on the environment—deforestation, water pollution (caused by the discarding of used chemicals into waterways and by ground leaching), and erosion of hillsides and silting of rivers.

Colombia and Bolivia present prototypical cases in which the benefits and liabilities of production, trade, and drug-control laws are vividly seen. In this chapter I have looked into economic, social, and political/administrative impacts in Colombia and Bolivia and attempted to assess their ramifications, including some of the unintended consequences of policy initiatives. Many of the ramifications and consequences are evident in the other countries under study, and some of the lessons learned here also apply. The trick is to move beyond error and into concrete results.

Notes

1. See, for example, LaMond Tullis, *Handbook of Research on the Illicit Drug Traffic: Socioeconomic and Political Consequences* (Westport, Conn: Greenwood Press, 1991), Chapter 6.

2. David Kline, "From a Smugglers' Paradise Comes Hell," *Maclean's*, 8 November 1982, 14; David Kline, "The Khyber Connection," *Christian Science Monitor*, three-part series, 9–11 November 1982; U.S. Department of State, Bureau of International Narcotics Matters, *International Narcotics Control Strategy Report* (Washington, D.C.: U.S. Government Printing Office, (1989, 1990, 1991, 1993, 1994), hereinafter cited as *INCSR*.

3. Richard Weintraub, "Pakistani Drug Drive Seen in 2 Major Hauls; Military Officers Held in Seizure of Heroin," *Washington Post*, 31 July 1986, A27.

4. Yev Yelin, "Why the 'Golden Crescent' Still Flourishes," *New York Times*, weekly news summary, 28–31 July 1985.

5. Henry Kamm, "Afghan Opium Yield up as Pakistan Curbs Crop," *New York Times*, 14 April 1988, A16.

6. Rensselaer W. Lee III, "Why the U.S. Cannot Stop South American Cocaine," *Orbis* 32 (Fall 1988), 499–519.

7. Bruce M. Bagley, "The New Hundred Years War? U.S. National Security and the War on Drugs in Latin America," *Journal of Interamerican Studies and World Affairs* 30:1 (1988), 161–182.

8. John McBeth, "The Opium Laws," *Far Eastern Economic Review*, 29 March 1984, 40–43.

9. The early theoretical literature on these points is reviewed in LaMond Tullis, *Politics and Social Change in Third World Countries* (New York: Wiley, 1973); and LaMond Tullis, *Lord and Peasant in Peru: A Paradigm of Political and Social Change* (Cambridge, Mass.: Harvard University Press, 1970).

10. James A. Inciardi, *The War on Drugs: Heroin, Cocaine, Crime and Public Policy* (Palo Alto, Calif.: Mayfield, 1986).

11. Principal source on Colombia is Francisco Thoumi, *Political Economy and Illegal Drugs in Colombia* (Boulder, Colo.: Lynne Rienner Publishers, 1994).

12. Ibid., Chapters 1 and 2.

13. Ibid., 135.

14. Ibid., 182.

15. Ibid., 179–195.

16. Ibid., 197.

17. World Bank, *World Development Report 1992* (New York: Oxford University Press, 1994), Table 3, 166.

18. Thoumi indicates that these data come from the Interamerican Development Bank's data bank and are based on the official national accounts of Colombia.

19. Thoumi, *Political Economy and Illegal Drugs*, 197.

20. Ibid., 199.

21. The financial capabilities of the Medellín group have overpowered rural areas. Thoumi informs us that "the profits from a small planeload of cocaine that smuggled 250 kilos into the United States in 1985, after paying $150,000 to the pilot and ditching the $100,000 plane, were enough to purchase between 1,200 and 4,800 hectares. In other words, the size of illegal profits is so large relative to the value of many Colombian assets that, even if one accepts the lower estimates of drug income, their impact on the Colombian economy can be extraordinary" (Thoumi, *Political Economy and Illegal Drugs*, 199).

22. Ibid., 161.

23. Ibid., 241–249.

24. Thoumi draws on McGee and Feige, who argue that the growth of the underground economy in the United States during and after the Vietnam War resulted in overestimations of unemployment and inflation levels in the late 1970s, which induced policymakers to implement stronger policy measures than were necessary and that deepened the recession of the early 1980s (Robert T. McGee and Edgar L. Feige, "Policy Illusion, Macroeconomic Instability, and the Unrecorded Economy," in Edgar L. Feige, ed.,*The Underground Economies: Tax Evasion and Information Distortion* (Cambridge: Cambridge University Press, 1989), 81–109.

25. Thoumi, *Political Economy and Illegal Drugs*, 246.

26. Ibid., 200.

27. Ibid., 238.

28. Ibid.

29. Ibid., 247–248. Thoumi develops the seven categories summarized here.

30. Ibid., 247.

31. Thoumi cites Eduardo Sarmiento, "Economía del Narcotráfico," in Carlos G. Arrieta, et al., *Narcotráfico en Colombia: Dimensiones Políticas, Económicas, Jurídicas e Internacionales* (Bogotá: Tercer Mundo Editores-Ediciones Uniandes, 1990), 43–98; and Eduardo Sarmiento, "Economía del Narcotráfico," *Desarrollo y Sociedad* 26 (September 1990): 11–40.

32. Thoumi, *Political Economy and Illegal Drugs*, 249.

33. Ibid., 72. See also Richard B. Craig, "Colombian Narcotics and United States–Colombian Relations," *Journal of Interamerican Studies and World Affairs* 23:3 (1981), 243–270; Comisión Andina de Juristas, *Violencia en Colombia* (Lima: La Comisión, 1990); and *La Violencia en Colombia: 40 Años de Laterinto* (Bogotá, Colombia: Pontificia Universidad Javeriana, Facultad de Estudios Interdisciplinarios, Programa de Estudios Políticos, 1989).

34. Thoumi cites Rodrigo Losada and Eduardo Vélez, "Muertes Violentas en Colombia, 1979–1986," Informe de Investigación (Bogotá: Instituto SER de Investigación, April 1988).

35. Thoumi, *Political Economy and Illegal Drugs*, 72–73.

36. Ibid., 73–74.

37. Ibid., 238.

38. Ibid., 75, citing FEDESARROLLO and Instituto SER de Investigación, "Indicadores Sociales," *Coyuntura Social* 2 (May 1990): 36–37.

39. Thoumi, *Political Economy and Illegal Drugs*, 77.

40. Ibid., 77–78.

41. Ibid., 200.

42. Ibid., 236.

43. Ibid., 239.

44. Ibid., 239–240.

45. Ibid., 267, citing Augusto Pérez G., "Los Años Ochentas," in Augusto Pérez G. ed., *Historia de la Drogadicción en Colombia* (Bogotá: Tercer Mundo —Ediciones Uniandes), 111–116.

46. See, for example, John Ross, "Colombia: Judge's Murder Linked to Drug Mafias," *Latinamerica Press*, 4 September 1986, 6; and U.S. Congress, House Committee on Foreign Affairs, Hearing, "Recent Developments in Colombia," One Hundredth Congress, Second Session (Washington, D.C.: U.S. Government Printing Office, 1988).

47. See U.S. Congress, House Report of a Staff Study Mission to Peru, Bolivia, Colombia, and Mexico, 19 November to 18 December 1988 to the Committee on Foreign Affairs, "U.S. Narcotics Control Programs in Peru, Bolivia, Colombia, and Mexico: An Update," One Hundred First Congress, First Session (Washington, D.C.: U.S. Government Printing Office), 1989.

48. See, for example, "Clean-up Campaign Gives Poor Results," *Latin American Weekly Report*, 18 May 1984, 9; "President Turns Right for Support," *Latin American Weekly Report*, 8 June 1985, 5; and Alan Riding, "Shaken Colombia Acts at Last on Drugs," *New York Times*, 11 September 1984, 1.

49. Thoumi, *Political Economy and Illegal Drugs*, 139.

50. Ibid., 141.

51. Ibid., 141–142.

52. Ibid., 143–144.

53. Ibid., 144. See also Fabio Castillo, *Los Jinetes de la Cocaína* (Bogotá: Editorial Documentos Periodísticos, 1987), 14; and Guy Gugliotta and Jeff Leen, *Kings of Cocaine: An Astonishing True Story of Murder, Money and International Corruption* (New York: Simon and Schuster, 1989), 154.

54. Castillo, *Los Jinetes*, 19–25.
55. Robert D. McFadden, "Head of Medellín Cocaine Cartel Is Killed by Troops in Colombia," *New York Times*, 3 December 1993, A1.
56. Thoumi, *Political Economy and Illegal Drugs*, 159.
57. Ibid.
58. Ibid., 236.
59. Principal source on Bolivia is James Painter, *Bolivia and Coca: A Study in Dependency* (Boulder, Colo.: Lynne Rienner Publishers, 1994).
60. See, for example, "Colombianization," *World Press Review*, February 1989, 40.
61. Painter, *Bolivia and Coca*, 141.
62. Ibid., 140.
63. See Ibid., Chapter 4.
64. Ibid., 140.
65. Ibid., 35.
66. Ibid., 35. Painter cites as source José Antonio Quiroga, *Coca/Cocaína: Una Visión Boliviana* (La Paz: AIPE–PROCOM/CEDLA/CID, 1990), 34.
67. World Bank, *World Development Report 1994*, 162 and 166, Tables 1 and 3.
68. Painter, *Bolivia and Coca*, 34–40.
69. Ibid., 40.
70. Ibid., Chapter 3.
71. Ibid., 42.
72. LaMond Tullis, "Cocaine and Food: Likely Effects of a Burgeoning Transnational Industry on Food Production in Bolivia and Peru," in W. Ladd Hollist and LaMond Tullis, eds., *Pursuing Food Security: Strategies and Obstacles in Africa, Asia, Latin America, and the Middle East*(Boulder, Colo.: Lynne Rienner Publishers, 1987), 247–283.
73. Painter, *Bolivia and Coca*, 54.
74. Ibid., 55.
75. Ibid., 56.
76. Painter noted Jeffrey Frank's argument that coca production raises all incomes by an average of at least U.S. $43, or 6.4 percent, using a low estimate of the value of coca/cocaine revenue remaining in the country (p. 56). See Jeffrey Franks, "La Economía de la Coca en Bolivia: ¿Plaga o Salvación?" *Informe Confidencial* 64 (June 1991), 10.
77. Painter, *Bolivia and Coca*, 57, referring to Kevin Healy, "The Boom Within the Crisis: Some Recent Effects of Foreign Cocaine Markets on Bolivian Rural Society and Economy," in Deborah Pacini and Christine Franquemont, eds., *Coca and Cocaine: Effects on People and Policy in Latin America* (Cambridge Mass: Cultural Survival, 1985.)
78. Painter, *Bolivia and Coca*, 57.
79. Ibid., 60.
80. Interest earned on dollar accounts was around 14 percent, highly competitive by regional standards, and done as a conscious governmental policy by adoption of a neoliberal economic model. Painter says that by "mid-1991 deposits in the private banks had climbed to over U.S. $1 billion (of which around 85 percent were held in dollars rather than in *bolivianos*, a steady increase from a low of around $500 million in mid-1989" (Painter, *Bolivia and Coca*, 61).
81. Ibid., 61.
82. Ibid., 61–62.

83. Ibid., 63–65. See also Tullis, "Cocaine and Food."

84. Painter, *Bolivia and Coca*, 106.

85. Ibid., 106. Painter refers to C. Balderrama's criticisms in *Opinión* (Cochabamba), 23 July 1991. Balderrama was auditor for the Federación Especial de Trabajadores Campesinos del Trópico de Cochabamba (FETCTC) and a researcher at the Centro de Información y Documentación para el Desarrollo Regional (CIDRE).

86. Coca/cocaine does not require an equivalent infrastructure. The value/weight ratio of cocaine and even coca makes it entirely economical for animal and human "beasts of burden" to move them about for processing and pickup.

87. Painter, *Bolivia and Coca*, 107–108.

88. Ibid., 108–136 passim.

89. Ibid., 109.

90. Ibid., 111. Painter draws attention to Alvaro Moscoso's quotes in *La Razón* (La Paz), 6 December 1991. Moscoso was president of the Civic Committee in Cochabamba.

91. Painter, *Bolivia and Coca*, 114.

92. Ibid., 116–117.

93. Ibid., 117.

94. Ibid., 119–122.

95. Ibid., 127.

96. Ibid., 128. See, especially, Econométrica, *Análisis del proyecto AgroYungas: AD/BOL/84/405* (La Paz: Econométrica,1990).

97. Painter, *Bolivia and Coca*, 129. The data are presented in Table 1.1.

98. Ibid., 131.

99. Ibid., 58.

100. Ibid., 59. See also Arthur M. Shapiro, "Drugs and Politics in Latin America: The Argentine Connections," *The New Leader*, 27 June 1988, 9; Scott Armstrong, "U.S.-Bolivia Relations Further Strained as Cocaine Smuggling Charges Fly," *Christian Science Monitor*, 14 August 1980; "Cocaine: The Military Connection," *Latin America Regional Reports*, 5 August 1980; and, Gregorio Selser, *Bolivia: El Cuartelazo de los Cocadólares* (Mexico: Mexsur, 1982).

101. Painter, *Bolivia and Coca*, 71, citing *DEA Review*, December 1989, 58, quoted in U.S. Congress, House Committee on Government Operations, "United States Anti-narcotic Activities in the Andean Region" (Washington, D.C.: U.S. Government Printing Office, 1990), 41.

102. Painter, *Bolivia and Coca*, 71.

103. See, for example, "Bolivia under Paz Estenssoro," *Latinamerica Press*, 20 October 1988, 6.

104. Painter, *Bolivia and Coca*, 70–74. See also Anturiano Hurtado, *La Hiena: Drama Social Sobre la Droga, Drogadicción, y Corrupción* (Santa Cruz, Bolivia: Empresa Editora El País, 1986); Shirley Christian, "Drug Case Raises Doubts in Bolivia," *New York Times*, 5 May 1988, A3; Richard B. Craig, "Illicit Drug Traffic: Implications for South American Source Countries," *Journal of Interamerican Studies and World Affairs* 29 (Summer 1987), 18; and David Kline, "How to Lose the Coke War," *Atlantic* 259:5 (1987), 22–27.

105. Painter, *Bolivia and Coca*, 66, referring to U.S. Congress, Senate Committee on Governmental Affairs, *Cocaine Production, Eradication, and the Environment: Policy, Impact and Options* (Washington, D.C.: U.S. Government Printing Office, 1990), passim.

106. Painter, *Bolivia and Coca*, 67.

... 6 ...

What Ought to Be Done? Consequences of Action and Inaction

What ought to be done? What *can* be done? What would the consequences be? These questions are scaldingly debated nationally and internationally. It is not just drug policy but the values underlying it that create the mischief. Judgments about what *can* be done are therefore inexorably tied to judgments about what *ought* to be done. Perspectives on both vary, ranging from militaristic annihilation of producers and consumers alike to full tolerance of "harmless" vices. Further complicating the discussion, at every bend in the policy river the "oughts" and "cans" meet the political whitecaps of consequences, both intended and unintended.

The turbulence deriving from the intermeshing of "oughts," "cans," and "consequences" frequently puts the interests of net producer and net consumer countries on a collision course. Understandably, therefore, hardly anyone is happy about either the world's present drug-control/drug-consumption condition or any of the recommendations to ameliorate it.

The purpose of this chapter is to advance at least one reasonable "ought" and to look into some of the likely intended and unintended consequences of achieving it, showing not only how far apart the interests of net producer and net consumer countries are but also how net producers' interests are pitted against each other. The analysis offers modest suggestions for two case-study countries—Colombia and Bolivia.

The observations about "oughts," "cans," and "consequences" advanced in this chapter will not appeal either to moral zealots or absolute relativists. They rest on an important "ought," embedded in the following question: How might harm associated with the production, consumption, and trade of psychoactive substances and the laws designed to control them be reduced? The focus is therefore on pragmatic approaches to *harm reduction*,[1] particularly as this concept may apply to illicit drugs' socioeconomic and political impacts on such net producer countries as those reviewed in this study.

We begin with one virtually proven premise: Regardless of one's values and the "oughts" that derive from them, the country studies on which this report is based universally acclaim that North America, Europe, and other net consumer regions are unlikely to solve their illicit-drug consumption problems by continuing or intensifying existing supply-suppression strategies. The lack of alternative income-earning possibilities among rural people in net producing countries is too substantial; the price differential between licit and illicit crops is too great; the astronomical profits traffickers may acquire in a moderately risky, illegal business are too enticing; and traffickers' abilities to elude law-enforcement efforts are too abundant (or replacements for those caught in law-enforcement nets too readily available). Even if supply suppression is successful in one area, new plantings and production quickly find a more congenial home elsewhere—the phenomenon of "problem migration." Clearly, on the foundation of failure alone, a mandate exists for a new course.

Because the present global supply-suppression strategy continues to be so vigorously advanced in some quarters, as a prelude to discussing other options it is useful to review why this failed approach cannot in almost any of its proffered permutations be a prescription for future drug-control success, regardless of the spin politicians may put on it. If an intensified supply-suppression strategy is to work as a credible international consumption-control strategy, it must be globally applied so as not to allow "balloon effects" or problem migration to occur. Yet global application would require income replacements for farmers; otherwise, they can simply move to areas outside central government control to continue or to initiate production of drug crops. Such an application would also necessitate the virtual dismantling of trafficker networks (in order to suppress farmgate prices and thereby create overwhelming economic disincentives to growers).

To implement such a policy or policies globally, sufficient money, domestic and international political will, and regimes of substantial political incorruptibility must exist. It is widely (and correctly) believed that insufficient domestic and international money, political will, and incorrupt polticians and political systems have been marshaled so far. Behavioral incentives of major political actors all pull in the wrong direction. Hardly any drug-prohibition policy (including alcohol prohibition) tried anywhere in the world over the past 250 years would offer a convincing alternative view from historical precedent.

Although supply suppression is unlikely to solve global illicit-drug problems, certain regions may nevertheless solve some of their own supply problems—principally by exporting them to other countries or regions. Thailand has been successful in suppressing production (although not trafficking). Through vigorous law-enforcement and alternative development and crop-replacement programs, the country has managed to send most of its drug-production problems to Laos and Myanmar/Burma. Since 1989, cultivated hectares of opium poppy in Thailand have been cut in half.[2] But *global* production has not been affected by these regional supply-suppression successes.

Although there has been no global dent in opium or heroin production, Thailand at least has been able to alter the mix and reduce the intensity of its own illicit-drug-production problems. Unfortunately, this progress has not reduced the country's drug-consumption difficulties or made much of a dent in traffickers' use of Thailand's excellent transport infrastructure to move drugs from Laos and Myanmar/Burma into the world market.

Bolivia has embarked on supply-reduction programs similar to Thailand's, emphasizing alternative development in order to give growers adequate income replacement for their eradicated drug crops. A principal intent in Bolivia's case is to reduce growers' incentives to migrate and raise drug crops wherever conditions are most favorable. Regardless, since 1989 there has been an increase in the amount of Bolivian coca produced, from an estimated 78,200 metric tons in 1989 to 84,400 metric tons in 1993—and this increase occurred on 5,700 fewer hectares of land.[3] Growers' agronomic abilities are improving. In Peru, where propitious conditions for alternative development schemes do not exist, coca production also increased between 1989 to 1992 by an amount equivalent to nearly 50 percent of Bolivia's total production.[4] The substantial decline in Peru's 1993 harvest (30 percent by U.S. State Department estimates) was due less to any supply-suppression strategies than to a "debilitating coca fungus, as well as cultivation shifts from traditional areas with high yield coca fields to new cultivation areas where leaf yields have yet to reach mature levels."[5] Unless the fungus takes everything out, look for Peru's coca harvests to rebound as long as a strong international market for cocaine exists. Alternative development programs or not, coca production continues to expand as long as a good market exists.

One frequently hears not only that the theory of supply suppression is sound but that its successful application hinges only on one factor—force. Put enough force in place, and the matter will be resolved.[6] According to this view, a more-vigorous-than-ever drug war can turn supply-suppression failure into success, weakness into strength. It plays to people's sense of faith that existing procedures can work if they are just carried out in a more organizationally integrated and forceful way.

Consider some of the likely consequences of intensifying a conventional drug war in Colombia and Bolivia, two of the principal sources for the world's cocaine. In Colombia, the supply-suppression strategy has failed so far, causing aggravated endemic violence, political corruption, social stress, cultural distortions, and a further delegitimation of the state. Still, the government could launch an all-out assault on traffickers and work more diligently to suppress growers.

Doing so would require enhancing military and police capabilities for search-and-destroy missions, strengthening the judiciary professionally and protecting it from corruption and intimidation, formalizing extradition treaties and making them operable, securing the prisons from internal corruption and dry-rot, identifying and stopping money laundering regardless of its impact on Colombia's foreign-exchange or capital-accumulation position, and taking on highly visible international operatives as well as their money, paramilitary organizations, and domestic political organizations. All these approaches have an obvious appeal among some people. Most of them do not live in Colombia.

In other words, Colombia would face obvious drawbacks in escalating the war against traffickers. Foremost among them, aside from the expected retributive violence from the traffickers, is that most of the war's financial costs and much of Colombia's domestic monetary and fiscal policy would require considerable external input. Principal institutions such as the military, police, and judiciary would come under increasing influence from the United States or other principal consumer countries, thereby raising an issue Colombians do not take lightly: They are already sensitive to the core about their sovereignty.

If done vigorously enough, implementing a more ambitious war on drugs in Colombia could put domestic traffickers out of business, although not necessarily Colombian traffickers operating elsewhere. However, there are four additional strikes against a bigger war's succeeding in Colombia. First, there is every indication that the Colombian electorate would throw out any government that allowed itself to be colonized by the United States for purposes of the drug war. The first post-drug-colonization elections, which the United States would be loath to try to get canceled because of its commitment to democratic proceedings, would destroy any Colombian politician supporting U.S. colonial venture. Understandably, Colombian politicians are not anxious for that to happen. Moreover, it is doubtful that the United States could sustain support for such an interventionist option politically with its own electorate.

Second, traffickers would work harder to undermine the state, and the level of violence would no doubt increase. Traffickers would have further reason to ally themselves with guerrilla movements, sabotage the oil industry, destroy infrastructure, and snuff out an increasing number of civilian lives in an effort to weaken political will. The Colombian state could not survive the drug running of too many more Pablo Escobars. Already, Cali has begun to take on the specter of Medellín in the wake of the latter's demise in the drug trade—a macho bravado that glories in violence, conspicuous displays of wealth, and gauntlet throwing as people jockey for position. It is doubtful that institutions claiming democratic foundations could sustain this atmosphere for long if the intensity continually spiraled upward. Colombia's domestic priorities should call for political reforms to enhance democracy, incorporate guerrillas into mainstream politics, improve social services and amenities such as education, health, and urban infrastructure, boost the GNP, more equitably distribute wealth, lower the inflation rate, and rein in out-of-control bureaucrats.

Third, unless a bigger war were regionalized to include Bolivia and Peru, traffickers would simply take up temporary or permanent residence there, just as they did in 1989–1990, when for a short time the Colombian government managed to raise the ante on their activities. This outcome would be to Colombia's advantage but hardly to anyone else's.

Fourth, implementing a bigger war would require more from the Colombian state than it appears able to deliver, even with outside help. It is clear that Colombian institutions are ill prepared to enforce administrative nonmarket policies, one of the reasons the illicit-drug industry got a toehold in the country in the first place. As Thoumi has observed, the "large underground economy, regime delegitimation and the weakening of the state, the high rent-seeking propensity of most Colombians, increasing illegality and corruption, and the political clientelist system, are all factors that increase the difficulty of the Colombian government to implement its own policies."[7]

If a bigger war on Colombian traffickers in Colombia is not in the country's best interests, regardless of how much the United States argues otherwise, how about launching greater efforts to suppress Colombia's coca, opium poppy, and cannabis growers? Going after the growers with both positive and negative sanctions would no doubt successfully reduce coca production in Colombia. But it would also impoverish many rural Colombians without making a single contribution to reducing world coca supplies. Coca production in Peru and Bolivia would simply replace Colombia's lost output, and many Colombian growers would migrate and replant in other countries, probably under the protection of Colombia's drug traffickers. Operators in Bolivia, Guatemala, Mexico, Paraguay, Brazil, and perhaps Argentina would work hard to pick up the slack in opium poppies and cannabis. Failing that, the Golden Crescent appears prepared to meet any shortfall in opium poppy supplies.

Thus, crop suppression must be carried out on, at a bare minimum, a regional level. But a regional approach would depend on eradication capabilities in Bolivia and Peru, at least as far as coca is concerned. Bolivia could not handle a precipitous reduction economically; Peruvian growers, who produce the most coca, would not respond favorably for economic reasons and would likely be protected by resurgent terrorist groups. Thus, a regional coca-reduction strategy is unlikely to work. Without a successful regional strategy, Colombia would pay a heavy political price for nothing. Thus, Colombia would have little incentive to adopt a more vigorous crop-suppression strategy, and it could expect additional rural unrest if it did.

If a more vigorous drug war on traffickers and growers is not in Colombia's best interests, how about Bolivia's? Bolivia has few traffickers of global significance. An all-out drug war would therefore need to be focused on the country's coca growers. This strategy is not practically possible because it would entail declaring war not only on the Chapare—where most of Bolivia's coca is grown—but also indirectly on a majority of Bolivia's rural villages, as angry migrants to the Chapare would return to their ancestral homes, where they could no longer be accommodated economically. This approach would radicalize the labor unions and perhaps drive them to solicit aid from such groups as Peru's Sendero Luminoso, however defunct this group is now thought to be. This is the great fear associated with the potential "Colombianization" of Bolivia. It is not something that Bolivia can—or will—do.

Thus, however much U.S. politicians of moment may call for death, destruction, and mayhem to drug suppliers, Colombia and Bolivia—and many countries like them—cannot be faulted for resisting. Pursuing U.S. interests in this way can only lead to further domestic travesty and instability. Absent regional if not global strategies, it is most likely that one country's success in reducing production or supplies may simply become another's problem as growers, traffickers, refiners, and middlemen migrate to places of least resistance and most opportunity. Migration or not, one may expect heightened violence and more concerted efforts to form counterstates, complete with regional taxing authority and paramilitary defenses.

A proper mix of national and international money, political will, and reasonably uncorrupted and incorruptible bureaucracies and law-enforcement agencies can be—and perhaps will yet be—found in several countries. However, these cases have not had a global impact, nor will they likely do so. Even aside from the country studies affirming the failure of the present supply-suppression strategy, most observers do not believe this approach can succeed under any feasible set of circumstances.

Despite regional successes, then, supply suppression is not a prescription for solving the world's illicit-drug problems. It is a prescription for funding drug mafias, peasant growers, petty traffickers, and smugglers. Its socioeconomic and political consequences, as outlined in Chapter 5, are generally hurtful to societies, economies, and polities alike. There is an unfortunate "law" in all this—the law of unintended consequences. Whether for philosophical reasons the present course *ought* to be pursued, doing so is obviously fruitless. What else, then, ought to be tried, or tried more vigorously? What *can* be done that *ought* to be?

Such a question requires that we specify our "oughts." Let me suggest two that appear reasonable from the standpoint of harm reduction: First we ought to try to reduce global consumption abuse and its deleterious externalities in socially productive ways; second, we ought to eliminate and avoid drug-control policies that produce unacceptable unintended consequences (or, at least, reduce those consequences as much as possible). Approaching drug-control policies from differing countries' perspectives along the lines of a harm-reduction model may at least help to shift the supply-suppression discussion to productive policy ends. The underlying presumption is that the world will not be free from psychoactive drugs but that it is both possible and desirable to reduce their negative impacts on peoples and countries.

In the balance of this chapter I look at the prospects for reducing consumption (principally in net consumer industrialized countries) as a prelude to examining likely impacts that any significant success would have on net producer countries. Aside from this pragmatic connection to the countries under study, reducing consumption is one element that should be emphasized in a general harm-reduction model instead of simply being assumed to be unattainable. I then explore options and consequences for net producer countries, first under conditions in which the present international drug-control regime remains basically unchanged, and then with specified changes assumed. Two countries, Bolivia and Colombia, are advanced as illustrations.

Reducing Drug Abuse and International Demand

Efforts to reduce demand and drug abuse may entail both negative and positive sanctions. Negative sanctions include general law-enforcement initiatives aimed at apprehending consumers and making life tough for them—through fines, jail, and/or loss of privileges. Positive sanctions, by contrast, offer people incentives to cease, or at least greatly to reduce, illicit-drug taking. The combination of positive and negative sanctions helps to create a climate wherein nonusers are reluctant to take up the habit.

Aside from general law-enforcement initiatives designed to raise risks for consumers and thereby deter them from consuming illicit drugs, principal consuming countries have engaged in popular education through programs in the classroom, appeals in the mass media, initiatives in the workplace, civic action, anticontagion treatment programs, and efforts to develop an antidrug ethos.

Prohibition with an accompanying general law-enforcement strategy that is increasingly tough, flexible, and direct on users is likely to reduce the abuse of and demand for illicit drugs only among two types of people: those who have something of value to lose and those who see themselves as having a future worth sacrificing for. Crack cocaine and heroin users in the United States seldom fall into this category, and might not be much affected. Members of the "underclass" of other countries may likewise be resistant. There is widespread realization that education within the classroom must be coupled with community-wide integrated efforts and explicit antidrug values disseminated with peer and hero modeling while children are fairly young.[8] The mass media in several consuming nations have for some time targeted selective audiences for antidrug campaigns. Some research has inquired into their success.[9] In some instances, selective audience targeting has appeared to be beneficial.

Initiatives in the workplace principally include drug testing, with threats of dismissal if results are positive. The drawback to a workplace model in the United States and perhaps elsewhere is that it is unlikely to reduce demand among the burgeoning number of inner-city crack and heroin users. For effective application, the model presumes that the drug user wants employment and has employment, that the employer values that specific employee, and that both employee and employer have an incentive to work together to create a drug-free workplace. All these factors are unlikely to coalesce among unskilled, minimum-skilled, or minimum-wage employees, who may be quickly replaceable as soon as a problem arises and are likely to drift from job to job. Nevertheless, when targeting the skilled, the wanted, the scarce, and those who really desire to retain their employment, the workplace presents an unmatched opportunity to initiate positive incentives to accompany the usual array of antidrug deterrents.[10]

Civic action is also advanced as a way to reduce demand and consumption abuse. Communities tend to know what their own difficulties are and frequently have some of the best ideas on how to resolve them. Helping people build homes, cleaning up vacant lots, assisting the hardcore unemployed in acquiring skills and finding jobs, creating educational and other opportunities for children of the deprived—these are activities in which some communities have engaged profitably and which have somewhat ameliorated their drug problems. It is becoming more and more evident that without instrumental community attention to the problems, outside agencies are unlikely to deal with them successfully. Concerted community involvement with support from diverse civic organizations may help reduce illicit-drug demand. It is usually acknowledged that collaboration with law-enforcement officials (to continue to increase individual risks for traffickers and users) is required.

Treatment programs are advanced for a variety of reasons—to reduce criminality, to undercut organized crime, to express humanitarian care, and to reduce ultimate costs to society. Few people speak of treatment programs per se as a means to reduce overall illicit-drug demand, although certainly they help drug abusers rehabilitate their lives. There is at least one exception, deriving from "anticontagion" addiction theories. The model is the epidemiology of a contagious disease; the underlying assumption is that most people become drug users and eventually, perhaps, addicts because friends have introduced them to the practice. Some of the friends may have been pushing drugs in order to support their own addictions. Thus, successfully treating addicts removes their economic need to market drugs to acquaintances and therefore eliminates a large cause of the spread of drug addiction. Accordingly, initiatives are made, even from highly placed law-enforcement officers,[11] for considerably more treatment funding for anticontagion purposes. Anticontagion treatment programs may thus help to reduce demand and consumption.

Finally, efforts to develop an antidrug ethos as a means of reducing illicit-drug demand and consumption abuse are attempted. A strong deterrent to illicit drugs is people's conviction that it is inappropriate to use them. Reasons may be moral or utilitarian. They may derive from fear, economic calculus, or perhaps even from acquisitiveness, greed, and avarice. For whatever reason, if people decline to consume illicit drugs, it seems clear that the demand and consumption abuse problems have been addressed, at least as far as those specific people are concerned.

However, unless the decision not to consume illicit drugs is driven by an inner conviction, the abstinence may be ephemeral. Change the calculus, remove the police, elect or appoint drug-disposed leaders, or sell an alternative educational curriculum to the schools, and the problem may return. But changing the disposition, character, fundamental values, culture, or political ideology of a specific people so as to disfavor illicit drugs will likely result in a more lasting reduction in consumption. Clearly, however, the value change must occur through persuasion rather than coercion—something the Chinese have discovered as drugs emerge once again in their society after being largely absent for the better part of two generations.

Some people believe that without fundamental social change or the development of a pervasive antidrug ethos, contemporary principal drug-consuming nations are essentially lost to psychoactive drug consumption. Indeed, harking on "rise and fall of civilization" themes, some people predict that future historians will look upon the inevitable fall of the United States and Western Europe in light of the anticivilization values generally associated with illicit drugs. That is fairly pessimistic talk. It need not necessarily be so.

More optimistic observers, by contrast, are looking into values and taking a longer view of the drug problem than is usually politically expedient, exploring cultural totems and taboos and the social context of drug use to come up with drug-policy options involving social change. Calls are made for strong mobilization of all positive forces to reestablish damaged social values and thereby turn back the drug onslaught. One device is to present substantial incentives for people to change their lifestyles, eventually leading to the establishment of antidrug controls that derive not from law but from custom and social preference. Another is simply to create alternative images worth pursuing.

Direct demand-reduction proposals or options all concentrate on users (as opposed to producers and traffickers) and suggest that people's propensity to indulge in illicit-drug consumption may be reduced by approaches that invoke fear, self-interest, or value change. In explicating these categories, it is useful to focus on the world's principal illicit-drug-consuming nation, the United States of America. So far, fear has underlain the United States's consumer-focused demand-reduction policies—fear of jail, fear of notoriety (with attendant loss of status or employment), fear of property losses. Not surprisingly, fear strategies work as a function of intensity and operate best on people who have personal freedom, good employment, and property at risk—in the United States, mostly the middle class. But fear has not reduced drug consumption among the economic underclass, where much hard-core drug abuse currently transpires. And such strategies plague nations with an assortment of socioeconomic and political costs. Comparative examples at the extreme are instructive. Singapore, Malaysia, and Saudi Arabia exhibit encouraging drug-consumption indicators. But liberal democracies have difficulty both in applying the attendant fear-invoking penalties and in accepting all the enforcement mechanisms' socioeconomic and political consequences. Thus, the United States's fear regime—its current principal consumption-reduction strategy—is controversial as to philosophy, effectiveness, and appropriateness. The struggle continues.

Self-interest, an alternative consumption-reduction strategy, may also be driven by a calculus of fear (as in fear of losing one's employment). However, much self-interested behavior is driven less by fear than by a calculus of desires. Thus, many drug-treatment centers successfully entreat addicts' concerns about their health, family, friends, economic well-being, and happiness. Significantly appealing to self-interest by many means could remove large segments of new underclass generations from a drug-abuse culture. Certainly, there are complex psychological issues here, as well as the complications of unstable or defective family structures and a lack of appropriate role models. But self-interest properly nurtured creates its own role models. On the whole, self-interested youth brushed with pragmatic alternatives are appropriately motivated.

Problems and imponderables abound, of course. Neither present nor future policies are free of this burden. But a substantial public effort on a self-interest strategy would produce consumption-reduction results. Moreover, consumption-reduction outcomes based on self-interest as opposed to fear have the prospect of being more durable. There is an additional advantage. Many of the costs that fear regimes externalize to the larger society would be eliminated.

Obvious caveats exist. Although a voluntary self-interest regime will likely produce quick gains among many children of the present underclass, such gains may not be sustainable across generations. New efforts lose momentum as novelty ages, and implementing bureaucracies tend to corrupt their original goals as their work becomes institutionalized. Within a generation cohort affected by a regime of self-interest, demand-reduction sustainability will depend on the extent to which nondrug-abusing, educationally prepared children from the underclass ultimately find a society that assimilates them economically, socially, and politically.

Whereas self-interest is judged favorably as a regime strategy to reduce drug demand and consumption abuse, neither it nor a regime based on fear will produce desirable long-term drug consumption results in the absence of value change—the general development of generations of people who desire to sustain their lives without abusing drugs. The best of prospects is also the hardest to achieve.

That substantial illicit-drug consumption still exists in the United States, for example, despite punitive laws is compelling evidence that large numbers of people have adopted strong drug-taking values. As even strong authoritarian states (e.g., post–World War II China) have not been able to eliminate illicit drugs completely from within their borders, it seems unlikely that other drug-using nations can be made completely drug free. No doubt attainable, however, are a vast reduction in drug abuse, if not use, and a substantial reduction in the public's burdens deriving from individual consumption and illegalizing laws. The best long-term prospects lie in value initiatives that are credible.

Both drug-taking and antidrug-taking values will require more public-policy scrutiny than they have yet received. The reasons are twofold: Campaigns among the middle classes are more easily undertaken than among the underclasses, where drug-taking values are thought to be more pervasive; and the art of engineering social values, whether from induced structural change or from its absence, is unpredictable.

Other Harm-Reduction Efforts in Net Consumer Countries

Left unexplored in efforts to reduce consumption abuse and illicit-drug demand are three imponderables: (1) the prospect that any of the consumption- and demand-reduction programs might be successful enough to make a substantial dent in the international drug traffic; (2) whether the programs may have cross-national applicability outside industrialized countries; and (3) the degree to which there is political will or resolve to carry them out. Failing any one of the three, it is doubtful that programmed or planned direct demand reduction is possible.

As the preceding section demonstrates, directly reducing demand or consumption via general policy strategies is problematical. Moreover, such initiatives return all the political costs to home base rather than externalizing them to net producer countries, as does a supply-suppression strategy. It is therefore a tough question for most politicians. Understandably, some people's attention has turned to alternative models for dealing with consumption abuse and its externalities, ranging from decriminalization to regulated availability.[12]

In the wake of problematic global consumption-reduction efforts on the one hand and supply-suppression failures on the other, alternative means of selectively controlling psychoactive drugs and their abuse have been and are being explored. One approach calls for a selective moratorium on the application of drug laws as they apply to drug users.[13] Regulating purity levels may decrease the number of overdoses and lower drug-related medical spending. Another approach is to allow medical practitioners to prescribe maintenance drugs for addicts. This step does not destroy the illicit market for new users, but it does take addicts and abusers out of the underworld. England took this approach for a number of years but has since largely abandoned it, in part because of physician abuse and a host of new users entering the market.[14]

Other observers have proposed legalizing drugs, with controls similar to those presently exercised on alcohol and tobacco in the United States and a prohibition on advertisements and glamorization.[15] Still others propose making a regulated volume of drugs available through a state monopoly, keeping the user fees as high as possible without triggering a black market. This system could be accompanied by a program of social disapproval and research to find out who is abusing drugs and how to get them help, reducing harms both to users and to society. For example, not only would purity levels be controlled, but drug mafias would be severely crippled as well. Nevertheless, these proposals currently appear to be politically inexpedient for many countries, although the discussions are receiving increasingly serious attention.

Regardless of generalized political expediencies, the try-a-new-idea mood is highly visible in some countries. The Netherlands, Switzerland, Denmark, and even Australia are cases in point. Here several governments—municipal, state, and national—have accepted that drugs are a way of life for some people and have searched for ways to reduce harm to them and to their communities. Thus, piece-by-piece harm reduction has entered drug-policy discussions as an alternative to failed demand-reduction or supply-suppression campaigns and to politically inexpedient initiatives such as outright legalization or decriminalization. A harm-reduction alternative will likely enter popular political discourse in the United States as it already has in several European countries. The approach is discussed in numerous publications[16] and is surveyed generally in an April 1994 unpublished report originating at the Woodrow Wilson School of Public and International Affairs, Princeton University.[17]

Assuming that direct demand reduction or abuse reduction through value change will not be forthcoming—or, if so, not quickly enough—harm-reduction discussions in industrialized principal user countries call for immediate steps to put drug abusers into circumstances where they are likely to do less harm to society and themselves than under present circumstances. Thus, harm-reduction initiatives call for the ready availability of needles and syringes (to reduce HIV transmission); the creation of outreach programs to work with drug users (to help them control their abuse); the development of informal community zoning (to give drug users room for "harm-reduction centers"); the extension of methadone maintenance programs (to wean abusers from heroin); the liberalization of cannabis use (to offer a drug less harmful than heroin or cocaine to committed drug users); the inclusion of tobacco in the harm-reduction program (to reduce some of its horrifying health effects and to set a nonhypocritical stage for harm-reduction policies); and the relaxation of criminal features of most drug-control laws, at least as applied to consumers (in order to disgorge the jails, cut law-enforcement expenses, unclog the judiciary, and bring otherwise useful people into a legitimate rather than illegal economy so they may make a normal contribution to a country's welfare).

Harm reduction acknowledges that the best way for people to avoid the deleterious consequences of drug abuse, and for countries to avoid the unintended consequences of drug control, is abstinence. However, its proponents accept that psychoactive drugs will be used to a greater or lesser extent in most countries, laws notwithstanding. The key effort is to reduce risks to users and to society. Each harm-reduction initiative is controversial as to its philosophy and ultimate impact on society.

The political acceptability, ethical appropriateness, or success or failure of current harm-reduction proposals notwithstanding, it must be emphasized that the current harm-reduction literature focuses almost exclusively on consumers (users and abusers) and their societies. *Harm reduction is a largely undeveloped concept for most of the net producer countries mentioned in this volume.* To be relevant for countries studied here (other than Thailand and Pakistan, which have large drug-abuse problems), harm reduction would have to focus on the regime of international drug control, which has contributed little to suppressing the illicit-drug trade and much to social dislocations, corruption, militarization, abuse of human rights, and a general disregard for human decency. It is the consequences of the international prohibition laws, not drug abuse, that have created most of the harm in principal producer countries. A fair question, therefore, particularly for the interest of this book, is how one may prevent drug-control policies from causing more harm to the principal producer countries than drug use itself causes to the principal consumer countries.

Assume that principal user countries continue efforts to reduce illicit-drug demand—one form of harm reduction—but that, in order to undercut the drug mafias and mitigate their corrosive impact on society, they adopt a supplemental public-health, domestic-harm-reduction package. What would its impact on principal producer countries be? Unless the approach, basically engineered for the industrial North, were accompanied by a change in the international regime of drug control, the benefits would be negligible on countries such as those surveyed in this volume. Indeed, harm reduction in the North conceivably could accompany harm *creation* in the principal producers of the South, which illustrates an important point: Most discussions about drug-policy reform say very little for principal producer countries even though these countries suffer considerable socioeconomic and political fallout from the drug-control laws designed to protect the North. The question arises: Do principal producer countries not have any options that might reduce *their* harm—in some instances the harm of drug consumption, but mostly the harm imposed by supply suppression?

Let us now turn to a consideration of such options, first within the context of existing international drug-control policies and without regard to potential success any of the new harm-reduction initiatives may have in principal consumer countries. Following that discussion, I look into the matter assuming a changed international drug-control regime.

Principal Producer Countries' Options to Reduce Harm

Assuming that international prohibition remains intact, reducing harm starts with a realization that any given drug-control policy may produce intended and unintended consequences. When over two decades ago supply suppression was envisioned and implemented as the principal international drug-control strategy, no doubt its creators did not anticipate the horrendous outcomes—no aggregate reduction in supplies (the intended consequences) and, as explained in Chapter 5 and elsewhere in this volume, considerable social and political mischief worldwide (the unintended consequences).

Such realization notwithstanding, bureaucratic and political momentum make change difficult. Although we ought—and many are trying—to reduce demand and consumption abuse and their externalities in principal consuming countries, and although we ought to eliminate and avoid drug-control policies that produce unacceptable unintended consequences on principal producer countries, it is unlikely in the short run that consumption will dramatically decrease or that hurtful international control policies will be radically altered. The political position of the United States, though evolving, is still fairly rigid. And even if countries such as the United States were to institute domestic reforms that may reduce harm domestically, these measures would not necessarily have much impact on net producer countries. Thus, net producer nations wishing to extricate themselves from hurtful socioeconomic and political consequences of illicit drugs and drug-control policies are left with a large question. What can *they* do to reduce harm to themselves under present conditions? Consider illustrations from two countries: Colombia and Bolivia.

Colombia

Before examining Colombia's harm-reduction options in the existing supply-suppression regime, it is useful to review how Colombia has been integrated into international prohibition practices and how any altered demand factors in principal consumer countries might affect the country.[18] Further, it is important—more than just a caveat—to reflect on Colombia's institutional strengths and weaknesses that have aided or limited full integration.

One starts with the premise that the Colombian state is unlikely to be a flourishing participant in the present international supply-suppression regime, certainly not to the satisfaction of principal consumer countries. Colombia's past and present efforts have been largely unsuccessful (the assassination of Pablo Escobar notwithstanding), and they have been undertaken at tremendous national cost. Limitations derive from both governmental weakness and illicit-drug-trafficker strength. The general lack of governmental legitimacy and Colombia's clientelist political system have combined to foster decades of political violence and guerilla activity. This is part of the problem. The traffickers' ability to work in—indeed, to accentuate—an underground economy, to corrupt officials, and to launch violent attacks on industry and government increases the difficulty of implementing internationally sanctioned drug-control policies, including supply suppression. These factors, coupled with the fact that the government is not really free to pursue national policies independent of the international environment, place major constraints on what Colombia is able to do.

Supply suppression and extradition have been Colombia's principal policy initiatives. With a weak government, strong drug industry, and economic pricing factors all reinforcing the vigorous production of cocaine for an illegal market, small wonder that the government's efforts have largely been a failure. The result has been high social costs for Colombia and nothing better than a stalemate in the war on drugs. Accordingly, the present policy mix, however much it may have benefited the United States, has hurt Colombia.[19]

What about demand reduction in the United States and other principal consumer centers as a considered measure that might help Colombia? Even within the current supply-suppression strategy, demand reduction in net consumer nations is a policy goal. But if progress were actually made, demand reduction would probably have an ambiguous effect on Colombia as long as a significant number of people somewhere wanted cocaine. Consumption reduction would have to be significant worldwide, and countries that are not now principal consumers would have to avoid becoming so. Overall, this scenario is unlikely. Absent a significant global reduction (e.g., through value change) in cocaine use, the Colombians, through intrigue and violence, would manage to pull in most of the profit-making transactions, putting Bolivians and Peruvians and almost everyone else out of work. Others, for the foreseeable future at least, would simply be outclassed in the business. Colombian traffickers have the experience, the networks abroad, and the constitutional will to employ violence to maintain their supremacy. Colombia's principal scourge—traffickers and their business behavior—would be little affected by even a significant reduction in illegal-drug demand in net consumer countries. They would simply become as predatory, violent, and aggressive as necessary to maintain their markets against competitors or interlopers.

From Colombia's vantage, harm-reduction policy options are few, and some may be worse than the present supply-suppression strategy that has created so much mischief for the country. Harm-reduction options that Colombia might consider include (1) calling a truce with traffickers but leaving supply-suppression laws in place (reducing violence and undermining the strength of the informal economy without becoming, necessarily, an international pariah); (2) unilaterally seceding from the existing international drug-control regime (for the same purpose but ignoring the difficulties of likely international sanctions); and (3) between what is analytically desirable and politically possible, struggling with long- and short-term benefits and liabilities of current policies to choose a policy mix that will reduce domestic harms—a mix that would be less costly socially, economically, and politically for the country than is the present supply-suppression course.

Harm-reduction option number 1—calling a truce with traffickers and abandoning drug-law enforcement, but leaving prohibition laws in place (a form of de facto decriminalization) to keep risk factors and uncertainties alive and to avoid becoming an international pariah—would legitimize both traffickers and their money. It would reduce traffickers' motivation to fund a counterstate or ally themselves with guerrillas and terrorists or become such themselves. Trafficker competition would still exist, and that could result in some violence and mayhem, but the Colombian state would not be the principal target, and the loss of uninvolved civilian life would probably decrease. These results would seem to offer something in the way of harm reduction for Colombia.

However, calling a unilateral truce with traffickers within an existing international-prohibition regime has all the prospects of frightful unintended consequences for Colombia. As risk factors would remain, "crime-tax" profits from abroad would likely still be high, thereby continuing to give Colombia's traffickers the wherewithal to infiltrate the state and its institutions and to acclerate the repatriation of enormous amounts of money into the economy, restructuring thereby not only national income shares but also national society. That would likely lead to considerable resentment and political hostility, perhaps even a lot of instability. Traffickers would become extremely aggressive in pursuing legitimation, a long-sought goal, precisely because they would be emboldened to come out into the open. On balance, harm-reduction option number 1 would therefore seem to offer the worst of several worlds—continued high profits to the traffickers and de facto legitimation of their activities, their persona, and their money, with the attendant negative consequences to economy and society that such trends would entail.

Harm-reduction option number 2—unilateral secession from the international drug-control regime—would deliver many of the benefits of option number 1 but would produce all its ills, with the added difficulty of Colombia's becoming an official international pariah. That would be a heavy price to pay, likely including an international freeze on loans and a boycott of Colombia's exports, if not an outright economic embargo on most of its formal-economy international transactions, all as punishment for unilaterally divorcing itself from the drug war.

Harm-reduction options number 1 and number 2 imply short-term initiatives. Neither is both attractive and politically feasible; on balance, neither is probably attractive or politically feasible in the existing international prohibition regime. Thus, in the short run, Colombia does not have meaningful harm-reduction policy options. That leaves option number 3—choosing a long-term policy mix within a regime of international prohibition that would reduce domestic harms.

Independent of what short-term policies the government follows, perhaps Colombia needs to follow Thoumi's advice and work incrementally and indirectly where it can politically for the longer term.[20] First, the government needs to involve nongovernmental organizations (NGOs) in its antidrug initiatives. The government cannot suppose that the problem is its responsibility alone. Inasmuch as long-term solutions imply strengthening other Colombian social institutions that have become weakened through time, involving NGOs in the effort is wise and conserves time and money. The Catholic Church, other churches, political parties, the government teachers' union, business clubs, neighborhood organizations, and other social groups are candidates to assist Colombian institutional reconstruction and antidrug policies. Thoumi puts it this way:

> It must be clear that this policy goal is very ambitious: its goal is to build strong social cohesion and social controls that would discourage anti-social behavior—which includes illegal drug production, marketing and consumption. This policy requires an assimilation into the Colombian mainstream of large parts of the population, to build strong communities, and to make people feel that they have a stake in the establishment. In many ways it is inseparable from a nation building project, but it reflects the systemic crisis faced by the country.[21]

Second, whatever international cooperation remains, especially between Colombia and the United States, must be targeted not simply to activities that have short-term goals and are ineffective anyway but rather toward strengthening Colombian organizations capable of assisting the country's institutional reconstruction.[22]

In the long run, under an international prohibition regime it appears that Colombia basically has two imperatives: (1) the strengthening of legitimate institutions of government, society, and the economy; and (2) the elaboration of help from principal consumer countries in doing so. Absent the realization of these goals, there is no long-term solution to Colombia's illicit-drug crisis. In a prohibition regime, there is no short-term solution. Period.

Colombia illustrates the dilemma that many producer/trafficker countries have when they do not also suffer significant domestic illicit-drug consumption. Participating in an international drug-control regime improves their international standing but harms them domestically. Domestic harm-reduction under these conditions is extremely difficult. Domestic harm-reduction and a supply-suppression strategy appear to be in substantial conflict in countries like Colombia.

Bolivia

Bolivia has begun to take on a full range of illicit-drug activities (coca production through cocaine trafficking).[23] However, in contrast to Colombia, Bolivia remains a principal producer of coca, not cocaine. Bolivia's own cocaine industrialists are still relatively few. Only when refiners and traffickers were driven out of Colombia did they come in large numbers to Bolivia. Colombians stay no longer than necessary and return quickly to domiciles in their native land as soon as it is safe to do so.

As a principal coca-growing but not cocaine-producing area, Bolivia's harm-reduction options within an international prohibition regime include (1) establishing both the requisite procedures and appropriate institutional strength to assure that traffickers and cocaine industrialists do not get a strong foothold in the country; (2) giving lip service to international prohibition but officially abandoning serious efforts to suppress coca supplies; (3) decriminalizing or legalizing all of the coca-growing industry within Bolivia;[24] and (4) continuing on—even enhancing—present supply-suppression efforts via a combination of crop eradication and alternative development.

Harm-reduction option number 1—establishing both the requisite procedures and appropriate institutional strength to assure that traffickers and cocaine industrialists do not get a strong foothold in Bolivia—would help to avoid the "Colombianization" of the country. Traffickers, their paramilitary forces, and their money have created more institutional damage in Colombia than can possibly be attributed to growers or users. Keeping the traffickers in Colombia and avoiding a comparative home-grown variety would be in Bolivia's best harm-reduction interests, at least in terms of the future. Implementing this option would require at least two things: First, that no drug-enforcement activities be undertaken in Colombia or Peru that would drive traffickers into Bolivia (this would certainly work against any drug-control "regional strategy"); and, second, that the United States or another rich country provide massive amounts of resources, including operational military personnel—not unlike the days when the world was looking for Ché Guevara in the Bolivian jungle.

There are two major political problems with option number 1. Not only would Bolivians object to a 1990s invasion of their sovereignty— U.S. Operation Blast Furnace against Bolivian drug traffickers having already sensitized them—but it is uncertain that the U.S. electorate could support U.S. military adventures in countries such as Bolivia for the length of time such operations would require. In October 1994 powerful members of Congress—and perhaps not just for political gain—were calling for a date-certain for U.S. troop withdrawal from Haiti, only three weeks after the soldiers arrived. It seems quite certain, then, that option number 1, even if it were a good idea, could not be implemented for practical, political, and economic reasons. In a prohibition regime, therefore, the potential for the "Colombianization" of Bolivia—with its attendant assault on institutions and society—must be viewed as a distinct possibility, one for which Bolivia has little harm-reduction defense.

Harm-reduction option number 2—giving lip service to international prohibition but officially abandoning serious efforts to suppress coca supplies—would reduce the country's internal stress with labor and coca-growers' unions and perhaps reduce the potential attractiveness to Bolivia's peasants of such radical terrorist groups as Sendero Luminoso. However, this option would be particularly difficult for Bolivia to implement. In contrast to Colombia, Bolivia is in constant and desperate need of foreign aid to subsidize its budget, supply foreign exchange, and feed its people. The United States has been a principal aid donor, although the whole world (through the United Nations and the European Union) has participated. Should Bolivia ease up on coca growers, aid would likely be cut for punitive reasons, presenting a national financial crisis with which the country would be ill equipped to deal.

There is a remote chance that complete domestic legalization of coca trade and production would stimulate a repatriation of drug profits now held abroad, but that would probably not offset the other liabilities of pursuing harm-reduction option number 2. For all practical purposes, therefore, it is unlikely that option number 2 will be formally attempted, although unofficially it is to this option that Bolivia currently most adheres.

Option number 3—decriminalizing or legalizing all production and trafficking—is not possible in Bolivia for the same reasons that it is not possible in Colombia. Implementation would require authorization from the U.S. government in order not to jeopardize Bolivia's foreign aid (on which Bolivia is much more dependent than Colombia) and to avoid international sanctions that the country can ill afford. The United States will not provide such authorization any time soon. But this is not a critical matter for Bolivia. The mix of international prohibition and domestic tolerance of growers in the absence of Colombian-style traffickers has not produced domestic drug-related crime and social violence, which legalization best addresses. Thus, there is little political motivation to adopt a legalization position.

That leaves option number 4—continuing on the present course, perhaps enhanced, of supply-suppression efforts via a combination of crop eradication and alternative-development activities. This approach holds the best continued harm-reduction prospects for Bolivia and could indeed turn to its long-term benefit. The country should work to minimize the political damage associated with crop eradication and get from the international community all it can for alternative development. This could reduce harms over the long term, despite the evidence that neither crop eradication nor alternative development has so far reduced aggregate coca supplies. By the time principal consumer countries finally realize that their supply-suppression strategy cannot achieve the goal of forcing consumption down, Bolivia, if it invests its resources well, may extract enough surplus from the international community to improve permanently its food-production capabilities and raise the living standard and economic position of hundreds of thousands of its peasants. Multiplier effects would help to improve economic conditions in the whole country, including the major cities. Unfortunately for drug-control planners, aggregate coca plantings would be largely unaffected.

James Painter shows that large-scale electrification of the Chapare, now undertaken by the UNDCP, would improve opportunities for income-generating agroindustrial projects there.[25] Enhanced farmer participation, under conditions wherein the coca price is decreasing, would boost participation in alternative income-earning projects that could not only survive the age of coca but give farmers viable alternatives now. The coca unions are willing to talk,[26] the politicians are anxious, and the international community is putting a lot of trust and faith in alternative development. Now is the time for Bolivia to strike.

The United States and other countries are increasingly aware of the role markets play in development—they have been preaching the virtues of such to Africa and Latin America for at least fifty years. Funds to identify and support the development of income-generating activities through the marketing of profitable crops (rather than simply ones that can be grown in the Chapare) should be not only vigorously sought but expected. This strategy will allow a greater emphasis on economic growth, with more social spending and more income redistribution; both will likely return to strengthen democracy as well as improve the human condition. The UNDCP calls for $100 million a year for eight years in international transfers, which would amount to just over 1 percent of the $9 billion total U.S. drug-control budget for 1990, or nearly the equivalent of two years of U.S. military aid earmarked for the Bolivian army for 1991 and 1992.[27] It is within reason and expectation. Bolivian enthusiasts should keep in mind Painter's closing words:

> Even if it proved impossible to find economic alternatives to coca, even if coca production were to move elsewhere, and even if a successful [supply-suppression] policy [in Bolivia] did little to stop the availability of cocaine in the United States, at least policy makers favoring alternative development could be left with the honorable objective of contributing to Bolivia's efforts to escape underdevelopment and helping poor farmers in their efforts to escape poverty—which was, after all, why most of them started growing coca in the first place.[28]

Net consumer nations' continued pursuit of supply suppression through a program of economic incentives (alternative development) could now turn to Bolivia's benefit, not because supply-suppression goals are achieved but because economic development is occurring. Vigorous participation in the current international supply-suppression regime could be a great benefit to Bolivia, although it is hurtful to Colombia.

In summary, it is clear that a harm-reduction package for Bolivia and Colombia within the context of an existing international prohibition regime must be tailored to each country's problems and needs. Colombia has a distressing need to build institutional legitimacy, reduce violence, rein in traffickers and their cohorts, and restore (or create) confidence among the citizenry that the government has its best interests at heart, that it is not beholden to a shadow state through corruption and terrorism.

For Colombia, no really attractive short-run policy options within an international prohibition regime can be found because drug profits capitalize on historical legacies inimical to any relatively quick solutions. Long-run options in an international prohibition regime reside almost exclusively in the strengthening of legitimate institutions of government, society, and the economy. This is a very large task, precisely for the reason that short-term challenges are so great—because of what illicit-drug profits have done to contribute to the delegitimation of Colombia's public institutions. Colombia may not be up to pursuing a long-term harm-reduction effort with a supply-suppression strategy intact. The international war on drugs has created domestic dynamics that do not augur well for the Colombian state or its people. A really satisfactory harm-reduction package for Colombia and perhaps other principal trafficker/refiner countries within the present international prohibition regime does not appear to exist.

By contrast, Bolivia, being mostly an agricultural producer of coca (but with increasing tendencies toward refining) has a great need to find labor-intensive employment for its burgeoning peasantry, especially at a time when the remarkable tin mines of Potosí and elsewhere have given up the last of their concentrated treasures. Bolivia's problem is not violence, excessive drug profits that threaten to destroy the state through corruption and intimidation, or serious sociopolitical dynamics that would turn the country into, say, a Peru. Rather, Bolivia's problems are feeding its people, finding them (or allowing them to get) productive employment, and employing resources productively. Thus, contrary to Colombia, Bolivia may best achieve harm reduction in the present prohibition regime. The task is to pursue the present course of nominal crop eradication and more aggressive alternative development as a way of attracting international money that might enter competitive, labor-intensive, market-oriented activities.

Bolivia and Colombia, like other net producer countries entertaining a harm-reduction orientation, find themselves at odds with each other on possible solutions and certainly at odds with whether or not to keep the present international prohibition regime intact.

Harm-Reduction Consequences of Altering the International Prohibition Regime

What if a radical change were made in the *international* regime of illicit-drug control? What impact would that have on harm reduction in principal producer countries such as Colombia and Bolivia? The most likely course such change would take—if change were to occur at all—is a move away from supply suppression toward some form of de facto decriminalization or legalization of production and trade of currently illicit drugs in the wake of a relaxation of absolute prohibition in net consumer countries. This would be a natural course should significantly more major consumer countries adopt domestic harm-reduction packages—ranging from selective moratoria (as practiced in the Netherlands) to regulated availability of the drugs in a legal market to actual reduction of domestic drug abuse and heavy consumption. The supply-suppression strategy, at least outside principal consumers' own borders, would fade as a significant policy initiative. Once it faded from international concern, most certainly it would fade from principal producer countries' domestic policy agendas as long as the drug business did not pose a national security challenge.

Decriminalization (removing penalties, or at least looking the other way) and legalization (officially sanctioning currently illegal behavior) may occur at the user, producer, or trafficker levels in the drug chain. Interestingly, most arguments in favor of some kind of liberalizing policy concentrate on decriminalizing or legalizing drug *consumption;*[29] a few advocate the same policies for producers;[30] hardly any are in favor of relieving traffickers from a potential confrontation with the law. Yet it is precisely decriminalization of production and trafficking that would severely cripple the drug mafias, the principal source of drug-related difficulties in countries such as Colombia.

Decriminalizing production and supply—or at least abandoning international efforts at supply suppression—would have an immediate impact on traffickers but perhaps a delayed impact on consumers. International decriminalization or legalization are therefore advanced not as strategies to reduce consumption—consumption in net consumer countries would likely increase[31]—but rather as initiatives to reduce drug-related crime and violence in all countries linked to the drug chain. They are a response to the evidence that neither supply-suppression nor direct demand-reduction policies will be significantly successful in reducing consumption and that the continued existence of an international prohibition regime imposes unacceptable overhead costs on many societies and peoples, especially in some net-producer countries.

Nearly all decriminalization or legalization proposals address larger moral issues such as reducing crime, enhancing public health and safety, and invigorating a sense of community. Thus, an outright libertarian preference for unfettered freedom to produce, consume, or sell psychoactive drugs is hardly ever advanced; most proposals are not necessarily so much in favor of unqualified personal drug liberties as they are against the most feared consequences of prohibition policies and their law-enforcement implementation—drug-related crime and the funding of international drug mafias capable of challenging a state's very existence. Most proposals for drug-user decriminalization focus on marijuana, several on cocaine, a few on heroin. Some do not differentiate policies on the basis of a specific target drug. Some would legalize all but crack cocaine. Thus, several kinds of drug-specific decriminalization and legalization options are advanced for principal consumer countries.

In considering both drug-consumer and drug-producer countries, several decriminalization or legalization permutations are apparent. For example, production could be legalized in a net producer country, or consumption could be decriminalized in a net consumer country. A net producer country, if it could recover from international sanctions from unilateral legalization, would probably see crime-syndicate assaults decline and enjoy something of an economic boom as drug profits now squirreled away in more or less secure financial repositories abroad were brought home for investment on native soil. Of course, absorbing those funds could create externalities of their own, as seen in the case of Colombia.

If net user countries decriminalized consumption, there would be no crime tax for traffickers, smugglers, and pushers to reap and therefore no reason for them to carry out turf wars, assault police, terrorize neighborhoods, undermine countries' institutional integrity, or repatriate laundered profits to their homelands (e.g., Colombia) to carry on their assaults there. The analogy is the fate of the alcohol-related crime syndicates in the United States after that country ended Prohibition in 1933. The syndicates faded away and went into other criminal pursuits or invested their alcohol-acquired profits in legitimate businesses.

The concerns among those not converted to a legalization position are many and intense. Would consumption increase? Probably so, at least in current principal user countries, where supply may serve to create its own demand (e.g., as with crack cocaine). Would the social, political, and economic externalities that societies suffer independent of illegalizing laws and policies therefore worsen? If the answer is a plausible "yes" and legalization turned out to be both disingenuous and counterproductive, could a country recover? Would these concerns be sufficiently worrisome and empirically verifiable to make the futility and destructiveness of prohibition appear less onerous than the futility and destructiveness of legalization? Would attacking international crime by depriving drug mafias of their profits through legalization or decriminalization hurt some countries while helping others? If so, why change? These and related concerns justifiably weigh heavily on the unconverted.

Arguments for and arguments against decriminalization and legalization compel thoughtful engagement with the troubling issues of crime and consumption and their related socioeconomic and political costs. There are many imponderables in these policy issues, matters incapable of being evaluated or weighed with precision. Nevertheless, the flurry of recent events may dictate policy initiatives that produce consequences that are both helpful and hurtful, intended and unintended. In the long term, encouraging people voluntarily to turn away from drugs that are harmful to self and society would appear to be the only option with consequences that are largely predictable and that international public policy can then address with reasonable precision. Clearly, it is a difficult task.

Nevertheless, with supply suppression rejected, demand reduction encouraged, harm reduction likely, and a fallback position on international decriminalization or legalization plausible, the implications and prospects in two test countries—Colombia and Bolivia—are now reviewed.

Under a prohibition regime, our analysis has shown, principal trafficker countries such as Colombia suffer as powerful counter-states, funded by repatriated laundered profits from abroad, challenge national security and undermine governmental institutions. By contrast, principal producer (grower) countries such as Bolivia appear to reap considerable distributed benefit from the illicit-drug trade. Hundreds of thousands of peasants otherwise out of work are employed in some form. Additionally, tens of thousands of others receive benefits from the international community's efforts to suppress production through alternative-income programs, crop substitution, human and community development, and the creation of new markets (including greater access to principal consumer countries' markets) for licit goods and commodities. And countries such as Bolivia have not experienced the murderous assaults by trafficker organizations that put such a burden on other countries.

Principal consumer countries' shifting their drug-control emphasis away from supply suppression abroad to harm reduction at home (which may conceivably include decriminalization) would likely reverse this matrix of benefits and liabilities for principal producer countries. The shift would weaken the international prohibition regime, reduce international transfers to principal producer countries in support of supply suppression, and thereby change the environment of benefits and liabilities that each net producer country may experience as a result of either being caught up in the drug trade or tendering efforts to suppress it. In the wake of such events, most net producer countries would probably choose to relax domestic controls on production and consumption. No one would be subsidizing their suppression efforts. Many of these countries have already calculated that there is precious little otherwise in it for them. After all, their principal rationale for participation in the prohibition regime came in the first place from international pressure (foreign aid and economic sanctions) and fears that counterstates would emerge on drug-money profits. With international pressure gone and a precipitous reduction in drug profits severely weakening the ability of most counter- or antistates to function, the pressure would be off.

Consider Colombia. Given that it is not a great consumer and that the principal problems for the country derive from illegal refining and trafficking, one is inevitably forced to consider the potential impact of international decriminalization or legalization. Some mix of decriminalization in net consumer countries and legalization of the coca/cocaine industry in Colombia would eliminate the huge profits traffickers reap from their industry and would at the same time obliterate overnight a major source of violence—Colombia's principal social problem. The drug-funded counterstate would largely be destroyed.

There would be unwanted side effects elsewhere: Addiction rates would probably increase in net consumer countries such as the United States as people otherwise deterred by criminal sanctions and social notoriety decided to try out the "trips" that for so long have been the subject of conversation in both polite and impolite society. However, a decriminalization mix would not likely increase the use/abuse rate much in Colombia. Supplies would be "normalized" and prices would fall, but petty drug criminals and sicarios have given bazuco and cocaine such a bad name domestically that, except among small societal segments, drug taking is not a desirable thing to do. Moreover, as pricing is not a factor in Colombian consumption (cocaine is already cheap), price declines brought on by legalization/decriminalization would not likely affect national consumption.[32] It is therefore not expected that large numbers of additional Colombians would rush to consume their home-grown drug. Thus, by considerably reducing the funding for social violence without significantly increasing consumption, an international decriminalization mix would be in Colombia's favor.

With Bolivia, almost the opposite is to be expected from a radical alteration in the international prohibition regime. Small peasant growers would likely be put out of business as coca plantations (reminiscent of tea plantations in the South Pacific) replaced small-scale coca farming. The price of coca would fall to its open-market price, further adding to the distress of small farmers who do not participate in an integrated industry (through cooperatives or share holdings). Most ominously, international transfers now coming into Bolivia to suppress production would be curtailed or stopped. This combination would occasion considerable economic distress throughout at least 20 percent of Bolivian society and provoke political manifestations that most people would consider threatening.

Under the present prohibition regime, Colombia is hurt and Bolivia is helped. Under a relaxed regime, Colombia is helped and Bolivia is hurt. Bolivia's hurt could be mitigated, of course, if significant aid were to be tendered for development rather than as a surrogate for a failed effort to suppress global drug supplies.

Summary and Conclusions

Should anything be done? Can anything be done? Clearly they should and can, but conventional wisdom about prospects and possibilities needs to change. A realization must develop that supply suppression will not solve consumption problems. The economics are against it, risk-taking operatives are too plentiful, and the corrupting influence of drug money is too pervasive. Moreover, some of the harm-reduction initiatives being considered in principal consumer countries may actually hurt as well as help principal producer countries.

If a country's harm-reduction policy choice is a direct contraction of consumption, its strategy must be multifaceted and, in democracies at least, accompanied by the development of an antidrug ethos. If the policy choice is some other kind of harm-reduction package, the politics may be easier, but the outcomes are not entirely known, no doubt highly subject to each principal consumer country's idiosyncratic mix of history, social structure, and social values. If the policy choice is decriminalization/legalization in order to undercut drug-related crime and remove monstrous life-sustaining profits from the drug lords, a likely increase in consumption and the proposals' political impracticality at the present time must be fully understood.

Ideas associated with raising risks or invoking fear, enhancing rewards that appeal to self-interest, and working vigorously for an underlying change in societal values show some promise in reducing consumption. Unfortunately, successes, insofar as they have been noted, have been possible because they benefit small target groups otherwise inextricably linked to structural features of society that create poverty, despair, and resignation. Thus, the challenge for reducing demand among people of the underclass appears to be in figuring out how, in fact, to remove them from the underclass. The prospects strike to the very core of a society's structure and the cultural predilections of its ruling classes. Drug change implies social change, not just of drug users but of societal features that contribute to drug use.

Harm-reduction proposals may help to address the structural problems associated with consumption in net consumer countries. They may even succeed in reducing harm. However, most say nothing about reducing harm for principal producer countries because the proposals are focused domestically on principal consumer countries and are not internationally linked in the sense of articulating a socioeconomic and political impact on net producer countries. Serious harm-reduction proposals intended to include principal producer countries would have to address the international prohibition regime itself—perhaps in some form of de facto decriminalization—*and* the question of economic development in some sensible way.

An examination of the above policy options in various "mixes" was made for Colombia and Bolivia and, by implication, the United

States. The present international policy mix that emphasizes supply suppression is perceived to benefit mainly the U.S. middle- and upper-middle classes, who are most dissuaded from drug taking by illegality. Pursuing supply suppression via alternative development policies has been beneficial to Bolivia. The big losers are all Colombians other than drug traffickers, growers, and intermediaries.

Various harm-reduction packages were explored in terms of political feasibility and outcomes for Colombia and Bolivia. Colombia's options within the existing international prohibition regime are highly constrained and are thrown into a long-term perspective. The country, following Thoumi's advice, will need to build strong social cohesion and social controls that would discourage antisocial behavior, including illicit-drug production, marketing, and consumption. To aid or accelerate this process, the United States will need to take a careful look at whether it can continue to justify an international supply-suppression policy that accomplishes nothing at home and great mischief abroad. Ultimately, some mix of decriminalization in principal consumer countries and legalization in Colombia would destroy the "crime tax" on which traffickers depend and would eliminate a major source of violence in the country. The great virtue would be in putting the traffickers out of business.

Bolivia's concerns are different. Bolivia remains a principal coca-producing nation, not a cocaine-trafficking one, although more Bolivian nationals appear to be getting involved in the refining stages of the industry. Bolivia's problems are therefore not traffickers or refiners but growers and the economic and social conditions that attract them to the drug trade. Supply suppression in combination with vigorous policies to enhance the country's overall development, especially for those who are drawn into the illicit-drug industry, can be beneficially pursued under the existing international-prohibition regime. The present supply-suppression strategy that includes alternative development initiatives has had a positive impact on economic conditions for some Bolivian growers. However, the strategy has not necessarily dampened their general enthusiasm for coca growing.

Demand reduction, decriminalization, and perhaps even other kinds of harm reduction—the three basic policy orientations beyond supply suppression—would depress Bolivia's farmgate coca prices, particularly where it has been politically impossible to carry out vigorous crop-eradication programs. This would turn people's interest to alternative crops and alternative development—if they were available. Bolivians started growing coca for the international market in the first place because they needed alternative development. Peasants may well end the practice when they no longer need coca in order to sustain life for self and family. Absent both coca and alternative development, however, Bolivian peasants would turn much more to political agitation and, probably, ultimately to another civil war. Desperate people with no alternative income possibilities sometimes do that.

These are not happy conclusions. Although alternative development has few negative moral and social overhead reverberations, it is difficult and costly and would have to be applied globally. Decriminalization or legalization advances unknowns that can only be imagined but never determined definitively until after the fact. The immediate impact would be to hurt hundreds of thousands of growers and others who are tied economically to the illicit-drug trade. It would also undo the international drug mafia.

Nevertheless, at some point, as the current drug-control regime continues to deteriorate, some principal consumer countries may decide that the risks of the unknown are worth taking. Decriminalization/legalization would be exceptionally beneficial to Colombia and countries like it. The current prohibition regime—when accompanied by alternative development strategies—immensely aids Bolivia and its producer equivalents around the world. One country stands to win, the other to lose, if a radical change in international prohibition were to occur.

This set of conditions obviously pits principal consumer and principal producer countries' interests somewhat against each other and even differentiates among producers themselves. Nevertheless, the cries of frustration are more and more understandable: "The present course has produced no good end. Try something else." What will the intended and unintended consequences be? Better than the present ones, we hope.

I return to the opening sentences of this chapter: What ought to be done? What *can* be done? What would the consequences be?"

This study demonstrates the pragmatic attractiveness of at least two "oughts." First, globally, in socially productive ways we ought to try to reduce consumption abuse and its deleterious externalities; second, we ought to eliminate and avoid drug-control policies that produce unacceptable unintended consequences, or at least reduce those consequences as much as possible.

Direct demand reduction and other harm-reduction strategies can help to reduce consumption abuse and its deleterious externalities. Abandoning international supply-suppression strategies can help net producer countries such as Colombia in their lethal struggle with drug-funded counterstates. This approach may hurt countries such as Bolivia, but the hurt can be ameliorated by significant compensatory international finance that actually helps accomplish one of the most elusive tasks of our time—distributive economic and human resource development.

The international drug-control policy signals seem clear enough: reduce consumption in principal consumer countries, abandon supply suppression in principal producer countries, and initiate significant compensatory development in countries that would be catastrophically hurt by this reorientation.[33]

The unintended consequences of this domestic and international harm-reduction strategy cannot be known before implementation. Some of the consequences could be unfortunate, but the prospects for positive results are good. We do have ample evidence of some of the unintended consequences of the existing prohibition regime—global illicit-drug consumption largely unchanged if not increasing; a further delegitimation of the state; and aggravated endemic violence, political corruption, social stress, and cultural distortions. Those costs are fairly high. It is hard to imagine that a domestic and international harm-reduction alternative could be anything but an improvement.

Notes

1. This concept was first advanced as a new way of thinking about alternative drug-control strategies affecting industrialized net consumer nations. Here I have adapted the term for thinking about options open to net producer nations. For other people's usage, see, generally, P. A. O'Hare, R. Newcombe, A. Matthews, E. C. Buning, and E. Drucker, eds., *The Reduction of Drug-related Harm* (New York: Routledge, 1992); and Nick Heather, Alex Wodak, Ethan Nadelmann, and Pat O'Hare, eds., *Psychoactive Drugs and Harm Reduction: From Faith to Science* (London: Whurr Publishers, 1993).

2. From approximately 4,000 hectares to 2,000 hectares. United States, Department of State, Bureau of International Narcotics Matters, *International Narcotics Control Strategy Report* (Washington, D.C.: The Bureau, 1993), 307, hereafter cited as *INCSR*.

3. *INCSR 1994*, 94.

4. *INCSR 1993*, 96, 126.

5. *INCSR 1994*, 118.

6. Of the three—product interdiction at various stages of refining, crop suppression, and asset forfeiture (traffickers' money)—the latter is held up as having good prospects. With new bilateral and multilateral agreements (see David A. Andelman, "The Drug Money Maze," *Foreign Affairs* [July/August 1994], 94–108), and a little political will—enforced if necessary—as much as U.S. $100 billion could be sequestered. But Andelman ends his proposal with an interesting imponderable: "Ultimately, if all these moves prove as effective as they promise, one final determination will need to be made. At what point have the good guys won? Or, as one enforcement agent put it, 'How much money do we have to take out of the system for how long a period of time to destabilize or neutralize the drug cartels?'" (108). Under

present conditions of demand and supply, the "how much?" will unlikely ever be enough.

7. Francisco Thoumi, *Political Economy and Illegal Drugs in Colombia* (Boulder, Colo: Lynne Rienner Publishers, 1994), 280.

8. See, for example, Kirk J. Brower and M. Douglas Anglin, "Developments, Trends, and Prospects in Substance Abuse," *Journal of Drug Education* 17:2 (1987), 163–180.

9. See, for example, Patricia Bandy and Patricia Alford President, "Recent Literature on Drug Abuse Prevention and Mass Media: Focusing on Youth, Parents, Women and the Elderly," *Journal of Drug Education* 13:3 (1983), 255–271; and Reginald G. Smart, Glenn F. Murray, and Awni Arif, "Drug Abuse and Prevention Programs in 29 Countries," *International Journal of the Addictions* 23:1 (1988), 1–17.

10. The logic of such motivation has now filtered into police departments in the United States, some of which routinely report drug arrests to employers. See "Miami Beach's New Approach to Drug Arrests: Tell the Employers," *New York Times*, 23 November 1990, B21.

11. For example, in December 1989, Washington, D.C., police chief Isaac Fulwood, Jr., called the U.S. federal government's emphasis on law enforcement "absolutely wrong" and solicited increased funding of drug-treatment programs (Philip Shenon, "Bush Officials Say War on Drugs in the Nation's Capital Is a Failure," *New York Times*, 5 April 1990, A1).

12. See Greg Chesher and Alex Wodak, "Evolving a New Policy for Illicit Drugs," *Journal of Drug Issues* 20:4 (1990), 555–561; and Ethan A. Nadelmann, "Should We Legalize Drugs? Yes," *American Heritage* (February/March 1993), 42–48.

13. This is the approach the Netherlands has taken. For Dutch officials, drug use is mainly a health and welfare issue rather than a criminal issue. See, for example, Ed Leuw, "Drugs and Drug Policy in the Netherlands," In Michael Tonry and James Q. Wilson, eds., *Crime and Justice: A Review of Research*, vol. 14 (Chicago: University of Chicago Press, 1991), 229–276.

14. For basic historical information see Justine Picardie and Dorothy Wade, *Heroin: Chasing the Dragon* (Harmondsworth, Middlesex, England: Penguin Books Ltd., 1985).

15. This and other basic proposals are reviewed in Chesher and Wodak, "Evolving a New Policy."

16. See, for example, O'Hare et al., eds., *The Reduction of Drug-related Harm*, and Heather et al., eds., *Psychoactive Drugs and Harm Reduction*.

17. Ethan Nadelmann, Peter Cohen, Ernest Drucker, Ueli Locher, Gerry Stimson, and Alex Wodak, "The Harm Reduction Approach to Drug Control: International Progress," unpublished paper, April 1994.

18. The principal source on Colombia is Thoumi, *Political Economy and Illegal Drugs*.

19. According to Thoumi, the policies have also been biased against U.S. inner cities. Thoumi observes that the "benefits of the current policy are perceived to be mainly accruing to the American middle- and upper-middle classes for whom the probability of addiction declines with PSAD illegality." Ibid., 283.

20. Ibid., 278–281.

21. Ibid., 288.

22. Thoumi argues that this must also involve institutional reconstruction in the United States, "strengthening community organizations and assimilating

into the mainstream of the consuming countries their underclasses who do not have much at stake in the system" (*Political Economy and Illegal Drugs*, 288–289). Clearly, such a long-term initiative calls for the United States to re-examine its own social policies in light of drug consumption in its inner cities.

23. Principal source on Bolivia is James Painter, *Bolivia and Coca: A Study in Dependency*, vol. 1 of Studies on the Impact of the Illegal Drug Trade (Boulder, Colo.: Lynne Rienner Publishers, 1994).

24. Some coca production is legal in Bolivia, meant to satisfy the international demand for soft-drink flavoring (e.g., Coca-Cola) and domestic coca-leaf chewing. However, legal production is a small percentage of illegal production.

25. Ibid., 143.

26. Ibid.

27. Ibid., 144–145.

28. Ibid., 146.

29. A sampling of the literature on decriminalizing or legalizing drug consumption is reviewed in LaMond Tullis, *Handbook of Research on the Illicit Drug Traffic: Socioeconomic and Political Consequences* (Westport Conn.: Greenwood Press, 1991), 240–246.

30. Ibid., 244, n. 8.

31. This certainly happened with the repeal of alcohol prohibition in the United States.

32. One needs to keep in mind that consumption rates in Colombia, where cocaine is relatively cheap, are much lower than in the United States. There is a cultural predilection for alcohol in Colombia but apparently not for cocaine and its precursors. Consumption is not Colombia's aggregate problem. Illegal production and trafficking are.

33. Compensatory development need not necessarily be thought of in zero-sum terms. Pragmatic effects are viewed as being helpful to all countries. See, for example, discussions by Phillips Foster, *The World Food Problem: Tackling the Causes of Undernutrition in the Third World* (Boulder, Colo.: Lynne Rienner Publishers, 1992); World Bank, *The Challenge of Development; World Development Report 1991* (New York: Oxford University Press, 1991); and UNDP, *Human Development Report 1994* (New York: Oxford University Press, 1994).

Bibliography

• • •

Abel, Ernest L. *A Comprehensive Guide to the Cannabis Literature.* Westport, Conn.: Greenwood Press, 1979.
———. *Drugs and Sex: A Bibliography.* Westport, Conn.: Greenwood Press, 1983.
———. *Narcotics and Reproduction: A Bibliography.* Westport, Conn.: Greenwood Press, 1983.
Adams, James. *The Financing of Terror.* London: New English Library, 1986.
Aguiló, Federico. "Movilidad Espacial y Movilidad Social Generada for el Narcotráfico." In *Efectos del Narcotráfico.* La Paz: ILDIS, 1988.
Akira, Suehiro. *Capital Accumulation in Thailand: 1855–1985.* Tokyo: Centre for East Asian Cultural Studies, 1989.
Alvarez, Elena. "Illegal Export-Led Growth in the Andes: A Preliminary Economic and Socio-political Assessment for Peru." A Study For UNRISD and UNU, draft of 25 January 1993.
Ammar, Siamwala, and Chaiyut Pannyasawatsut. *Botbat Kanlaklop Kha Yaseptit To Sethakit Thai* [The Impact of Narcotics Smuggling on the Tai Economy]. Bangkok: Thailand Development Research Institute Sectoral Economics Program, 1991.
Andelman, David A. "The Drug Money Maze." *Foreign Affairs.* July/August 1994, 94–108.
Armstrong, Scott. "U.S.–Bolivia Relations Further Strained as Cocaine Smuggling Charges Fly." *Christian Science Monitor.* 14 August 1980, 5.
Asociación de Estudios Peruanos sobre la Paz (ADEP). *Cocaína: Problemas y Soluciones Andinos.* Lima: ADEP, 1990.
Bacon, John. "Is the French Connection Really Dead?" *Drug Enforcement.* Summer 1981, 19–21.
Bagley, Bruce M. "Colombia and the War on Drugs." *Foreign Affairs* 67:1 (1988), 71–92.
———. "Colombian Politics: Crisis or Continuity." *Current History* 86 (1987), 21–41.
———. "The New Hundred Years War? U.S. National Security and the War on Drugs in Latin America." *Journal of Interamerican Studies and World Affairs* 30:1 (1988), 161–182.
Bandy, Patricia, and Patricia Alford President. "Recent Literature on Drug Abuse Prevention and Mass Media: Focusing on Youth, Parents, Women and the Elderly." *Journal of Drug Education* 13:3 (1983), 255–271.
Baratta, Robert Thomas. "Political Violence in Ecuador and the AVC." *Terrorism* 10 (1987), 165–174.
Bedoya, E. "Las Causas de la Deforestación en la Amazonia Peruana: Un Problema Estructural." Clark University Institute for Development Anthropology: Cooperative Agreement on Human Settlements and Natural Resource Systems Analysis, 1990.

Blachman, M. J., and K. E. Sharpe. "The War on Drugs: American Democracy Under Assault." *World Policy Journal* 7:1 (Winter 1989–1990), 135–163.

Bohlen, Celestine. "For New Russia, New Breed of Swindler." *New York Times.* 17 March 1994, A1.

"Bolivia under Paz Estenssoro." *Latinamerica Press.* 20 October 1988, 6.

Booth, Cathy. "Tentacles of the Octopus; The Mafia Brings Europe's Worst Drug Epidemic Home." *Time.* 12 December 1988, 48.

———. *The Chinese Mafia: An Investigation into International Crime.* New York: Stein and Day, 1981.

———. *The Trail of the Triads: An Investigation into International Crime.* London: Weidenfeld and Nicolson, 1980.

Brooke, James. "One Victory, A Long War." *New York Times.* 3 December 1993, A7.

———. "The Rebels Lose Leaders, but Give Peru No Peace." *New York Times.* 5 February 1993, A3.

Brookes, Stephen. "Chinese Mafia Takes Vice Abroad." *Insight.* 24 April 1989, 34–36.

Brower, Kirk J., and M. Douglas Anglin. "Developments, Trends, and Prospects in Substance Abuse." *Journal of Drug Education* 17:2 (1987), 163–180.

Brownstein, Henry H., Hari R. Shiledar Baxi, Paul J. Goldstein, and Patrick J. Ryan. "The Relationship of Drugs, Drug Trafficking, and Drug Traffickers to Homicide." *Journal of Crime and Justice* 15:1 (1992), 25–44.

Buddenberg, Doris. "Illicit Drug Issues in Pakistan." A Study For UNRISD and UNU, draft of May 1993.

Castillo, Fabio. *La Coca Nostra.* Bogotá: Editorial Documentos Periodísticos, 1991.

———. *Los Jinetes de la Cocaína.* Bogotá: Editorial Documentos Periodísticos, 1987.

Chambers, Carl, James A. Inciardi, David M. Petersen, Harvey A. Siegel, and O. Z. White. *Chemical Dependencies: Patterns, Costs, and Consequences.* Athens: Ohio University Press, 1987.

Chesher, Greg, and Alex Wodak. "Evolving a New Policy for Illicit Drugs." *Journal of Drug Issues* 20:4 (1990), 555–561.

Chirot, Daniel., ed. *The Crisis of Leninism and the Decline of the Left: The Revolutions of 1989.* Seattle: University of Washington Press, 1991.

Christian, Shirley. "Drug Case Raises Doubts in Bolivia." *New York Times.* 5 May 1988, A3.

Clayton, Richard, and William Estep. "Marijuana Cultivation and Production in the United States, Appalachia, and Kentucky: The Context and Consequences." A Study for UNRISD and UNU, draft of 25 January 1993.

"Clean-up Campaign Gives Poor Results." *Latin American Weekly Report.* 18 May 1984, 9.

"Cocaine: The Military Connection." *Latin American Regional Reports.* 29 August 1980, 5–6.

Collins, James J. "Summary Thoughts About Drugs and Violence." In Mario De La Rosa, Elizabeth Y. Lambert, and Bernard Gropper, eds., *Drugs and Violence: Causes, Correlates, and Consequences.* NIDA research monograph 103. Washington, D.C.: U.S. Government Printing Office, 1990.

"Colombianization." *World Press Review.* February 1989, 40.

Comisión Andina de Juristas. *Violencia en Colombia.* Lima: La Comisión, 1990.

Corry, James M., and Peter Cimbolic. *Drugs: Facts, Alternatives, Decisions*. Belmont, Calif.: Wadsworth Publishing Company, 1985.

Cox, Terrence C. *Drugs and Drug Abuse: A Reference Text*. Toronto: Addiction Research Foundation, 1983.

Craig, Richard B. "Colombian Narcotics and United States–Colombian Relations." *Journal of Interamerican Studies and World Affairs* 23:3 (1981), 243–270.

———. "Illicit Drug Traffic and U.S.–Latin American Relations." *Washington Quarterly* 8 (Winter 1985), 105–134.

———. "Illicit Drug Traffic: Implications for South American Source Countries." *Journal of Interamerican Studies and World Affairs* 29 (Summer 1987), 1–35.

———. "La Campaña Permanente: Mexico's Anti-drug Campaign." *Journal of Inter-American Studies and World Affairs* 20:2 (1978), 107–131.

———. "Operation Condor: Mexico's Anti-drug Campaign Enters a New Era." *Journal of Inter-American Studies and World Affairs* 22:3 (August 1980), 345–363.

Cribb, Robert. "Opium and the Indonesian Revolution." *Modern Asian Studies* 22:4 (1988), 701–722.

Day, Mark. "Peru: Battle Intensifies over Renewed Drug Eradication Plan." *Latinamerica Press*. 7 September 1989, 1.

de La Rosa, Mario, Elizabeth Y. Lambert, and Bernard Gropper, eds. *Drugs and Violence: Causes, Correlates, and Consequences*. NIDA Research Monograph 103. Washington, D.C.: U.S. Government Printing Office, 1990.

de Soto, Hernando. *The Other Path: The Invisible Revolution in the Third World*. New York: Harper & Row, 1989.

DEA Review. December 1989, 58.

DESCO. "Coca: La Realidad que se Ignora." *Quehacer* 52. May–June 1988, 44–50.

Dickens, Charles. *Oliver Twist*. Paris: Hachette, 1870.

Econométrica. *Análisis del proyecto AgroYungas: AD/BOL/84/405*. La Paz: Econométrica, 1990.

Elliott, Michael, et al. "Global Mafia." *Newsweek*. 13 December 1993.

Faison, Seth. "U.S. Says 17 in Bronx Gang Rented Rights to Sell Heroin." *New York Times*. 27 May 1994, A12.

FEDESARROLLO and Instituto SER de Investigación. "Indicadores Sociales." *Coyuntura Social* 2 (May 1990), 36–37.

Fialka, John J. "Death of U.S. Agent in Mexico Drug Case Uncovers Grid of Graft." *Wall Street Journal*. 19 November, 1986, 1.

———. "How the Mexican Trail in Drug Agent's Death Yields Cache of 'Crack.'" *Wall Street Journal*. 20 November, 1986, 1.

Flynn, Stephen E. *The Transnational Drug Challenge and the New World Order*. Washington, D.C.: Center for Strategic and International Studies, 1993.

Foster, Phillips. *The World Food Problem: Tackling the Causes of Undernutrition in the Third World*. Boulder, Colo.: Lynne Rienner Publishers, 1992.

Franks, Jeffrey. "La Economía de la Coca en Bolivia: ¿Plaga o Salvación?" *Informe Confidencial* 64 (June 1991).

Ghai, Dharam. Preface to LaMond Tullis, "Illicit Drug Taking and Prohibition Laws: Public Consequences and the Reform of Public Policy in the United States." UNRISD Discussion Paper. April 1991.

Goldstein, Paul J. "The Drugs-violence Nexus: A Tripartite Conceptual Framework." *Journal of Drug Issues* 15 (1985), 493–506.

Grapendaal, Martin, Ed Leuw, and Hans Nelen. "Drugs and Crime in an Accommodating Social Context: The Situation in Amsterdam." *Contemporary Drug Problems.* (Summer 1992), 303–326.

Groedidler, Camille. "Mexico Becoming Center of Drug Traffic Despite Anti-Drug Drive." *Christian Science Monitor.* 11 January 1984, 9.

Gugliotta, Guy, and Jeff Leen. *Kings of Cocaine: An Astonishing True Story of Murder, Money and International Corruption.* New York: Simon and Schuster, 1989.

Harrison, Lana D. "International Perspectives on the Interface of Drug Use and Criminal Behavior." *Contemporary Drug Problems.* (Summer 1992), 188–189.

———. "The Drug-Crime Nexus in the USA." *Contemporary Drug Problems.* (Summer 1992).

Headly, Bernard D. "War in 'Babylon': Dynamics of the Jamaican Informal Drug Economy." *Social Justice* 15:3–4 (1988), 61–86.

Healy, Kevin. "Coca, the State, and the Peasantry in Bolivia, 1982–1988." *Journal of Interamerican Studies and World Affairs* 30:2–3 (Summer 1988), 105–126.

———. "The Boom Within the Crisis: Some Recent Effects of Foreign Cocaine Markets on Bolivian Rural Society and Economy." In Deborah Pacini and Christine Franquemont, eds. *Coca and Cocaine, Effects on People and Policy in Latin America.* Boston: Cultural Survival, 1986.

Heather, Nick, Alex Wodak, Ethan Nadelmann, and Pat O'Hare, eds. *Psychoactive Drugs and Harm Reduction: From Faith to Science.* London: Whurr Publishers, 1993.

Henning, Daniel. "Production and Trafficking of Opium and Heroin in Laos." A Study for UNRISD and UNU, draft of 26 May 1993.

Hersh, Seymour M. "The Wild East." *Atlantic Monthly.* June 1994, 61–82.

Hurtado, Anturiano. *La Hiena: Drama Social Sobre la Droga, Drogadicción, y Corrupción.* Santa Cruz, Bolivia: Empresa Editora El País, 1986.

Inciardi, James A. "Beyond Cocaine: Basuco, Crack, and Other Coca Products." *Contemporary Drug Problems* 14:3 (1987), 461–492.

———. "Editor's Introduction: Debating the Legalization of Drugs." *American Behavioral Scientist* 32:3 (1989), 233–242.

———. *The War on Drugs: Heroin, Cocaine, Crime and Public Policy.* Palo Alto, Calif.: Mayfield, 1986.

Inciardi, James A., and Duane C. McBride (1989). "Legalization: A High-Risk Alternative in the War on Drugs." *American Behavioral Scientist* 32:3 (1989), 259–289.

Informe Final de la Evaluación del Proyecto AID No 527–0244, Desarrollo del Area del Alto Huallaga. Lima: ECONSULT, 1986.

Isikoff, Michael. "Peruvian Coca Fields Sprayed in Test of Plan." *Washington Post,* 22 March 1989, A16.

Kamm, Henry. "Afghan Opium Yield up as Pakistan Curbs Crop." *New York Times.* 14 April 1988, A16.

"Kanfin" [Opium Matters]. *Samitsan* [Excise Department Journal; Myanmar] 1:2 (November 1941), 38.

Kendall, John. "Drugs, Money Add up to Temptation for Police." *Los Angeles Times.* 20 December 1988, 3.

Kerr, Peter. "Chinese Now Dominate New York Heroin Trade." *New York Times.* 9 August 1987, B1.

Kline, David. "From a Smugglers' Paradise Comes Hell." *Maclean's*, 8 November 1982, 14.

———. "How to Lose the Coke War." *Atlantic* 259:5 (1987), 22–27.

———. "The Khyber Connection." *Christian Science Monitor.* Three-part series, 9–11 November 1982.

Kolata, Gina. "In Cities, Poor Families Are Dying of Crack." *New York Times.* 11 August 1989, All.

Kozaczuk, Wladyslaw. *Enigma: How the German Machine Cipher Was Broken, and How It Was Read by the Allies in World War Two.* Trans. by Christopher Kasparek. Frederick, Md.: University Publications of America, 1984.

Krauthausen, Ciro, and Luis F. Sarmiento, *Cocaína y Co.: Un Mercado Ilegal por Dentro.* Bogotá: Tercer Mundo Editores, 1991.

Kumarasingha, D. P. "Drugs—A Growing Problem in Sri Lanka." *Forensic Science International* 36 (1988), 283–284.

Kwitny, Jonathan. "Money, Drugs and the Contras." *The Nation.* 29 August 1987, 1.

La Violencia en Colombia: 40 Años de Laterinto. Bogotá: Pontificia Universidad Javeriana, Facultad de Estudios Interdisciplinarios, Programa de Estudios Políticos, 1989.

Lao Peoples Democratic Republic, National Commission for Drug Control and Supervision (LNCDCS). *Drug Control in 1990.* Vientiane: LNCDCS, February 1990.

Larmer, Brook. "Colombians Take Over 'Coke' Trade in Mexico." *Christian Science Monitor.* 9 January 1989, 1.

———. "Mexico's Corruption Clampdown: Arrest of Corrupt Officials Along with Drug Baron May Root out Graft." *Christian Science Monitor.* 13 April 1989, 1.

Latin America Weekly Report. 11 August 1994, 354–355.

Lee, Rensselaer W., III. "The Drug Trade and Developing Countries." *Policy Focus* 4 (May 1987), 2–10.

———. *The White Labyrinth: Cocaine and Political Power.* New Brunswick, N.J.: Transaction Publishers, 1989.

———. "Why the U.S. Cannot Stop South American Cocaine." *Orbis* 32 (Fall 1988), 499–519.

Leuw, Ed. "Drugs and Drug Policy in the Netherlands." In Michael Tonry and James Q. Wilson, eds., *Crime and Justice: A Review of Research.* Vol. 14. Chicago: University of Chicago Press, 1991, 229–276.

Lintner, Bertil. "Opium War." *Far Eastern Economic Review.* 20 January 1994, 22–26.

Losada, Rodrigo, and Eduardo Vélez, "Muertes Violentas en Colombia, 1979–1986." Informe de Investigación. Bogotá: Instituto SER de Investigación, April 1988.

Lupsha, Peter A. "Drug Trafficking: Mexico and Colombia in Comparative Perspective." *Journal of International Affairs* 35:1 (1981), 95–115.

MacDonald, Scott B. *Dancing on a Volcano: The Latin American Drug Trade.* New York: Praeger, 1988.

———. *Mountain High, White Avalanche: Cocaine and Power in the Andean States and Panama.* New York: Praeger, 1989.

———. "Slaying the Drug Hydra." *SAIS Review* 9:1 (1989), 65–85.

McBeth, John. "The Opium Laws," *Far Eastern Economic Review.* 29 March 1984, 40–43.

McBride, Duane C., and Clyde B. McCoy. "The Drugs-Crime Relationship: An Analytical Framework." *The Prison Journal* 73:3–4 (September/December 1993), 257–278.

McClintock, Cynthia. "The War on Drugs: The Peruvian Case." *Journal of Inter-American Studies and World Affairs* 30:2–3 (Summer/Fall 1988), 127–142.

McFadden, Robert D. "Head of Medellín Cocaine Cartel Is Killed by Troops in Colombia." *New York Times.* 3 December 1993, A1.

McGee, Robert T., and Edgar L. Feige. "Policy Illusion, Macroeconomic Instability, and the Unrecorded Economy." In Edgar L. Feige, ed., *The Underground Economies: Tax Evasion and Information Distortion.* Cambridge: Cambridge University Press, 1989, 81–109.

McGuire, Phillip C. "Jamaican Posses: A Call for Cooperation Among Law Enforcement Agencies." *Police Chief.* (January 1988), 20.

McWeeney, Sean M. "The Sicilian Mafia and Its Impact on the United States." *FBI Law Enforcement Bulletin.* (February 1987), 1–9.

Mecham, Michael. "Drug Smugglers Prove Elusive Targets for Interdiction Forces." *Aviation Week and Space Technology.* 30 January 1989, 34–36.

Medina-Mora, María Elena, and María del Carmen Mariño. "Drug Abuse in Latin America." In Peter H. Smith, ed., *Drug Policy in the Americas.* Boulder, Colo.: Westview Press, 1992.

Méndez Asensio, Luis. *Caro Quintero al Trasluz.* Mexico City: Plaza & Janes, 1985.

"Miami Beach's New Approach to Drug Arrests: Tell the Employers." *New York Times.* 23 November 1990, B21.

Miller, Dave. "Drug Mafia Arms Campesinos." *Latinamerica Press.* 14 July 1988, 6.

"Money Laundering: Who's Involved, How It Works, and Where It's Spreading." *Business Week.* 18 March 1985, 74.

Morales, Edmundo. "Coca and Cocaine Economy and Social Change in the Andes of Peru." *Economic Development and Cultural Change* 35:1 (1986), 143–161.

———. "Coca Culture: The White Cities of Peru." *Thesis* (CUNY graduate school magazine) 1:1 (Fall 1986), 4–11.

———. *Cocaine: White Gold Rush in Peru.* Tucson: University of Arizona Press, 1989.

———. "Comprehensive Economic Development: An Alternative Measure to Reduce Cocaine Supply." *The Journal of Drug Issues* 20:4 (Fall), 629–637.

———. "Land Reform, Social Change, and Modernization in the National Periphery: A Study of Five Villages in the Northeastern Andes of Peru." Ph.D. dissertation, City University of New York, 1983.

Mugford, Stephen. "Licit and Illicit Drug Use, Health Costs and the 'Crime Connection' in Australia: Public Views and Policy Implications." *Contemporary Drug Problems.* (Summer 1992).

Nadelmann, Ethan A. "Should We Legalize Drugs? Yes." *American Heritage.* (February/March 1993), 42–48.

———. "The DEA in Latin America: Dealing with Institutionalized Corruption." *Journal of Interamerican Studies and World Affairs* 29 (Winter 1987), 1–39.

———. "U.S. Drug Policy: A Bad Export." *Foreign Policy* 70 (Spring 1988), 97–108.

Nadelmann, Ethan A., Peter Cohen, Ernest Drucker, Ueli Locher, Gerry Stimson and Alex Wodak. "The Harm Reduction Approach to Drug Control: International Progress." Unpublished paper, April 1994.

National Institute of Drug Abuse (NIDA). *National Household Survey on Drug Abuse.* Rockville, Md.: NIDA, 1988; 1990.

O'Hare, P. A., R. Newcombe, A. Matthews, E. C. Buning, and E. Drucker, eds. *The Reduction of Drug-related Harm.* New York: Routledge, 1992.

Orjuela, Luis J. "Narcotráfico y Política en la Década de los Ochenta: Entre la Represión y el Diálogo." In Carlos G. Arrieta et al., eds., *Narcotráfico en Colombia: Dimensiones Políticas, Económicas, Jurídicas e Internacionales.* Bogotá: Tercer Mundo Editores—Ediciones Uniandes, 1990, 216–219.

Orozco, Jorge Eliécer. *Lehder . . . el Hombre.* Bogotá: Plaza & Janes, 1987.

Ortíz Pinchetti, Francisco, Miguel Cabildo, Federico Campbell, and Ignacio Rodríguez. *La Operación Cóndor.* Mexico City: Proceso, 1981.

Painter, James. *Bolivia and Coca: A Study in Dependency.* Vol. 1 of Studies on the Impact of the Illegal Drug Trade. Boulder, Colo.: Lynne Rienner Publishers, 1994.

———. "Bolivian Military Leader Questions DEA's Role in Drug Bust Gone Awry." *Christian Science Monitor.* 12 July 1991, 6.

Peña, R. Análisis Agroeconómico de la Producción de Coca en la Región del Alto Huallaga. Lima: Project AD/PER/86/459-PNUD, 1987.

Pérez G., Augusto. "Los Años Ochentas." In Augusto Pérez G., ed., *Historia de la Drogadicción en Colombia.* Bogotá: Tercer Mundo—Ediciones Uniandes, 111–116.

Perl, Raphael Francis. "Congress and International Drug Policy." *Extensions* (A Journal of the Carl Albert Congressional Research and Studies Center [U.S.]), Fall 1993, 6–9.

Picardie, Justine, and Dorothy Wade. *Heroin: Chasing the Dragon.* Harmondsworth, Middlesex, England: Penguin Books Ltd., 1985.

President's Commission on Organized Crime. *The Impact: Organized Crime Today.* Report to the President and the Attorney General. Washington, D.C.: The Commission, 1986.

"President Turns Right for Support." *Latin American Weekly Report.* 8 June 1985, 5.

"Probing into the Underworld." *Latin America Regional Reports.* 4 March 1983, 3–4.

Quiroga, José Antonio. *Coca/Cocaína: Una Visión Boliviana.* La Paz, Bolivia: AIPE–PROCOM/CEDLA/CID, 1990.

Ramírez, Sergio García. *El Narcotráfico: Un Punto de Vista Mexicano.* México: Miguel Angel Porrúa, 1989.

Renard, Ronald D. "Socioeconomic and Political Impact of Production, Trade and Use of Narcotic Drugs in Burma." A Study for UNRISD and UNU, draft of 3 November 93.

Reuband, Karl-Heinz. "Drug Addiction and Crime in West Germany: A Review of the Empirical Evidence." *Contemporary Drug Problems.* (Summer 1992), 327–349.

Reuter, Peter, and Mark A. R. Kleiman. "Risks and Prices: An Economic Analysis of Drug Enforcement." In Michael Tonry and Norval Morris, eds., *Crime and Justice: An Annual Review of Research.* Vol. 7. Chicago: University of Chicago Press, 1986.

Richburg, Keith B. "More Heroin Said to Enter U.S. from Asia; Chinese Gangs Replacing Traditional Organized Crime Networks." *Washington Post.* 16 March 1988, A16.

Riding, Alan. "Shaken Colombia Acts at Last on Drugs." *New York Times.* 11 September 1984, 1.

Robertson, Frank. *Triangle of Death: The Inside Story of the Triads—The Chinese Mafia.* London: Routledge and K. Paul, 1977.

Robinson, Carl. "The Day of the Triads: Hong Kong's Gangs Move in on Australia." *Newsweek.* 7 November 1988, 72.

Rohter, Larry. "Mexicans Arrest Top Drug Figure and 80 Policemen." *New York Times.* 11 April 1989, 1.

———. "Mexico Is Accusing a Slain U.S. Agent." *New York Times.* 16 January, 1990, A7.

Ross, John. "Colombia: Judge's Murder Linked to Drug Mafias." *Latinamerica Press.* 4 September 1986, 6.

Ross, Timothy. "Colombia Goes after Drug Barons." *Christian Science Monitor.* 12 January 1987, 9.

Rubin, Roberta Louise. "International Agreements: Two Treaties Between the U.S. and Italy." *Harvard International Law Journal* 26 (1985), 601–607.

Sarmiento, Eduardo. "Economía del Narcotráfico." *Desarrollo y Sociedad* 26 (September 1990), 11–40.

———. "Economía del Narcotráfico." In Carlos G. Arrieta, et al., eds., *Narcotráfico en Colombia: Dimensiones Políticas, Económicas, Jurídicas e Internacionales.* Bogotá: Tercer Mundo Editores—Ediciones Uniandes, 1990, 43–98.

Satchell, Michael. "Narcotics: Terror's New Ally." *U.S. News and World Report.* 4 May 1987, 30–37.

Schachter, Jim. "Customs Service Cleans House in a Drive on Drug Corruption." *Los Angeles Times.* 16 June 1987, 3.

Selser, Gregorio. *Bolivia: El Cuartelazo de los Cocadólares.* Mexico: Mexsur, 1982.

Shapiro, Arthur M. "Drugs and Politics in Latin America: The Argentine Connections." *The New Leader.* 27 June 1988, 9.

Shenon, Philip. "Bush Officials Say War on Drugs in the Nation's Capital Is a Failure." *New York Times.* 5 April 1990, A1.

———. "Thai Legislators Are Enmeshed In Drug Charges by the U.S.." *New York Times.* 26 May 1994, 5.

Singhanetra-Renard, Anchalee. "Socioeconomic and Political Impact of Production, Trade and Use of Narcotic Drugs in Thailand." A Study for UNRISD and UNU, draft of 23 April 1993.

"Slice of Vice: More Miami Cops Arrested." *Time.* 8 January 1986, 72.

Smart, Reginald G., Glenn F. Murray, and Awni Arif. "Drug Abuse and Prevention Programs in 29 Countries." *International Journal of the Addictions* 23:1 (1988), 1–17.

Spain, James W. "The United States, Turkey and the Poppy." *Middle East Journal* 29:3 (1975), 395–409.

Steinitz, Mark S. "Insurgents, Terrorists, and the Drug Trade." *Washington Quarterly* 8:4 (1985), 141–156,

Sterling, Claire. "Redfellas: The Growing Power of Russia's Mob." *The New Republic.* 11 April 1994, 19–27.

Strug, D. "The Foreign Policy of Cocaine: Comments on a Plan to Eradicate the Coca Leaf in Peru." In Deborah Pacini and Christine Franquemont, eds., *Coca and Cocaine: Effects on People and Policy in Latin America.* Cambridge, Mass.: Cultural Survival, 1985, 73–88.

Thailand, Office of Narcotics Control Board (ONCB). *Thailand Narcotics Annual Report.* Bangkok: Office of the Prime Minister, 1988.

Thak, Chaloemtiarana. *Thailand: The Politics of Despotism*. Bangkok: Social Science Association, 1979.

Thornton, Mary. "Sales of Opium Reportedly Fund Afghan Rebels." *Washington Post*. 17 December 1983, A32.

Thoumi, Francisco. *Political Economy and Illegal Drugs in Colombia*. Boulder, Colo.: Lynne Rienner Publishers, 1994.

Tokatlián, Juan G. "La Política Exterior de Colombia Hacia Estados Unidos, 1978–1990: El Asunto de las Drogas y su Lugar en las Relaciones Entre Bogotá y Washington." In Carlos G. Arrieta, et al., eds., *Narcotráfico en Colombia: Dimensiones Políticas, Económicas, Jurídicas e Internacionales*. Bogotá: Tercer Mundo Editores—Ediciones Uniandes, 1990.

Tonry, Michael, and James Q. Wilson, eds. *Drugs and Crime. Crime and Justice: A Review of Research*. Vol. 13. Chicago: University of Chicago Press, 1990.

Toro, María Celia. "Mexican Drug Control Policy: Origin, Purpose, Consequences." A Study For UNRISD and UNU, draft of 9 June 1993. In press, Lynne Rienner Publishers, Boulder, Colorado.

Treaster, Joseph B. "U.S. Altering Tactics in Drug War." *New York Times*. 17 September 1993, A7.

Tullis, LaMond. "Cocaine and Food: Likely Effects of a Burgeoning Transnational Industry on Food Production in Bolivia and Peru." In W. Ladd Hollist and F. LaMond Tullis, eds., *Pursuing Food Security: Strategies and Obstacles in Africa, Asia, Latin America, and the Middle East*. Boulder, Colo.: Lynne Rienner Publishers, 1987.

———. *Handbook of Research on the Illicit Drug Traffic: Socioeconomic and Political Consequences*. Westport, Conn.: Greenwood Press, 1991.

———. *Lord and Peasant in Peru: A Paradigm of Political and Social Change*. Cambridge, Mass.: Harvard University Press, 1970.

———. *Politics and Social Change in Third World Countries*. New York: Wiley, 1973.

UNDP, *Human Development Report 1994*. New York: Oxford University Press, 1994.

UNESCAP. "Proceedings of the Meeting of Senior Officials on Drug Abuse Issues in Asia and the Pacific." Bangkok, 1991.

United Nations. Conference Room Paper No. 1. 13 October 1989. Prepared for the Joint Meetings of the Committee for Programme and Co-ordination and the Administrative Committee on Co-ordination, 24th series. New York, 16–18 October 1989. Ref. No. 89–24360.

United Nations. *The United Nations and Drug Abuse Control*. New York: UN, 1987.

U.S. Congress, House Committee on Foreign Affairs. Hearing. "Narcotics Review in South America." One Hundredth Congress, Second Session. Washington, D.C.: U.S. Government Printing Office, 1988.

———. Hearing. "Recent Developments in Colombia." One Hundredth Congress, Second Session. Washington, D.C.: U.S. Government Printing Office, 1988.

———. Hearing. "Review of Latin American Narcotics Control Issues." One Hundredth Congress, First Session. Washington, D.C.: U.S. Government Printing Office, 1987.

———. Hearing. "The Role and Activities of the National Drug Enforcement Policy Board." Ninety-ninth Congress, Second Session. Washington, D.C.: U.S. Government Printing Office, 1986.

————. "Turkish Opium Ban Negotiations." Ninety-Third Congress, Second Session. Washington, D.C.: U.S. Government Printing Office, 1974.

U.S. Congress, House Committee on Government Operations. "United States Anti-narcotic Activities in the Andean Region." Washington, D.C.: U.S. Government Printing Office, 1990.

U.S. Congress, House Committee on International Relations, Subcommittee on Future Foreign Policy Research and Development. "The Effectiveness of Turkish Opium Control." Ninety-Fourth Congress, First Session. Washington, D.C.: U.S. Government Printing Office, 1975.

U.S. Congress, House Report of a Staff Study Mission to Peru, Bolivia, Colombia, and Mexico, November 19 to December 18, 1988 to the Committee on Foreign Affairs. "U.S. Narcotics Control Programs in Peru, Bolivia, Colombia, and Mexico: An Update." One Hundred First Congress, First Session. Washington, D.C.: U.S. Government Printing Office, 1989.

U.S. Congress, Senate Committee on Governmental Affairs. "Cocaine Production, Eradication, and the Environment: Policy, Impact and Options." Washington, D.C.: U.S. Government Printing Office, 1990.

U.S. Department of State, Bureau of International Narcotics Matters. *International Narcotics Control Strategy Report.* Annuals of 1989, 1990, 1991, 1993, 1994.

"U.S. Interdiction Efforts Forcing Coke Shipments to Europe, OC Commissioners Report." *Crime Control Digest.* 21 October 1985, 2–3.

U.S. News and World Report. 17 January 1994, 22–41.

Vichai, Poshyachinda, et al. *Epidemiologic Study of Drug Dependence Patients at the Buddhist Temple Treatment Center: Tam Kraborg.* Bangkok: Chulalongkorn University Institute of Health; Research Technical Report No. DD-1/77, 1977.

Wardlaw, Grant. "Linkages between the Illegal Drugs Traffic and Terrorism." *Conflict Quarterly.* (Summer 1988), 5–26.

Washington Office on Latin America (WOLA). *Clear and Present Dangers: The U.S. Military and the War on Drugs in the Andes.* Washington, D.C.: WOLA, 1991.

Watson, Russell. "Death on the Spot." *Newsweek.* 13 December 1993.

Weintraub, Richard. "Pakistani Drug Drive Seen in 2 Major Hauls; Military Officers Held in Seizure of Heroin." *Washington Post.* 31 July 1986, A27.

Welch, Mary Ellen. "The Extraterritorial War on Cocaine: Perspectives from Bolivia and Colombia." *Suffolk Transnational Law Journal* 12 (1988), 39–81.

Westermeyer, Joseph. *Poppies, Pipes and People: Opium and Its Use in Laos.* Berkeley: University of California Press, 1982.

Wichian, Saengkaeo. "Yaseptit Hai Thot Kap Khwammankhong Chat Bangkok." *Nitayasan Ratchataphirak* 18:3 (3 July 1976), 39–40 (Thesis, Thailand National Defense College).

Wilson, James Q. "Against the Legalization of Drugs." *Commentary* 89:2 (February 1990), 21–28.

Wilson, James., and John J. DiIulio Jr. "Crackdown." *The New Republic* 201:2 (10 July 1989), 21–25.

Wines, Michael. "Traffic in Cocaine Reported Surging Weeks after Colombian Crackdown." *New York Times.* 1 November 1989, A10.

Wirpsa, Leslie. "Colombian Mafia Hurt by Testimony of Key Deserter." *Miami Herald.* 12 June 1989, 4A.

Wolman, Karen. "Europe's Cocaine Boom Confounds Antidrug War." *Christian Science Monitor.* 19 June, 1989, 1–2.

Yang, Dali L. "Illegal Drugs, Policy Change, and State Power: The Case of Contemporary China." *Journal of Contemporary China* 4 (Fall 1993), 28.

Zinberg, Norman. *Set and Setting: The Basis for Controlled Intoxicant Use.* New Haven, Conn.: Yale University Press, 1984.

Index

• • •

Afghanistan, opium trade in, 36, 117, 118, 119, 137

Alternative development: and crop eradication, 162–163; and economic development, 98–99, 103, 110–111, 198; foreign aid for, 98, 163, 164–165; and strengthening of legal markets, 98–99; and supply-suppression efforts, 206–207

Andean Strategy, 91, 102, 130 (n.31)

Asset seizure, 119, 121

Australia, drug-traffic organizations in, 21

Bazuco, 29 (n.26), 36, 52, 126

Bhutto, Benazir, 118

Bolivia, 155–167; alternative development in, 103, 162–166, 179, 198, 206–207; coca production and processing in, 6 (n.8), 26, 36, 37, 39–41, 155–156, 179; cocaine consumption in, 49–50; drug-control efforts in, 99–104, 156, 163, 164, 182–183, 196–197; drug involvement of rural elites in, 72–73; drug-related crime and violence in, 14; economic impact of drug industry in, 99–100, 155–157, 167–168; environmental impact of drug industry in, 169–170; guerrilla groups in, 155; harm-reduction options in, 196–200; interdiction and forced eradication in, 100–103, 162–163, 198; and international decriminalization/legalization proposals, 204; migration to coca-growing regions in, 165, 168; money laundering in, 160–161; peasant growers in, 72, 155; public corruption in, 168–169; small-scale

building societies in, 160, 161; trafficking in, 14, 71–74; U.S. military involvement in, 101–103, 155, 156, 196–197

Britain: colonial drug policies of, 114, 116–117; drug abuse approach in, 189

Bush administration, drug-control policies of, 102, 130 (n.31)

Cali cocaine syndicate, 21, 31 (n.63), 66, 68, 73, 143, 152, 181

Camarena, Enrique, 105

Cannabis. *See* Marijuana

Cardona, Pardo, 75

Caro Quintero group, 75

Chile, cocaine processing in, 37

China: Chinese Triads in, 21, 31 (nn.60, 61); drug production in, 37; trafficking and drug-related crimes in, 12

Coca/cocaine: increased production of, 4, 6 (n.8); legal production of, 142, 210 (n.24); major producers of, 2, 4, 6 (n.8), 26, 36, 37, 42–43, 37, 59 (n.1), 60 (n.17), 71–74, 95, 99, 179; syndicates, 21, 22, 24, 31 (nn.62, 63), 66–68, 73, 95, 143, 145, 173 (n.21); value of, 142, 156–158. *See also* Bolivia; Colombia; Peru

Colombia, 140–154; Cali cocaine syndicate in, 21, 31 (n.63), 66, 68, 73, 143, 152, 181; crop eradication in, 93; drug consumption in, 52–53, 149–150, 210 (n.32); drug money in, 2, 92–93, 142–146; drug syndicates and drug "families" in, 21, 31 (nn.62, 63), 66–68, 73, 143, 152, 181; drug-control laws and policies in, 92–94; drug-related

crime and violence in, 14, 22–23,
95, 146–148, 151, 152–153;
economic consequences of drug
industry in, 141–146;
environmental impact of drug
trade in, 169; escalated drug-
control efforts as policy option in,
180–182; extradition in, 93, 94–95,
193; governmental ambivalence
toward illicit-drug industry in, 92;
governmental delegitimation in,
66, 67, 70, 141, 150–154, 192;
harm-reduction options in,
193–196, 199–200; interdiction and
anti-money-laundering activities in,
93–94; and international
decriminalization and legalization,
203–204; marijuana industry in, 93,
94, 95; Medellín syndicate in, 21,
22, 66, 68, 73, 95, 143, 145, 152,
173 (n.21); narco-guerrilla alliance
in, 68–69, 154; rural social decline
in, 149; social impact of drug trade
in, 146–150; trafficking in, 2, 4, 6
(n.8), 14, 36, 42–43, 66–70, 92–93,
95, 146–150, 152–153; value of
illicit-drug trade in, 2, 157
Commission of the European
Communities (CEC), 118
Consumption, 36, 49–58; increase in,
49; socioeconomic and political
effects of, 135–136. *See also specific
countries*
Consumption reduction. *See* Drug-
control strategy(ies); Harm-
reduction strategy(ies)
Corruption, drug-related, 8–9, 11, 15,
138–139, 168–169. *See also specific
countries*
Costa Rica, drug use in, 51
Crack cocaine: crime and violence by
users, 8, 11, 14; increased
production of, 4
Crime and violence, 7–24; and *bazuco*,
29 (n.26), 36, 52, 126; corruptive-
criminality dimension in, 8–9, 11;
and crack cocaine, 8, 11, 14; by
drug abusers, 8, 11–13, 14;
economic-compulsive dimension
in, 8, 9–10; and organized crime,
14–18, 20–21; and political
terrorism, 13–14, 19, 22–23, 32
(n.70), 71, 96, 98, 182; by
producers, 19, 24–27;
psychopharmacological dimension
in, 8, 9; and traffickers, systemic
violence of, 10–11, 13–24, 65,
66–67, 146–148, 151, 152–153; of
youth gangs, 12–13
Crop-reduction measures, 93, 97,
100–103, 110–111, 112, 117, 123,
124–125, 126, 162–163, 166–167,
198

Decriminalization and legalization,
194, 197, 200–204
Drug-control strategy(ies), 89–133;
asset seizure, 119, 121;
consumption reduction, 91; crop
reduction, 93, 97, 100–103,
110–111, 112, 117, 123, 124–125,
126, 162–163, 166–167, 198; direct
consumption reduction, 126–127;
drug abuse prevention, 184–188;
economic development, 98–99,
110–111; effectiveness of, 122–127,
178–180, 183; eradication, 96,
100–103, 123, 166–167;
extradiction, 93, 119, 193;
interdiction, 96, 100–103, 123,
124–125, 166–167; international
agreements, 90–91; law
enforcement, 139–140, 184,
189–190; in principal consuming
vs. principal producing countries,
122–123; supply-driven consumption formula in, 122–127; trafficker
disruption, 92, 123–124, 125–126.
See also Alternative development;
Harm-reduction strategy(ies)
Drug industry, illicit: as business
enterprise, 4–5; as vertically
integrated, 71, 82, 84
Drug profits: and conspicuous
consumption of traffickers, 92–93,
139, 167–168; effect of illegality on
drug value, 143; estimates of, 2,
142, 156–158; laundering of, 15,
17, 18, 68, 160; and peasant
growers, 13, 25, 30 (n.52); and
public corruption, 139, 168–169

Economic development, as drug-
control approach, 98–99, 110–111

Ecuador, drug-related political
terrorism in, 23
Escobar, Pablo, 66, 68, 95, 151
Europe, Eastern, as new market,
16–17, 18
Europe, Western, trafficking in,
17–18
Extradition, 93, 94–95, 119, 193

Finsa (Firma Integral de Servicios
Arévalo), 161
French Connection, the, 20, 30
(n.58)
Fujimori, President Alberto, 71

Gacha, Gonzalo Rodríguez, 66, 67
Gallardo, Ángel Félix, 75
García Meza, Gen. Lucas, 168
Germany, drug-related crime in,
11–12
Golden Crescent, opiate trade in, 3
Golden Triangle, illicit-drug
production in, 36, 46–47, 75, 76,
84
Guatemala: drug production in, 36,
37; drug-related political terrorism
in, 22–23

Harm-reduction strategy(ies), 5,
183–204; community involvement
as, 185; consumption reduction as,
184–188; decriminalization and
legalization, 200–204; and drug
laws, 189–190; fear as motivation
in, 186–187, 188; and
nongovernmental organizations
(NGOs), 195; prohibition, 184;
self-interest drive as, 187–188;
treatment programs, 185;
workplace initiatives, 184–185, 209
(n.10)
Heroin: China White, 79;
consumption, 36, 109–110; crime
by users, 11; increased production
of, 4
Herrera family, 75
Hong Kong, heroin transit in, 37

Illegality, and retail value of drugs,
142
Insurgent movements, and drug
traffickers, 19, 22, 68–69, 71, 76–77,

79, 80–81, 84–85, 96, 98, 138–139,
154, 155, 182
Interdiction strategy, 96, 100–103,
123, 124–125, 166–167
Iran, illegal opiate trade in, 36
Italy, drug-traffic organizations in, 21

Jamaica, as cannabis exporter, 36
Jamaican Posses, 21, 31 (n.64)
Japanese Yakuza, 21
Juárez cartel, 75

Kempff Mercado, Noel, 169
Kentucky, U.S.: drug production and
trafficking in, 48–49; supply-
reduction attempts in, 120–122
Khun Sa, 80, 81

Laos: addiction and consumption in,
56–57; crop-substitution programs
in, 111, 112; drug production in,
46–47; drug trafficking in, 77–79;
government drug-control efforts in,
111–113; government-military
cooperation in drug trade, 77–78;
insurgent and organized-crime
movements in, 79; opiate trade in,
36
Lara Bonilla, Rodrigo, 94, 151
La Violencia, 146–147, 151
Law-enforcement initiatives, 184,
189–190
League of Nations, 90
Lebanon, illegal opiate trade in, 37
Lehder, Carlos, 67, 68
Lo Hsing-han (Luo Xinghan), 80, 81

Marijuana/cannabis: production, 4,
36, 42–43, 48–49, 121–122;
traffickers, in Mexico, 74–75;
traffickers, organization of, 24
Medellín syndicate, 21, 22, 66, 68, 73,
95, 143, 145, 152, 173 (n.21)
Mexico: drug consumption in,
50–52; drug-control efforts in,
104–107; drug "families" in, 75;
drug production in, 36, 43; drug-
related corruption in, 105–106;
marijuana trafficking in, 74–75;
Mexican mafia, 21, 31 (n.62); as
transshipment country, 17, 43,
105

Migration, drug-related, 99, 165, 168, 182

Myanmar/Burma, 113–116; Chinese Kuomintang (KMT) in, 80, 87 (n.43), 108; drug consumption in, 55–56; drug production in, 44–46; drug trafficking in, 80–81; drug-related political terrorism in, 23; government drug-control efforts in, 114–115, 116; history of narcotic drug use in, 113–114; opiate trade in, 36; State Law and Order Restoration Council (SLORC), 80–81

Netherlands, the: drug-related crime in, 11–12; drug-traffic organizations in, 21; drug-use approach in, 200, 209 (n.13)

Nuclear weapons, and drug trade, 15

Opiate trade, 36, 81–83, 107–108, 113–114, 118, 119

Pakistan: crop substitution in, 117–118; demand-reduction initiatives on, 118–119; drug-control efforts in, 117–120; drug organizations in, 83; drug production and consumption in, 36, 47–48, 57–58, 81–83; drug trade in, big business aspect of, 82; drug trade in, economic benefits of, 137; history of drug use and production in, 116–117; international trade routes in, 82; Narcotics Control Board, 118; opium production and trade in, 36, 81–83

Paraguay, coca production in, 37

Peasant growers, 13, 19, 25, 30 (n.52), 72, 155

Peru: coca production in, 37, 38–39, 41–42, 60 (n.17), 99, 179; drug consumption in, 53–54; drug-control efforts in, 95–99; drug trafficking in, 70–71; economic effects of drug production in, 26; environmental damage from drug production in, 26–27; integrated drug organizations in, 71; Sendero Luminoso in, 19, 22, 71, 96, 98,

182; supply-control programs in, 96–99

Production: drug-crime connections in, 19, 24–27; estimates, various countries, 36–39; socioeconomic and political effects of, 136–137; value-added, 70–71, 82

Prohibition: and decriminalization, 194, 197, 200–204; effectiveness of, 184

Rivera, Verónica, 67

Roca Suárez, Jorge, 73

Rural poverty, and illegal-drug growing, 19, 25, 30 (n.52)

Russia, as transshipment country, 17

Sendero Luminoso, 19, 22, 71, 96, 98, 182

Sicilian mafia, 21

Soviet Union, drug-traffic organizations in, 21, 36

Spain, drug-traffic organizations in, 21

Sri Lanka, drug-related political terrorism in, 23

Suárez Gómez, Roberto, 73

Supply-suppression strategies, 89, 96–97; and alternative development, 166–167, 206–207; crop-reduction measures, 93, 97, 100–103, 110–111, 112, 117, 123, 124–125, 126, 162–163, 166–167, 198; failure and successes of, 178–180, 183. See also Drug-control strategy(ies)

Terrorism, drug-financed, 13–14, 19, 22–23, 32 (n.70), 71, 96, 98, 182

Thailand: alternative development in, 162; crop-substitution and economic development programs in, 110–111; drug-control efforts in, 107–111; drug-financed ethnic warfare in, 76–77; drug trafficking in, 75–77; heroin consumption in, 109–110; history of opium use and trade in, 107–108; illicit drug consumption in, 36, 44, 55–55; political implications of drug trade in, 9, 138; supply-suppression success in, 179; Thailand

Development Research Institute (TRDI), 54–55; transshipment in, 36, 44

Thai village development model, 116

Trafficking, 65–87; advanced technology in, 16; corrupting influence of, 8–9, 11, 15, 138–139, 168–169; and crime, 7–27, 65, 66–67, 146–148, 151, 152–153; and crime tax, 139–140, 194; disruption of, as drug-control effort, 92, 123–124, 125–126; narco-guerrilla connection, 68–69, 76–77, 79, 80–81, 84–85, 138–139, 154, 155; and organized crime, 14–18, 20–21; and product improvement, 84

Trafficking organizations, 20–24; cocaine syndicates, 21, 31 (n.63), 66, 68, 73, 143, 152, 181; drug "families," 31 (n.62), 75; Medellín syndicate, 21, 22, 31 (n.63), 66, 68, 73, 95, 143, 145, 152, 173 (n.21); Mexican mafia, 21, 31 (n.62); and terrorist/insurgent groups, 19, 22–23, 69, 71, 96, 98, 182

Treatment programs, anticontagion, 185

Turkey, and the French Connection, 20, 30 (n.58)

United Kingdom, drug-traffic organizations in, 21

United Nations: development program financing, 111, 117–118, 163; drug-related agenda of, 90–91, 127 (n.1); 1961 Single Convention on Narcotic Drugs, 90, 109, 110, 117; UNDCP (United Nations Drug Control Programme), 99, 111, 115, 118, 165

United Nations Research Institute for Social Development/United Nations University (UNRISD/UNU) project, vii–ix, 35, 225

United States: Aryan Brotherhood and Texas syndicate in, 21; consumer-focused demand-reduction policies, 186–187; consumption of illicit drugs in, 36, 49, 58, 121, 127; domestic drug-control efforts, 122, 125, 186–187; drug-control aid to Laos, 111; drug-control policy in Bolivia, 100, 101–103, 155, 168–169; drug-control policy in Colombia, 93, 94, 180–181; drug-control policy in Mexico, 104, 105; drug-control policy in Peru, 96–99; drug-related crime in, 12, 14; drug use surveys in, 49, 62 (n.77); expenditures on illicit drugs in, 2; and international decriminalization/legalization, 204

USAID (U.S. Agency for International Development), 96, 97, 99, 118, 163, 164–165

Venezuela, drug production in, 6 (n.8), 37

Violence. See Crime and violence

Workplace drug-control initiatives, 184–185, 209 (n.10)

Youth gangs, drug-related crimes of, 12–13

About the Book and Author

• • •

Analyzing the socioeconomic and political impact of the illegal drugs industry in nine countries, this book also assesses the effectiveness and unintended consequences of the laws and policies designed to criminalize, thwart, or otherwise address drug production, consumption, and trade.

Tullis draws on studies of Bolivia, Myanmar/Burma, Colombia, Laos, Mexico, Pakistan, Peru, Thailand, and the United States to demonstrate that—though strategies for suppression of supplies and disruption of marketing networks continue to be pursued vigorously —aggregate global consumption and production of illicit drugs still are increasing. Considering what, if anything, can be done about this situation, he explores several options for the illustrative cases of Bolivia and Colombia.

LaMond Tullis is professor of political science at Brigham Young University. His principal publications include *Lord and Peasant in Peru, Politics and Social Change in Third World Countries,* and *Handbook of Research on the Illicit Drug Traffic.* He is director of the joint UNRISD–United Nations University multicountry project on the impact of the illicit drug trade.

The United Nations Research Institute for Social Development (UNRISD) is an autonomous agency that engages in multidisciplinary research on the social dimensions of contemporary problems affecting development. Its work is guided by the conviction that, for effective development policies to be formulated, an understanding of the social and political context is crucial. The institute attempts to provide governments, development agencies, grassroots organizations, and scholars with a better understanding of how development policies and processes of economic, social, and environmental change affect different social groups. Working through an extensive network of national research centers, UNRISD aims to promote original research and strengthen research capacity in developing countries.

Current research themes focus on the social dimensions of economic restructuring, environmental deterioration and conservation, ethnic conflict, the illicit narcotic drugs trade and drug-control policies, political violence, the mass voluntary return of refugees, and the reconstruction of war-torn societies, as well as ways of integrating gender issues into development planning.

A list of publications can be obtained by writing to the Reference Centre, UNRISD, Palais des Nations, CH-1211 Geneva 10, Switzerland.

 The United Nations University (UNU) is an international academic organization that provides a framework for bringing together the world's leading scholars to tackle pressing global problems of human survival, development, and welfare. It is an autonomous body of the United Nations, with academic freedom guaranteed under its charter to allow free collaboration with scholars worldwide. The University operates through a global network of its own research and training centers and programs and in association with individuals and other institutions throughout the world.

Currently, the University works in five program areas, each related to an area of major global concern: universal human values and global responsibilities, the world economy and development, global life support systems, advances in science and technology, and population dynamics and human welfare.